NATURAL RESOURCES
AND
PUBLIC RELATIONS

"Public sentiment is everything.
With public sentiment nothing can fail;
without it, nothing can succeed."

. . . . . Abraham Lincoln

NATURAL RESOURCES
AND
PUBLIC RELATIONS

(Second Edition)

DOUGLAS L. GILBERT
Professor of Wildlife Biology and
Head, Department of Fishery and Wildlife Biology
College of Forestry and Natural Resources
Colorado State University

Published by
The Wildlife Society
1971

THE WILDLIFE SOCIETY

The Wildlife Society has for its major objectives the establishment of high professional standards, the encouragement of management of wildlife along sound biological lines, and the dissemination of information to accomplish these ends. The members of The Wildlife Society believe that wildlife and other natural resources have a permanent place in our culture. The Society supports programs to enhance the esthetic, recreational, and economic values of wildlife and seeks to insure the wise use of this natural resource as part of our living standards.

These objectives, rising from unselfish motives, are directed toward the well-being of all occupants of our planet. They are carried out in a large number and variety of ways, primary among these being the publications of the Society, all edited by volunteers. *The Journal of Wildlife Management,* our 40-year old scientific quarterly, and Wildlife Society Bulletin, a new quarterly. Scientific papers too lengthy for inclusion in *The Journal of Wildlife Management* are published in the Society's *Wildlife Monograph* series. The Society, in meeting its obligations to enhance man's knowledge and to assist those within the wildlife profession, also has published a 589-page book, "The Wild Turkey and Its Management"; a 623-page manual, "Wildlife Management Techniques"; a 722-page "Readings in Wildlife Conservation," and a 200-page basic work-book entitled, "A Manual of Wildlife Conservation."

The Society's wide and diverse professional interests and responsibilities are reflected in its stylized hieroglyphic emblem adopted in 1937, the Society's first year of existence. The horizontal lines of figures, from top to bottom, may be translated as: beasts, birds, fishes, and flowering plants.

Fred G. Evenden
Executive Director

FOREWORD

Countless young people contemplating a professional career in conservation reached such an important decision because of their love for outdoor life and their interest in wild birds, fish and mammals. Both are certainly prerequisite to satisfaction in this type of life's work.

They will soon find, however, that most of their time will be spent working with people, rather than with the natural resources. Most of their days and nights will be spent in offices or indoor meeting places rather than tramping the fields, waterways and forests.

Thousands of others who have already started their conservation careers can attest to this fact. They have completed their formal training and have been successful in finding jobs as wildlife biologists, game managers, law enforcement officers, range managers, foresters, agronomists or administrators. Most of these professionals long since have realized their technical knowledge is of little avail if their publics do not understand their conclusions nor accept their recommendations.

No suitable management program for our nation's natural resources—soils, waters, forests, rangelands and wildlife—can succeed without public support. Technical knowledge in recent years has constantly been far ahead of public acceptance. This characteristic of American conservation efforts is epitomized by the imaginary (but typical) character who is reputed to have said, "Don't confuse me with the facts; my mind is already made up."

Dr. Gilbert has written this book to help conservation workers get the facts accepted by the average citizen. Although there are many excellent books and articles on public relations, as far as I know this is the only book designed and written specifically for professional conservationists.

Natural Resources and Public Relations has been written by a man well qualified to present such an important subject. I first came to know Doug Gilbert when we labored as co-workers in the Colorado Game and Fish Department. There he quickly was recognized for his talent and success in the public information and education program of one of the most effective state conservation agencies in the country. Later we came to rely on Professor Gilbert as one of conservation's best moulders of public opinion as he entered the teaching profession.

No government agency can fully exercise its authority and responsibility in resource management without the support of the people. Every career employee should receive public relations training as part of his formal education, as well as in-service training. Each member of a conservation agency, from the top administrator to the farthest field representative, must know how to effectively explain proper management techniques to the lay sportsman and citizen. Dr. Gilbert has done an exceptionally capable job of describing public relations techniques that are, or should be, used by conservation agencies and organizations. I am sure this book will win new friends and influence people to support the most important cause in America. It is my hope this book will find its rightful place among the many textbooks used by students of natural resource management, as well as on the required reading list for every conservation worker.

THOMAS L. KIMBALL
Executive Director, National Wildlife Federation
Washington, D. C.

DEDICATION

Dedications usually are not adequate. However, I would like to mention three persons or groups.

To my family; parents, brothers, and sisters for encouragement and help. Many times when my way erred, I was brought up short and put back on the right track.

To my students, colleagues, and fellow workers for inspiration in teaching public relations as pertaining to natural resource management and for seeing the need for such a book.

And to my wife, Dorothy, for being the impetus behind the entire operation. She constantly provided the encouragement needed for completion.

About the Author

A native of Colorado and the West, Doug Gilbert's roots are in the natural resource management professions. He has worked with several state and federal natural resource management agencies and taught at Colorado State and Cornell Universities and the University of Montana. Bachelor's and Master's degrees were earned at Colorado State University while his Ph.D. is from the University of Michigan. He belongs to many honorary and professional organizations and has written for popular and scientific publication in numerous magazines and journals.

Although his major efforts have been in wildlife science, and his degrees are in that field, he has a very strong interest in the people problems of natural resources management. His first book on "Public Relations in Natural Resources Management" won the Wildlife Society award for Conservation Education in 1964. He is widely known as a lecturer and a consultant in fields of wildlife biology and public relations efforts in natural resources management.

ACKNOWLEDGMENTS

Some of the material used in this publication is the result of Doctoral Study at the University of Michigan. Therefore, I wish to thank the members of my Doctoral Committee who were so tolerant in allowing me to pursue a subject greatly different from the usual. These gentlemen offered criticism, help, and condolence whenever needed. Drs. Warren W. Chase and Archibald B. Cowan, my major professors and committee chairmen, especially were patient and helpful.

The National Wildlife Federation was very generous in providing three grants of money. Without this help, the study would never have been possible. The Graduate School and the School of Natural Resources of The University of Michigan also provided financial assistance.

The aid of many conservation departments must be acknowledged. Their employees laboriously answered written questionnaires and personal questions concerning their organization and its operation. Personnel of the Colorado Wildlife Division were particularly cooperative. They supplied many of the photographs. Gratitude also must be extended to the many employees of this organization who helped so willingly with television and radio programs during and after my employment with the Colorado Department of Game and Fish.

Additional photographs are from the files of Colorado State and Cornell Universities. Others were supplied by my older brother, Paul F. Gilbert. Dr. Oliver H. Hewitt spent tedious hours editing the manuscript.

PREFACE

I believe that certain explanations must be made. I have taken liberties with set patterns of thought and actions established by knowledgeable people in the field of writing, radio, public speaking, television, public opinion and public relations. I ask their tolerance and understanding. My training is that of a natural resource manager and not that of a public relations practitioner.

Many of the suggestions which are presented are the result of trial and error in actual practice. When one method failed, another was tried. When one television or radio show did not produce results, other approaches to get the message across to a public were tried until one was successful. Perhaps the field of natural resources management requires different public relations techniques than do the standard areas of operation such as business and government.

Since my particular field of interest in the natural resource areas is wildlife biology, many of the examples are of wildlife management situations. However, the examples are usually equally applicable to other natural resource disciplines. I am sure that forest managers, range managers, soil managers, park managers and conservationists in general can find some analogous situation without too much difficulty.

If this publication puts some of the applicable techniques into a workable, concise form and into the hands of resource managers who are attemping to do the job of information-education and public relations; if the importance of human management is understood and stressed in the natural resource professions; if students of natural resource management are made to understand there is more to natural resource management than only managing the resource, that they are public servants and must maintain good relations with others; if the importance of communicating good management methods and ideas to the public is understood and carried out; and if employees and employers realize that the business of natural resource management must be considered as an entity, and fractions cannot stand alone; then I shall have partially succeeded.

DOUGLAS L. GILBERT

TABLE OF CONTENTS

LIST OF TABLES

LIST OF FIGURES AND PHOTO CREDITS

(Where not credited, photographed by the author)

FIGURE   PAGE

INTRODUCTION

Numerous natural resource administrators have indicated that their greatest problems originate in the field of human relations. Many echo the well-known phrases—"We know how to manage the resource but not the people," or—"Natural resource management is 90 per cent managing the public and 10 per cent managing the resource." If these statements are true, the necessity for natural resource management agencies to establish and maintain good public relations is obvious.

Everyone involved in management of natural resources, whether an individual or an agency, portrays an image to those with whom he or she comes in contact. This image is reflected to the various audiences and becomes the reputation of that individual or agency. This reputation, based upon deed and action, is the basis for the public relations of that person or organization. This process is constant and does not cease. The results are either positive or negative.

People who fail in the natural resource management professions, whether the failure is actually being fired from a job or simply not advancing in rank or responsibility, generally do so *not* because of a lack of technical knowledge or a corresponding ability to manage the resource. Will (1966) stated that 80 per cent of an organization's problems are public relations failures. Most of these failures are due to inability, or perhaps lack of desire, to get along with people. The word "people" as used here means either co-workers or those outside of the agency.

This ability to work with people and to get along with them partly is inherent. However, a cognizance of the importance of good public relations definitely is a step in the right direction. The days of the "timber beast," the "lone cowboy" and the "pioneer trapper" are over. In place of these individuals is the personable, well-dressed, well-mannered, natural resource manager who *must* strive for understanding and acceptance of his work. This is of absolute importance because most natural resource managers are public employees. They serve their publics, and their agency was created because of a public need.

With less and less of the natural resources for more and more people; with these people having more time for leisure, better modes of travel, and more money to spend for outdoor recreation, the need for good public relations will increase. Therefore, managers of our natural resources must make every effort to keep knowledge of their publics at the same level or at a higher level as knowledge of natural resource management.

Brief History of Natural Resource Management

Natural resource management is not a new field of science. References are made to various thoughts and deeds that occurred long before biblical times. Many of the laws for hunting probably originated with tribal taboos which evolved from superstitions concerning killing of females or young animals. Perhaps these superstitions resulted in obvious increases of wildlife. Biological techniques that appeared to be sound, such as "males only" hunting regulations resulted.

We know that aboriginal tribes used fire to move animals and to harvest large numbers of them. Unknowingly, they were practicing range and forest management by setting back ecological succession. Methods were observed and passed from father to son. Thus, the start of "management" almost is synonymous with human history.

The Mosaic Law, as reported in the Book of the Covenant, (Deuteronomy 22:6) is one of the first written restrictions regarding the harvesting of natural resources. In general, this law states that the dam shall be left on the nest and only the sire and young shall be harvested. One should note that the first attempts toward natural resource management dealt with the control of harvests rather than with the habitat or manipulation of it.

The problem of ownership of the natural resources developed with the Greeks and Romans in the First Century, A.D. Trees, grass, soil, and water always have belonged to the landowner, be it an individual or the government. With wildlife, however, ownership by an individual first was controlled by trespass laws. Later, in 1215, the Magna Carta took the right of ownership of wildlife from the Sovereign and gave it to the people. The King was to hold the wildlife "in trust" for the people. This was the nucleus for our present policies regarding ownership of wildlife in the United States of America.

In America the sequential changes in the handling of natural resources seem to fall into fairly definite eras or similarities of thinking. The first era, lasting until about 1850, can be termed the *Era of Abundance*. There was little or no worry about the supply of natural resources. Huge, unmapped, untouched supplies of trees, grass, water and wildlife were just around the next bend of the river or over the next ridge (Figure 1). This was the era of the rugged mountain men who depended directly on the natural resources, as we do now indirectly, for livelihood (Figure 2).

From approximately 1850 to 1900 the *Era of Exploitation* occurred. This was the time of depletion, destruction, and the start of restrictions. Forests and forested lands over wide areas were ruined by destructive logging and fire. Range lands were abused and erosion became common. Policies were to cut out and get out

Figure 1. *The Era of Abundance*. Natural resources were thought to be present in amounts that would never be depleted.

(Figure 3), graze out or farm out and move on (Figure 4), or kill off or fish out and look elsewhere (Figure 5).

This was the time of market hunting and over liberal regulations which brought the advent of legislative restrictions; such as bag limits, shorter seasons and otherwise curtailed methods of harvest. In the 1890's the bison, for all practical purposes, became extinct, and the pronghorn nearly so. It was during this era (1872) that Yellowstone National Park was established to perpetuate some of the natural beauty for future generations to enjoy. Then, the "panic button" was pushed, and in many instances it was high time.

The next era, *Preservation and Production*, lasted approximately from 1900 to 1935. Man did the preserving, and the animals took care of the production. Much happened during this time to establish many of the "conservation principles" that we know today. The names of two great conservationists stand out. Gifford Pinchot became the Chief of The Division of Forestry in 1898. This organization later was to become the U. S. Forest Service. Theodore Roosevelt was elected President in 1901. He was the first President to recognize the value of our natural resources and associated problems.

The Lacey Act (1900) regulated market hunting, controlled interstate transport of illegally killed game and controlled import of exotic species. The Bureau of Biological Survey was established in 1905 and later (1940) became the United States Fish and Wildlife Service. International treaties with Canada and Mexico regarding

Figure 2. Mountain men depended upon the natural resources for their livelihood.

waterfowl were ratified. The Migratory Bird Conservation Act in 1929 made wildlife refuges a reality, and in 1934 it became necessary to have a "duck stamp" to hunt waterfowl. Funds obtained from sale of duck stamps were used to operate the wildlife refuges.

Figure 3.   Cutover and abandoned forest area.

The United States Forest Service was created in 1905, primarily as a protection agency. Professional societies were organized (Society of American Foresters, 1900; The Wildlife Society, 1936; and The American Society of Range Management, 1948) to band together professional natural resource managers.

The job of preservation and production was done well. Restrictions became ever tighter. Laws where only males could be killed were the order of the day. Refuges became numerous for all species. Bounty laws, artificial propagation and stocking were thought to be good management. In short, wildlife crops were protected and the increase was not harvested.

Abandoned farm lands and cutover forests were in early second-growth stages and afforded excellent food and cover for game and domestic animals (Figures 6 and 7). As a result, many wildlife populations increased beyond expectations. Budding research programs concentrated on life history studies and ways to increase populations, in many instances already at capacity.

During this period "conservation" primarily meant protection rather than "wise use." Conservation was like a boomerang. New ideas of management were discovered, but the old ideas of preservation and protection had been sold so well that they couldn't be thrown away! In other words, such a good job was done of "selling" males only seasons, artificial propagation and stocking, bounties on

Figure 4.   Farmstead abandoned as a result of land abuse and erosion. Eroded
material has inundated the dwelling.

predators (Figure 8) and restricted hunting that many people simply
would not accept anything contrary as being good management.
Even today many state game agencies have difficulty getting authorization to permit harvesting of female deer and very few are
allowed seasons for hen pheasants. This is in spite of the fact that
very large numbers of both are wasted each year due to starvation
and other causes of death (Figures 9 and 10).

The ecological *Era of Harvest and Habitat* management started
in approximately 1935. The principles still continue to be practiced,
although we are launching into the next period or era.

The Taylor Grazing Act of 1934 was enacted to stop injury to
public grazing lands caused by overgrazing and soil erosion. Provisions also were made to rehabilitate these areas.

During the last 25 or 30 years, wildlife management and research
have been concentrated on environmental manipulation with the
premise that if the necessities of a species are present, such as food,
water and shelter in required amounts, the species will be able to
exist in proportion. Federal aid to the states for fish and wildlife
research and management, commonly called Pittman-Robertson
(1937) and Dingell-Johnson (1950) Acts, for game and fish, respectively, gave research and management by state conservation
departments the most important financial impetus yet to be realized.

Biologists in some enterprising states have been able to convince
others of the necessity for "either sex" seasons to reduce animal
populations compatible with what the habitat can carry. It has been

shown again and again that high reproductive abilities enable animals to populate an area beyond carrying capacity within a short time, and many areas were found to be badly. overpopulated (Figure 11).

With the realization that open areas were good for something besides planting trees the Forest Service became more than a protection organization or a saw-log producing agency. The concepts of "multiple use" and "the greatest good for the greatest number in the long run" were discussed (Figure 12). Watershed management and good land management were accepted as basic to good stands of grass, timber, and populations of wildlife, and the resource area was evaluated as a unit (Figure 13).

New agencies concerned with land management came into existence. Franklin D. Roosevelt created the Civilian Conservation Corps in 1933. This group of young men did much to bolster management of natural resources and to heal scars that had been left on the land.

The Soil Conservation Service was created in 1935, and the Bureau of Land Management came into being in 1946 through a combination of the General Land Office and the Grazing Service. Effects of the Soil Bank Act (1956) upon restoration of habitat and better land management are still being realized. Legislation of the last

Figure 5. During the *Era Of Exploitation,* overharvest was the rule rather than the exception.

Figure 6.   Second growth of vegetation in previously cut-over and burned-over areas afforded excellent wildlife habitat.

Figure 7.   Opening of timber stands also aided stockmen. Too many animals often were grazed on an area to the detriment of the vegetation and the land.

decade, such as The Wilderness Act and The Land and Water Conservation Fund Act, shows an increasing interest in recreational uses of wildlands.

Figure 8.   Bounties on predators were thought at one time to be wise management. Now we are not so sure that predators even should be killed.

And so we come to the present era, one that can be called the
Era of Technology, Sophistication and of Human Management. Sophistication in methods of natural resources management mark this
era. Computers, programming, biometrics, telemetry, animal behavior studies, systems ecology, biochemistry and nutrition are bywords of today's natural resource manager. More accurate, random
and finite methods are used in gathering data; and much more
sophisticated criteria and technology are used in analysis of those
data. Instead of reason and result, or observation and correlation,
the modern manager is interested in the cause and effect of natural
phenomena.

For years natural resource managers have concentrated on the
resource and the users of the resource have been pretty much neglected. Only within the last few years have public relations, cooperative agreements, and user communications also become bywords
in natural resource management. The professional natural resource
managers now have pretty well proven the soundness of ideas on
how to manage the range, forests, soils, water and wildlife, but this
information has been gained at the expense of neglecting knowledge
about the users of these resources.

We are in the midst of a population boom, one that probably
will never slow down, certainly never stop. Increasing numbers of
people will use the natural resources and there will be a corresponding per capita decrease in natural resources (Figure 14), including
those needed for energy or where a conflict with energy producing
materials is involved.

It is necessary, therefore, that the resources be used more wisely
than ever before. There is a corresponding increase in misuse, litter-
ing, and pollution (Figure 15). The obvious answer is to communi-

Figure 9.   Starving deer. The result of too many deer and too little food.

cate, inform, and to educate the people who harvest the benefits from the resources, whether the method be by gun, bow and arrow, fly rod, grazing of domestic stock, axe, saw, camera or just looking. Resource management agencies are now making progress in this critical area. The United States Forest Service appears to be moving ahead with plans to have a public relations man on the staff of each National Forest. Only two state conservation agencies do not have an information and education department of some type. The U. S. Fish and Wildlife Service has an information specialist in each region (about eight states each). The Bureau of Land Management has been a leader in publishing materials and generally in leading the way in public relations work.

And so efforts to influence, inform, and instruct the users of our natural resources are increasing. The future? The cycle may start over. With increasing human pressure, we may again enter an era of depletion or shortages, of increasing protection and of greater restrictions. Indications are that this is already happening.

Definitions of Public Relations

Definitions of public relations are as varied as the practice itself. It is a field that includes diverse ideas and involves concepts as well as activities. Rules, standards and patterns are still being established, and the profession is broad, complex and disorganized. Semantics, advertising, selling, publicity, communications, influencing thought and reaction and much common sense are incorporated.

Figure 10. Aftermath of a hard winter. Mother Nature's way of harvest is rather sad.

Good public relations is a phenomenon necessary for the success and acceptance, or support of any program. It is a two-way system of contact and understanding between organizations and individual publics. A certain amount of manipulation of thought or "engineering of consent" is involved. This is neither illegal nor dishonest, and techniques of selling ideas are now known and accepted.

Published definitions are nearly as many as the authors who write in the profession. Some of the current definitions are as follows:

1. "Those functions and policies designed to bring about the communications and interpretation of ideas and information to all various publics of an enterprise; and the communication and interpretation of information and ideas from these publics to the enterprise in an effort to bring the two into harmonious and fruitful adjustment" (Schoenfeld, 1954).

2. "The management function which evaluates public attitude, identifies policies and proceedings of an individual or organization with the public interest, and executes a program of action to earn public understanding" (Public Relations News, in Cutlip and Center, 1964).

3. "The planned effort to influence public opinion through acceptable performance and two-way communication" (Cutlip and Center, 1964).

4. "The art or science of developing reciprocal understanding and goodwill between a person, firm, or institution and the public." (Webster's Collegiate Dictionary, 1968).

5. "A suitable thing made up of many forces both inside and outside the individual organization" (Gerber, 1960).

6. "Part of the affairs aimed at keeping publics informed, keeping informed about public attitudes, and reacting to those attitudes" (Reynolds, 1966).

7. "Public relations strives by long range effort to build favorable public attitudes" (Will, 1966).

Figure 11.   Overused deer range. Dead shrubs and a browseline on the trees as high as the deer can reach are evidence of overpopulations.

Despite their differences, the preceding definitions have certain important things in common. They all stress the idea of good performance and the communication of that performance. More simply stated, this is the old idea of "not hiding your light under a bushel basket." If a private business or a government agency has performed well, it should let its publics know of its achievements. Another important inclusion, real or implied, which is found in all of the previously mentioned definitions is the emphasis on two-way communications. The publics communicate with the organization and the organization communicates with its publics.

It should again be pointed out that public relations are continuous and always present; good, bad or in-between. Public relations can be compared to a wagon. If allowed to coast, it can only go one way—downhill.

Figure 12. Multiple use of lands currently is practiced by most natural resource management agencies.

Other authorities have made an analogy between public relations and a bank. Frequent deposits and withdrawals are made in this "Bank of Good Will." Deposits are made deliberately or unconsciously, when an operation results in favorable opinion or high morale. These deposits can be accumulated. Withdrawals result when an effort brings unfavorable opinion or low morale. Again, this can be done knowingly or unknowingly. Withdrawals can exceed deposits, and the account can become overdrawn! The result is a loss of faith and confidence in the organization and its program, and worthy effort is blocked rather than supported (Figure 16).

Lesly (1962) pointed out that the value of good public relations is usually not realized until absent. It can be reflected in the morale of an organization; or be indicated by quality and quantity of goods or services produced; or be shown by the support, or lack of support of an organization by its publics.

Good public relations might be likened to health. Good health is not usually appreciated until an individual is ill. By the same token, we don't go to a dentist until pain makes it necessary. Good dental care would have prevented the effort. By comparison, good public relations are not missed until needed and would have prevented some of the catastrophies which stem from poor public relations.

Despite the high degree of truth and honesty which must be the basis of any public relations effort, there is no doubt that public relations is an effort to influence and in many cases, change public opinion. However this must be done by presenting the facts of the whole story and not by distorting the issue.

Problems in Public Relations of Natural Resource Agencies

There are many problems involved in the management of publicly owned natural resources. As important as any is the problem that some agencies and individuals working in the various natural

Figure 13. Many areas are categorized as to which type of use is best for the resources and the people. Note lower sign warning of cyanide guns set for coyotes.

Figure 14. More and more people are making increasing demands on a
dwindling supply of natural resources, including places to fish.

resource disciplines are not aware of the importance and necessity
of establishing and maintaining good communications and public
relations. If the people who are responsible for managing our resources do not recognize this need, it is difficult to imagine how
they can favorably influence public impressions.

Natural resource agencies differ from many businesses in that
they can sell only ideas, services and opportunities to enjoy, and
do not usually sell goods. The resources on public lands already are
owned by the people, and all public agencies must have support
from the people to succeed in their management programs. Schoenfeld (1957) wrote that "We must have public support, at least suffer-
ance, and the development of a favorable climate of public opinion
must even precede management."

Research in the natural resource professions must be explained
in simple terms so that it will be accepted by all of the employees of
the agency, as well as by people not belonging to the organization.
Natural resource management must be allowed to keep pace with
research. People must know and understand what is being done,

Figure 15. Suds from detergents are not readily broken down by bacterial
action and pollute many waterways.

how it is being done, and why it is being done, before they will give
the necessary support for changes. The problems associated with
managing deer in Michigan, rabbits in Pennsylvania, trees in Ore-
gon, bighorn sheep in Colorado, grass in Montana or grouse in
Minnesota, are not exclusively, or even primarily, biological problems. They are problems which stem from a lack of understanding
and support by people, not from the lack of research.

Public recognition of the necessity for good, sound, management methods and public confidence in the professional manager's
ability to do the job must be developed. Some people even suggest
registration of professionals in the natural resource management
professions. Mr. Charles A. Connaughton, a Regional Forester for
the U. S. Forest Service, said that we must show people that we
know how to manage resources properly because people now associ-

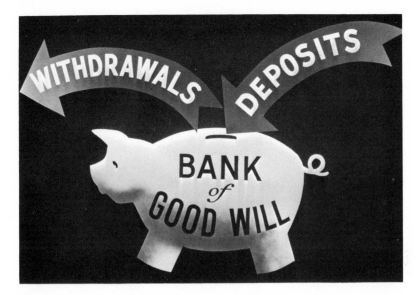

Figure 16. Public relations is analogous to "The Bank of Good Will." Deposits can be accrued and the account can be overdrawn.

ate "use" with "abuse." Cain (1960), former Assistant Secretary of The Department of Interior for Fish and Wildlife, stated that "Our management problems depend on habits, behavior, and views of the consuming public, . . . our knowledge of consumer patterns, and our ability, or lack of it, to educate people."

We must give conservation information public appeal. Competition for time and interest is great, and the lesson must be made attractive. You do not hear enough about natural resource management during the best radio or television times. Nor do you read enough about it in the most popular magazines. Costs are prohibitive and people frequently prefer to be entertained.

Swift (1961) pointed out that some people are interested only in profit, exploitation, and the economic use of resources. Leopold (1956) believed the solution is to educate people so that they will appreciate the opportunity to go hunting and fishing and the esthetic qualities of these activities. Therefore, it certainly seems that we must educate the people to harvest more of the less popular species of wildlife and to measure success by the thrill of pursuit rather than by a full bag limit.

Programs of human management seem to be greater in wildlife management than in the associated natural resource professions. Wildlife managers do not know their users, nor do they have as much control of them, as do forest and range managers. Public interest in hunting and fishing is inherent and is greater than in harvesting forest and range crops. Wildlife harvesters are more numerous

Figure 17. Harvesters of wildlife are more numerous, less controlled, and less is known about them. They cause more problems than harvesters of other natural resources.

than range and forest harvesters. With greater numbers, and often a lack of professional interest, hunters and fishermen may be less experienced and may have fewer scruples than users of other natural resources (Figure 17). Political influences appear to be stronger in wildlife agencies than in range and forest agencies. In the past, wildlife workers have often been less qualified for their jobs, due to less stringent employment qualifications, than professional foresters or outdoor recreationists. Also, hunters and fishermen, more than stockmen or timber cutters, use lands that are publicly owned and are thus less subject to agency control. Law enforcement problems certainly are greater in wildlife management than in forestry or other allied professions.

As stated earlier, some natural resource management concepts have been so well "sold" to the publics in the past that we now are having trouble "unselling" them. Practices currently outdated and unsound were promoted widely by natural resource managers in earlier times, and it has been learned that refuting an idea or policy that has been accepted and practiced is a very difficult operation. Hence, all attempts to mold thinking should be based on the soundest principles.

Public relations and communications problems internal to the agency, as well as external, must be recognized and solved. Employees at all levels, technicians and nontechnical workers, all must work together for the same goal. An organization's "house" must be in good order before that organization attempts to sell something to an outside public. If employees do not agree that the idea or policy is sound, how can customers, in this instance the natural resource users, be persuaded to accept that idea or policy?

Two-way communications must be maintained with all individuals and groups with whom the agency is concerned. This calls for the use of all media and methods at the right time and in the right way. The conservation agency must always have contact with the public so that the public's thoughts can be known and proper action taken. The agency must *sell itself* and *its practices* to the people and organizations involved.

It should be noted that the people may not want to be educated in conservation matters. Many show apathy and prejudice. Instances are known where sportsmen's club meetings have been attended by only a few sportsmen and many more natural resource agency employees.

Today's public relations efforts by most natural resource management agencies seem to be haphazard, token efforts. Low salaries, low budgets, lack of interest by administrators and policy makers, lack of adequate training of information and education personnel and lack of freedom, all handicap the individual who attempts to establish public relations work in a conservation agency.

Other big businesses (natural resource management is big business) have efficient and highly paid sales and public relations forces to promote the agency and its goods or services. How about the natural resource organizations? The information and education division may not even be consulted until after an effort has failed. Budgets of state or federal natural resource management agencies depend upon the ability of personnel to influence elected state and federal legislators. Most budgets are inadequate for resource management purposes; without including the costs of influencing people and an equally important public relations program.

Human pressures upon natural resources will become greater with increasing populations. Public understanding of resource problems is the most obvious solution to gaining support for reducing the effects of heavy use of the resources. We must work for better public understanding, or some of the natural resource professions will cease to exist. Shomon (1959) stated that national destruction is inevitable unless misuse of natural resources is stopped. He compared the potential of this misuse to the misuse of nuclear energy. The latter is fast and dramatic. The former is insidious and not dramatic; however, their ultimate effects can be equal.

Value of Good Public Relations to a Natural Resource Agency

What can any organization gain from good public relations? For any business the list includes prestige, good will, recognition, promotion of goods and services, community acceptance, few misconceptions and prejudices, prevention of misunderstanding and ill will, lack of apathy and ignorance and support from other businesses and agencies.

For a natural resource agency we can add desired legislation from politicians and beneficial policies and rules of operation from governing boards. Thus, the laws and regulations under which a public employee and a public agency operate depend upon good public relations with those who make the laws and formulate the regulations. Understanding of these policies and regulations, and acceptance of them by employees and those outside of the agency also depends upon good public relations.

Budgets of state or federal natural resource management agencies depend upon the ability of people to influence and "sell" their needs to lobbyists and to elected state and federal legislators. Therefore, adequate dollars to do the job and the presence or absence of enough, well-trained employees at all levels depends upon good public relations.

Administration is public relations. Someone leads, is the boss, and others follow, are lesser administrators or employees. Internal harmony, or the lack of it, between leaders and followers, is the result of good or bad public relations efforts. It can be said that the success or failure, or the very existence of any business, including natural resource management agencies, depends upon good public relations, or the lack of it, at all levels and with all groups and people they deal with.

Types of Public Relations Efforts

There are two distinct kinds of public relations ventures in the natural resource management professions. The first type is a constant, day-by-day, contact, deed, practice, appearance sort of thing, which results from all efforts of all workers in the organization. This type of public relations is not a one-man job and generally is unorganized except for its desired constancy. This type of public relations should include all employees at all times, because one slovenly, rude or incompetent individual can give the entire organization a poor reputation.

It is easy to see that the basic field man who contacts most of the people is "Mr. Organization" to those people. The ranger, biologist, or conservation officer represents the agency (Figure 18). As the contact goes, so go the impressions that an individual will have of the entire organization. Who can deny that daily appearances, even in the field, and constant courtesy at all times are important? Public confidence in any agency, based on good impressions, is a prerequisite to all other public relations activities.

Figure 18. The ranger, wildlife conservation officer or other field man is "Mr. Organization" to the people he contacts.

The second type of public relations work may be called the "engineered operation" or the "organized effort." One or a few experts plan the moves and the countermoves responsible for molding public opinion so that views toward an item or idea are favorable. This type of public relations involves planning well in advance, in definite sequences, and can be divided into two methods, mainly based on time.

The first method can be termed the traditional "hard sell." This technique employs the repetition of factors of current importance. The operation is planned well in advance, but the duration of operation is short.

For example, this technique has been used successfully in a safety program before a big game season. All communications media are used for two or three days before the season and during the first part of the season to get the message across to the sportsman public as frequently as possible. Safety articles and notices appear several places in each newspaper. Free safety stickers are distributed at service stations. Signs and posters are put up about hunter safety, and safety brochures are given free with each license sold. An often repeated, one-minute spot on the radio or television of a rifle shot, a terrified woman's scream and the voice of a man saying, "You must be sure of your target before pulling the trigger," will be remembered by the hunter in the field.

Another example where the "hard sell" technique might be applicable is when the fire danger is extremely high. Repeated warnings, posters in prominent places, and use of all of the methods of contact that are available would make campers and other users aware of the fire danger. It is obvious that some natural resource management operations fit very well into a "hard sell" public relations effort.

The second method is the "soft sell" technique. This method starts long before the actual event takes place and proceeds slowly. This is an attempt to create favorable public opinion toward an idea long before the proposal is presented to the public. Careful planning is needed. For example, if a grazing allotment cut is deemed necessary or if a hen pheasant season is wanted in an area, the work on the proposal should start a year, or even longer, in advance.

The question immediately arises, should outside consultants be hired to promote this effort or should the operation be engineered by the organization's own personnel? Both have advantages and disadvantages. The answer to this question depends upon the capabilities of the natural resource agency public relations men. Staff personnel will have a better knowledge than outsiders of the problem and of the capabilities of others in the organization. These staff men will be available constantly and already are considered part of the team. They also should have a personal interest in the operation.

Hodgson (1968) and Youel (1960) wrote in favor of outside specialists. They believed public relations practitioners from outside the agency would be less inclined to be influenced by prejudices. Outsiders should be more objective because they personally are less involved than organization personnel. In other words, they will be able to see both the forest and the trees. It appears that outside specialists currently are better qualified than most natural resource agency information and education people. Outside specialists have more experience and a "reputation" which lends authority. They also cost more.

Whether the job is handled by inside or outside public relations men, the client (organization and its administration) should not interfere. The agency's function is to provide the necessary factual information. The organization should know what is happening, and understand why, but must be only a spectator (Lesly, 1962).

HISTORY OF PUBLIC RELATIONS

The beginning of public relations is indefinite. Cutlip and Center (1964) wrote that the forces of public opinion have been known since ancient times. They stated the Romans used the phrase, "The voice of the people is the voice of God." The early Kings of England had individuals called "keepers cf the king's conscience" to facilitate communications with the people. Some early Polynesian tribes had a "talking chief" and the real monarch did not utter a word. The power of public opinion has been used in America since white men first traded with the Indians.

Early Concepts

Organized interest in public relations started with big business and government. Samuel Adams publicized biased accounts of the Boston Massacre and Tea Party. Thcmas Paine, Patrick Henry and John Adams were early mobilizers of public opinion and kept colonists aroused against British mercantilism. President Jackson, unlettered and inarticulate, employed one Amos Kendall to convey his ideas to the nation.

The development of public relations as a profession can be categorized into three periods (Bernays, 1952). The first period, prior to World War I is referred to as the time of *The Public Be Damned.* "Muckraking" and "whitewashing" were terms commonly associated with attempts to influence public thinking. This was a period of silence by organizations regarding both decisions and disasters. Agencies operated on the philosophy "what the people didn't know wouldn't hurt them." No one had an obligation to any public. The media, mainly newspapers, had to guess what was happening. Often they guessed wrong. They were forced, sometimes willingly, into "press agentry" and gross exaggeration by the unscrupulous. The business that made the most noise attracted the greatest attention. Medicine shows thrived on misrepresentation and P. T. Barnum methods were the order of the day.

Government business was handled in that same way. People were not even informed that President Taft had cancer. Now the President's backache or flu is news for the world. Election campaigns to influence public thinking were first used by Bryan and McKinley in the 1898 campaign and have been in use since then. One need merely to look at current governmental activities to see the effect of public relations in the political arena. P.R. can work either positively or negatively. The 1974 Watergate Scandal certainly is a notable example of poor public relations.

In this era the impression that public relations was sneaky and underhanded was understandable. Little material regarding public relations was published. Techniques for influencing people were guarded by the few who used them and were aware of the power available. Around 1900, a few business operators, mainly railroad magnates, started to realize the value of good public relations.

Transitions in Thinking

The second era began during the first World War and lasted until approximately 1930. This period can be termed the *Public Be Informed* era. Press conferences, where media representatives were treated festively, became popular.

John D. Rockefeller, Sr., in 1914, employed Ivy Lee to act as his public relations man. Mr. Lee gave information to the press concerning railroad accidents and problems in a mining controversy. Soon Mr. Rockefeller was pictured as a kindly old man who gave dimes to children. This is regarded as the first, well-planned, organized effort at public relations, and Mr. Lee is considered to be the "father" of public relations (Bernays, 1952).

President Woodrow Wilson said, "Anything crooked should be out in the open. It will either straighten out or disappear." It also was Wilson who said, "We should worry about telling the people what Washington thinks, but we should worry more about telling Washington what the people think." He employed the first press secretary and started the first White House conferences to tell of his actions and decisions. These conferences have been continued by all Presidents since and were the forerunners of F. D. Roosevelt's "Fireside Chats," Eisenhower's "State-Of-The-Nation" addresses, and Kennedy's, Johnson's, Nixon's and Ford's unrehearsed press conferences. People, presidents, and organizations were trying to humanize themselves as well as to inform and influence.

This was the time of large mailing lists and similar "broadside" efforts. Attempts to influence opinions and actions were not aimed at specific publics (which make up the total public), as they are now, and should be. Energies were used on "the public" instead of "a public." Liberty bond sales and war recruiting were increased by planned campaigns. Many of our current propaganda techniques were developed. Large scale industrial publicity was recognized as being important to big business success.

Radio was developed in the mid-1920's and, as another medium of mass contact, created competition for newspapers. The newspapers started doing a better, more thorough, unbiased job. Literature regarding public relations and public relations techniques began to appear.

Current Trends

The present, and third, stage in development started in the 1930's and may be called the era of *Publics Understand and Be Understood*. The big change is that an attempt is made to establish mutual agreement and understanding between an agency and its publics. It is now believed that an organization need not bare all, but something about failures as well as successes should be told. Truth is paramount, and to err is human. Agencies now try for a personal, humanistic image in the eyes of their publics.

The importance of knowing details about a *specific* public is realized. All possible information about individuals composing groups is considered necessary. This includes race, religion, culture, beliefs, political preferences, homogeneity, organizations belonged to, occupations, stresses, interests and charities, in addition to many other specific details. Research is necessary to obtain this information so that correct plans can be formed for management to follow and to create desired images in a specific public's mind. Polls, customer opinions and surveys were first used early in this era to learn the opinions of a public through the actions or impressions of a few component individuals who constitute a well chosen sample. The value of listening to an individual and drawing out his feelings was discovered.

Existing communications methods have been improved and new ones developed. Modern mass media methods make an interchange of facts and thoughts between organizations and their publics possible on a larger, more reliable and more complete scale than was formerly the case. Television has opened the door to countless new techniques of contact and has caused radio and newspapers to improve upon outmoded methods.

During World War II public maneuvering and propaganda were widely used by both sides. Psychological warfare was as lethal as any weapon. "Tokyo Rose" and "Axis Sally" were known by thousands of soldiers and sailors and influenced many. The United States painted pictures in the minds cf servicemen of evil, buck-toothed, sneaky, slant-eyed Orientals; or cruel, slow, stupid, ruthless Europeans. Some of these images were so firmly implanted that they still remain despite efforts to erase them. Both sides broadcast their gains widely and kept their losses quiet. The Office of War Information was created and did a spectacular job of propaganda and publicity, and the armed forces developed large public relations departments. Local angles were constantly stressed by business, and home morale was considered important. Army and Navy "E's" for excellence were awarded for extra production and effort on the home front.

At this time business was increasingly made aware that good communications and public relations were advantageous. Slogans that reached the consciousness of the people and showed the business was behind the war effort sold goods. One such example was "Lucky Strike Green Has Gone to War." There were many others.

New techniques of winning internal harmony were developed by business at the end of the war and the start of greater competition. Exit interviews, greater fringe benefits, employee attitude surveys, training programs and worker participation in management are all now considered mandatory for success.

Large businesses, including natural resource agencies, have delegated authority by developing regional headquarters in order to reach their publics at the "grass roots" level and to destroy the image of bureaucracy attached to big business by most people. Encouragement of local participation helps any organization to be accepted and to become a part of the area in which the business is located. With stockholders replacing single owners, with greater worker organization in the form of unions and civil service, and with more and stronger government influence on people, positions of leadership in public relations by big business and government have been retained.

Public interest has been put first with the idea that nearly all else for a successful operation will follow. This usually is true. Non-profit spending by large corporations is used widely to win favor and to reduce taxes. Many campaigns, grants, scholarships, endowments, research programs, community development projects and other worthwhile efforts are financed with a realization that, in the long run, total profits will be increased through the public favor that is won.

This is the age of personal diplomacy. Visits are made to see the housewife and to foreign countries to sell goods, services or ideas. Dictators and presidents try to outdo each other across the conference table. Free samples are passed out. This is all done to mold favorable public impression toward an item, action or idea. Yet, strikes and wars continue and businesses fail.

Much of the world turmoil, past and present, city-wide and state-wide, nationally and internationally, has been the result of poor public relations. The constant worldly confusion with us today is the result of trying to influence individuals, groups, races, and nations that certain ways of thinking and acting are right. Our leaders' power comes more from ability and position used to persuade and mold public opinion than from ability to command.

The American Public Relations Association was formed in 1944, and in 1948 the Public Relations Society of America was founded. In 1948, both organizations listed a total of 2,600 members and 21 consulting firms. Currently there are in excess of 2,000 firms and 100,000 members. Both organizations publish regular journals, and over 200,000 members are soon predicted. But not one natural resource agency is listed in the membership roster of either organization!

The subject of public relations now is taught at more than 250 colleges and universities (Hiebert, 1965). This is approximately 15 per cent of all institutions of higher learning. Harper's magazine recently included a statement that it is our fastest growing industry.

Over two billion dollars were spent on public relations work in 1960. This increased to nearly four billion by 1967 and five billion by 1969. Soon the total will be over ten billion dollars. General Motors has a public relations staff of over 100 people and an annual budget for public relations work of over one million dollars. Public relations has become a profession. The profession is young, but it is growing rapidly.

Public Relations in Natural Resources Management

Published information regarding the history of public relations in natural resources management is nearly nonexistent. Information specialists and information and education departments in state conservation agencies under various titles have been in existence since the late 1920's and early 1930's (Smits, 1937). By 1949, 41 of the 48 state conservation departments had information and education sections (Culbreath, 1949). These departments averaged a staff of only two people including the stenographer. They operated with 1.6 per cent of the total agency budget.

In 1949, 10 of the largest, eastern states spent 7 per cent of their budgets on information and education work. Eleven of the western states spent 1.7 per cent of their budgets on the same activity. Manpower percentages of total department personnel in information and education work for the eastern states was 3.5 per cent, and 1.8 per cent in the western states (Culbreath, 1949).

Shomon's (1952) study indicated that only 14 state conservation departments had well-established "I and E" programs. Great variation is shown between Culbreath's and Shomon's interpretation of results. This difference probably is due to what constitutes a "well-established" program.

A later study in 1962 showed an average of 11 employees in each state information and education section (Table 1). Only two states indicated they had no information and education department of some type. This analysis showed that only 5.8 per cent of the organization budget was spent by information and education sections.

In many states all employees are required to do some information and education work. Therefore, the 3.5 per cent of total employees in the department doing information and education work may not be a valid figure.

Table 1. State Conservation Information and Education Department Data, 44 states (Gilbert, 1962).

	No. Employees in Organization	No. Employees in I. and E. Department	I. and E. Budget Per Cent of Total
High	4,700 (California)	36 (Michigan)	20% (Mississippi)
Low	18 (Hawaii)	2 (four states)	less than 1% in many states
Average	477.4	11.2 (3.5% of total employees)	5.8%

States were categorized by per cent of total organization budget allotted to the information and education department. Twenty-nine states (69%) with information and education departments had *less than five per cent* of the total budget allocated to information and education work; 11 states (26%) had an information and education budget of from five to ten per cent of the total; and only one state (2%) had an information and education budget of more than ten per cent of the total organization budget (Gilbert, 1962). Periodic samples show that these data have not changed greatly since the study was done.

A study in 1966 by Alan M. Courtright of Alaska (personal communication) showed that 42 of 47 state conservation department agencies which replied to his questionnaire had an information and education program of some type in their organization. This is 89 per cent. However, Mr. Courtright pointed out that he queried 62 states and provinces and received 47 returns, or 77 per cent. Five of six Canadian Provinces which replied (83%) had an I and E program of some type. There are 10 Canadian provinces. It is probable that the five which did not reply to his questionnaire do not have I and E programs. It is probably true then, that only 5 of 10 provinces, or 50%, have I and E Departments.

Mr. Courtright gave an average budgetary expenditure for information and education work of 4.36 per cent of the total department budget. The number of people employed in I and E work in state conservation agencies ranged from 1 to 23, with an average of 8.2 (no percentage figure was given). Both budgetary and personnel percentages in 1966 show no increase over 1962 figures, but actually show a decrease (5.8% to 4.36%, budget; 11.2% to 8.2% personnel).

A study by the Wildlife Management Institute (1968) showed all of the 50 states (with the exception of Hawaii) had a full time

Information and Education staff and program. Numbers of personnel varied from 48 in New York and 42 in Texas to one in Ohio and Alaska.

Comparable figures for other businesses are difficult to obtain. Large corporations, however, show that the average public relations budget is between 10 and 20 per cent of the total money spent and their public relations staff is between 5 and 10 per cent of the total number of employees.

The natural resource agency must realize that it is a big business. Therefore, it seems logical that at least 10 per cent of the total budget and 5 per cent of the total staff should be allocated to information and education of public relations work for the agency to be comparable to other large businesses. This is about double current staffs and expenditures.

However, money and people are not a panacea. To do a good job of public relations the organization must be cognizant of the importance of good public relations. Good public relations simply do not "just happen." Planning and effort must be expended in the right directions.

Common problems of the natural resource agency information and education departments resulted in the formation of the American Association for Conservation Information Society in 1941. This organization offers a yearly opportunity for discussing mutual problems. But how many state conservation agencies have a *trained* public relations man on their staff? Probably not one! Jack Culbreath (1952), then of the U. S. Fish and Wildlife Service, said that, "It is not generally approved to initiate a program in state or federal service under the title of public relations." This attitude has changed but little. Recently a western state conservation department attempted to hire a qualified public relations man. The request never even passed the commission, and another information writer was hired instead.

Some of the State Information and Education sections did, and still do, an excellent job of communicating with their publics. Communications from the publics to management is virtually nonexistent, however, except by chance methods, and herein lies a difference between information and education and public relations. Information and education sections contact their many publics but often fail to communicate and influence. They do little or no research of the publics involved. They still use broadside efforts which allow the messages to fall where they may. Public relations involves more than contact. It includes understanding, two-way communications and action in the right direction.

What of federal natural resource management agencies? They seem worse off than state conservation departments. The Information and Education sections are greatly understaffed, if one exists. The public relations department of the Federal Extension Service employs approximately 300 people of which one-third are professionals. The closest division to natural resources in the Federal Extension Service is agriculture.

About 120 people work in the information office of the U. S. Forest Service in Washington, D. C. The information and education staff of the Soil Conservation Service in Washington, D. C. totals about 50 employees; and of the U. S. Fish and Wildlife Service, also about 50 employees. It must be pointed out that these figures include office help. This poor showing is stressed in an article in *Conservation News* which stated, "The Fish and Wildlife Service is doing a distressingly poor public relations job. Results are essentially nil, frequently negative" (Anonymous, 1959). The current budget of the U. S. Fish and Wildlife Service for public relations-information education work is less than two per cent of the total. They have no magazine, very few motion pictures, little work in radio and television, and less effort is put forth to do this important job than expended by most states.

It currently does seem, however, that most federal and state conservation agencies are starting to wake up to the need of good public relations work and are reacting with more personnel and increased budgets at both staff and line levels. A good example for this optimism is the outstanding job in public relations done by the Bureau of Land Management in the last few years. This agency has taken its place among leaders in natural resource management due to progressive public relations efforts.

Perhaps all natural resource agencies are on the threshold of realizing the importance of good public relations. Perhaps all are starting to use modern techniques to form public opinion to their advantage. With more posted lands, and with many more people who have more money and more time, it seems that there is no other choice.

PRINCIPLES OF PUBLIC RELATIONS

The principles of public relations, as such, are not delineated in the literature. These principles stem from the disciplines of psychology, social sciences, communications and other fields. Ideas and theories are profuse, but in many instances uniformity is lacking. However, the following principles are suggested as being the foundation of good public relations for any organization. Some are explained in this section. Other principles will be explained in detail in later sections. Other principles are self-explanatory. Where needed, the procedures for achieving the principles are also presented.

Every Group or Individual Dealing with People Makes an
Impression Which May Be Good, Bad, or Indifferent

This principle is basic to all others. The impression referred to in the above heading may not be of great significance nor may it necessarily be a lasting one. Nevertheless, each contact or deed, by an individual or attributed to a group, does influence or impress, to some degree, the person or persons contacted in some way. Thus, everything we say or do has a bearing upon the "image" people have of us or of our organization.

Honesty and Truth in Deed and Statement Are Necessary
for Good Public Relations

Every organization has a reputation, as does every individual. To be successful, an agency must have a good reputation and a degree of public confidence which must be earned. Smart publicity will never replace sound management policies and commendable performance in building a solid foundation of good will. Social lubricity and "bar room influence" will never replace open and "above-board" actions and efforts.

Problems and conflicts of an organization are often the result of misunderstandings between the agency and individuals or groups concerned with the agency. With mutual understanding, many of the problems between management and customer, or natural resource organizations and user, cease to exist.

Good Public Relations Is a Prerequisite of Success

No person or business will succeed very long or to any extent if not accepted as a reliable source of the goods sold or services performed. Many more people are unsuccessful because of a lack of "people knowledge" than for a lack of technical knowledge. Relative to a business or organization, if the agency has good relations with their many publics, success is often automatic and assured, assuming good business sense also is present.

Every Organization Deals Differently with Each of Many Publics

Rather than with the Total Public

A public can be defined as a group of people distinguished from other people by the factors held in common. A better definition, perhaps, a public is a group of two or more people with a common interest (Figure 19). A public behaves as a group, although it differs from a group in that the component individuals do not have to be at the same place at the same time.

Figure 19. A public is a group of two or more people with a common interest.

A public may or may not contain sub-publics. For example, biologists may include range biologists, forest biologists, game biologists and fish biologists. These can be divided further into lesser publics. For example, game biologists may include both big game biologists and waterfowl biologists, among others.

Publics fall into one of two categories, natural or unnatural. A natural public has an inherent interest in a situation or issue. An example for a game and fish department would be a sportsmen's club. An unnatural public is one that is not normally interested but may be won over through a planned effort. An example for a game and fish department would be a women's garden club.

Natural publics of an agency can be divided into internal and external publics. An internal public is unmistakably identified with the organization family. All internal publics should be natural publics. An external public is not directly connected with the organization.

Good Public Relations Depend on Favorable Public Opinion

Broadly defined, public opinion means what people think. Psychologists and sociologists have developed the techniques of influencing public opinion. These techniques are quite involved and some are difficult to comprehend. However, they are quite well delineated and are accepted as being valid and not dishonest or illegal. They will be discussed in detail under the heading *The Sociology of Public Relations* (Pages 83 to 96).

Public Opinion Is Based on Culture and Environment

The basis for all public relations techniques and processes is the way that people act and react (Cutlip and Center, 1964). The way we act as individuals, or as groups, primarily is a result of our society and its culture. Society controls our behavior, our progress and our constraints. Man is a creature of his culture or his social heritage. Culture is the man-made environment consisting of customs, traditions and beliefs which influence man's actions and feelings. Cultural tendencies and feelings are learned. They are not passed from generation to generation through biological inheritance. These attitudes are the result of associations and teachings from others in the society, from parents and from schools.

Culture constantly is changing. Cultural changes are forced by alterations in technology, ideology and majority beliefs. Exhaustion of natural resources can be added to this list. It currently seems that culture in our American way of life is considered less important than it used to be. Traditions now often appear to exist only to be broken. These same traditions may have been handed down through centuries and have been considered synonymous with law.

Adequate Communications Are Necessary for Good Public Relations

It is necessary for an organization to tell its publics of the good work being done as well as to determine services which are needed. This must be done to insure understanding and appreciation. When correct information is not furnished or received, false impressions and conclusions often are reached.

The Process of Furthering Good Public Relations

Is a Series of Complex, Intergraded Steps

Good public relations are not the result of a single act or deed. The public relations process requires careful planning of sequential step by step efforts and constant evaluation of results. This process is covered in a later section (Pages 222-226).

TOOLS OF PUBLIC RELATIONS

People who are not familiar with public relations often confuse the tools of public relations with the practice. Public relations, like most disciplines, is based on certain concepts and a philosophy which incorporates these concepts. It is a way of looking at, and handling, the problems which arise between an organization and its publics. Public relations is not advertising and press agentry or publicity, persuasion and propaganda, or even communications. These are the "tools" and are incorporated into the finished product or result. These tools are not the practice itself (Figure 20).

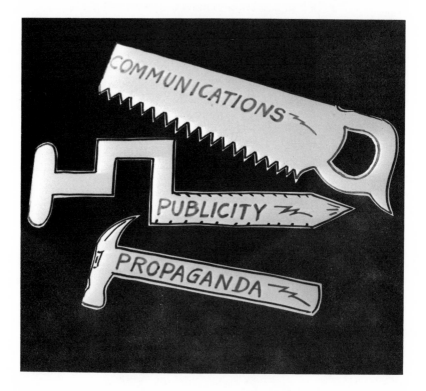

Figure 20. Tools of public relations.

Communications

In our daily lives we often take our ability to communicate for granted. However, the importance of communications and language in our daily lives and in the evolution of man as a social animal cannot be overstated. This is a visible part of public relations. The ability to communicate and to record knowledge sets man apart from the other animals.

36

Communications is a process that is changing constantly. There is no beginning or end (See Figure 44, Page 97). The result of good communication is *understanding*. Assuming the idea is good, if understanding is achieved, then acceptance and good public relations are the result. The principles of communication will be covered in depth in another section (Pages 97 to 108).

Publicity and Advertising

Publicity is not synonymous with public relations or communications, but can be thought of as a tool of public relations. It, too, is a visible part of public relations. Publicity is a contact technique used to obtain, or create, interest in a certain idea or subject, and can be good or bad, favorable or unfavorable. All publicity should be grounded in good public relations and is no more than a spotlight to focus attention (Figure 21). Some publicity is controlled, and some is not. Good publicity should be pursued constantly by a natural resource management organization. It is necessary to keep the publics aware of the agency in the most favorable light and as often as possible. Lesly (1962) stated publicity simply is the intelligent spreading of news, where it exists, and inventing news discriminately, where it does not exist. Bad news can be handled discreetly and good news can be spread widely.

Figure 21. Publicity is a spotlight to focus attention on something.

To illustrate with a wildlife management example, an overabundance of deer should be publicized. The point should be made that the conservation department is doing, and has done, all that is possible to prevent and control the problem. The herd should not have been allowed to increase beyond the capacity of the land to support it. Artificial feeding is not a solution to the problem. The story is not pleasant. There undoubtedly will be adverse publicity, but the wildlife department's position is cleared, and *it is on the offensive.*

Publicity should be carefully planned and controlled. So that nothing is overlooked that should be publicized, an events calendar should be used (Appendix A). The steps in planning are very similar to those presented in planning communications.

Advertising is publicity which is paid for. It is controlled in text and medium by the buyer, because he only purchases so much time or space to be used at his discretion. The agency or sponsor also is well defined since they want the advantages of, and the credit for, the advertising. The motive of advertising, or paid publicity, by the agency then is assumed by the public. Corporate advertising certainly has been important in attracting attention and in selling goods.

Little advertising is done by natural resource agencies. In some instances they are required by law to advertise notices of sales, seasons, and other happenings in local newspapers for a certain number of days. Other than this, a natural resource agency simply is not allowed to spend its allotted dollars on anything except that which is directly concerned with management of the resource. Advertising is not considered to be in this category.

Persuasion and Propaganda

It is necessary to obtain the attention of the individual or group and to hold their interest before techniques of persuasion and propaganda can be used. The story must be told appealingly and in accord with the physical, emotional and mental state of the public that is being approached with the idea of influencing them.

Propaganda (from the Latin "propagare" meaning to propagate or to generate) incorporates many techniques used to influence the attitudes, opinions and beliefs of others toward a specific goal. Propaganda is a conscious and deliberate effort on the part of the manipulator to persuade a public to accept a proposal (Lesly, 1962). Derring (1967) defined it as an attempt to influence others to some predetermined end by appealing to their thoughts or feelings.

War efforts have given an evil connotation to propaganda. Perhaps this is justly so, because many people believe that stressing only one side of an issue is not fair. However, this technique is used widely today by business and government in every day practices. Propaganda is the "engineering of consent," in the language of the public relations man and it is not necessarily bad (Figure 22).

Figure 22. Propaganda is "the willing and conscious effort to influence someone." Propaganda is not necessarily bad or dishonest.

Propaganda and education can be compared. Similarities are that both may be concerned with the creation or change of opinions, both rely upon symbolic methods, both are persuasive and both use truth and facts. Propaganda differs from education in that education is always considered good. Education has less intentional appeal, proposes to develop critical thinking and usually presents both sides without holding back facts. Propaganda often uses prejudices and hidden or disguised methods.

The techniques of propaganda cannot be distinctly separated. One or all can be used in an effort to influence. Albig (1956) listed over 12 different techniques. These are combined here where similarities appear to exist and an attempt is made to illustrate each with a natural resource management example.

The *Band Wagon* approach incorporates the suggestion that everyone is doing it. It is human nature to follow the masses. Many commercials which are heard or seen today use this technique. More people use brand X, take pill Y or drive car Z. Therefore, it must be the best product for the individual to use. As a natural resource example, many of the western states have had either-sex deer seasons. Some of the eastern states have also had them. Either-sex seasons worked for them, so they should work elsewhere.

The technique of censorship, or *Card Stacking*, implies that both sides of an issue are not told, or something is made to appear different than it actually is. This is willful deception. To illustrate, a field trip might be taken to the worst area of range where the most deer have starved. Or a concerted effort may be made to show only the data for the year with the worst deer starvation losses. Mention might not be made of the years when starvation did not occur. The other side of the story is not told or is curtailed greatly. Another example, the reproduction of 64 per cent of the deer was adversely affected, (but only two per cent died).

Name Calling or the use of "loaded" words is common. Many words have a positive or negative meaning. Two words can mean essentially the same thing but have entirely different connotations. To illustrate, "frugal" or "stingy," "elected official" or "politician," "earthy" or "dirty," and "information" and "facts," all have approximately the same meaning, but have different connotations. Some commonly used words in natural resource management and their loaded counterparts are "scent" or "stink," "tree" or "timber," "predator" or "killer," "female" or "doe," "over-used land" or "erosion," "visitor" or "non-resident," and "diet deficiency" or "malnutrition." These words have about the same meaning, but the meaning can be played up or down depending upon the desires of the communicator and the tendencies of the listening or viewing public. Loaded words are not noticed if the trend is to agree with the communicator. They are noticed, and branded as propaganda, if the recipient tends to disagree with the sender.

The *Red Herring* technique is to lead the public down a side track, to divert its attention to favorable conditions or information and away from an unfavorable situation. The manipulator attempts to make the public forget a bad situation (the last either-sex deer season that was not too successful) in the light of a new idea (the money coming into the community from increased numbers of deer hunters) favorable to the cause.

The *Testimonial* method uses the leader-follower idea. Doctors use brand X or take pill Y. They are professionals in relation to intricate workings and needs of the body. They should know which is the least harmful cigarette or best pill. A natural resource example, a person with prestige, knowledge and recognized ability (such as the head of the department of wildlife management at a local university) has accepted an either-sex season as being good game management. Thus, it follows that such a season must be good. A variation of this is the *Plain Folks* technique in which it is pointed out that the common man has accepted the idea. Because many people desire to be part of the group, they also conform. Another variation is the *Transfer* technique where an influential organization, such as the church, is asked to lead or approve of the campaign.

Emotional Appeal is used every day and is a stronger propaganda tool than logical or physical appeal. The weak spot of the audience is determined ahead of time. If the public is a sportsmen's group, the vulnerable area may be that those deer which will die of starvation could be harvested rather than be wasted. If the public is composed of non-sportsmen, the starvation and human decency approach might produce the best results.

Money has universal appeal. If it is possible to show how the loss of the deer will cause hunters not to come to that area in future years; how harvesting more deer, including does, will eventually produce more and larger deer; and how these factors will cause monetary loss or gain, the deer season is a long way toward acceptance in that locality.

Repetition has been used as a propaganda technique in recent wars. "Brain washing" methods employ repetition. Something repeatedly heard or seen makes an impression on the mind. Advertised items, slogans, billboard posters, radio or television announcements and articles in the newspapers will eventually penetrate the life sphere or inner consciousness of a public, if put in front of that public often enough. Repetition, however, can be overdone. The public may get sick and tired of seeing or hearing too much about something. What has been accomplished can be erased, and more, if such an operation is not stopped in time.

Is propaganda dishonest or bad? Not necessarily so. If the proposal is biologically sound and will be good for the resource and the people, it should be promoted so it will be accepted. Opposition to the proposal, and there will be some, will not hesitate to use all of the persuasion or propaganda techniques available. Many good, sound, natural resource proposals have been rejected by publics who were propagandized by unscrupulous groups or individuals with money and a strong desire to stop the proposal.

PUBLICS IN NATURAL RESOURCES MANAGEMENT

Components of each public have their own thoughts, characteristics, and actions. Each public must be treated differently depending upon current states of attitude and other characteristics revealed by research. As much as possible should be known about a public to correctly plan the action to be taken. Information about the people composing the public, such as experiences, culture, history, religion, family conditions, heterogeneity, political affiliation, financial status, who the leaders are and many other items is important.

This information prevents a public relations effort from being aimed at "the public" in general. Instead, the effort can be aimed directly at the target, at a "public," where an attempt to change public opinion will produce the greatest results. We can't shoot first and then draw a target around the hole. If we shoot at a flock of ducks, none fall. If we aim for a single bird, our chances of success are greater.

Each public is in a different state of readiness to accept or reject an idea. This readiness is based on past experiences and many other factors as listed in the preceding paragraphs. To give an example of the probable reaction of similar, yet different, publics, a certain pulping method accepted by loggers in Michigan may be turned down by the timber workers in Montana.

Internal Publics

The internal publics are as important as the external publics, perhaps more so, because the internal acceptance of an idea or item is necessary before the external operation can succeed. Strife or dissention within an organization easily can be detected by those outside the organization. If such is the case, the question is then asked by outsiders, "How can this thing or idea be good if they cannot agree on it themselves?" Hence the idea is rejected by those outside the agency whose concurrence and support are necessary. Many attempts at management, such as open seasons on female pheasants, have gone awry because people within the organization spoke against the idea. Some of the internal publics of three natural resource agencies are listed in Table 2.

Table 2. Internal Publics of Three Natural Resource Agencies

Game and Fish Department	U. S. Forest Service	National Park Service
Administrators: (Directors, Chiefs and Assistants)	Administrators: (National, Regional, Forest Supervisors and Assistants)	Administrators: (National, Regional, Superintendents, Chiefs and Assistants)
Wildlife Conservation Officers	Rangers and Assistants	Rangers and Naturalists
Pittman-Robertson and Dingell-Johnson Personnel	Forest and Range Experiment Station Personnel	Researchers and Biologists
Office Staff	Office Staff	Office Staff
Retired Employees	Forest Service Alumni Association	Retired Employees
License Agents	Dude Ranchers and Fire Wardens	Concessionaires
State Legislators	Federal Legislators	Federal Legislators
Game and Fish Commission	Forest Service Advisory Board	Park Service Advisory Board

Employees

Employees constitute a public that is as important as any other. A worker investing effort and time certainly is as important as is a customer that invests dollars. All workers in any agency, from the custodial help to the "big boss" are important because the outsiders expect an employee to answer questions about his company. One instance is known where the janitor of a Forest Service building also was the commander of the local chapter of the Veterans of Foreign Wars. It is easy to see that this man had contact with and influenced many people. He reflected impressions and attitudes gained while at his daily job. This illustration stresses the fact that all employees are important, and that it is possible to belong to several publics simultaneously.

Good employee relations are essential for a harmonious operation and are expressed in morale, conduct, and quality and quantity of production or services rendered. For internal happiness and efficiency, a climate of mutual understanding is necessary. This climate is built or destroyed by the day-to-day actions of those in charge.

If an employee is told why changes are being made, and if the reasons seem logical to him, the changes usually will be accepted. Any employee should have a chance to voice his opinions, especially if the action being considered will affect him. But once that policy or an action is adopted, and the worker has been included in the deliberations, it then is fair to insist that he comply without complaint.

Wooding (personal communication) presented the information in Table 3 at a lecture on public relations at the University of Michigan. In this table are nine items considered to be most important to employees for the well-being of an organization. These items were rated in accordance to their comparative importance by employee and employer. Others (Pfiffner, 1951; Morgan, 1956; Lesly, 1962) are not in complete agreement, but the general trend coincides.

Table 3. Employee and Employer Ratings of Nine Employee Requirements

Requirements	Employee Rating	Employer Rating
1. Wages and Fringe Benefits	5	1
2. Working Conditions	4	4
3. Stability or Security	9	2
4. Advancement Possibilities	7	3
5. Loyalty of the Organization	8	7
6. Recognition and Appreciation	1	8
7. Status and Participation	2	6
8. Interesting Work	6	5
9. Help on Personal Problems	3	9

The employee ranks recognition and appreciation first on the scale. It is rated eighth by employers. Workers need to know that hard work and good performance will be recognized and appreciated. They need to be needed. One way recognition and appreciation may be shown is for the agency to present merit awards for outstanding service or for years of performance. This shows, with a material gift, that recognition is present. The individual also is placed in the limelight for his accomplishments. Pfiffner (1951) suggested that it may be better to use objective performance than subjective judgment in choosing individuals for awards. Continual, active recognition of good performance of employees by administrative personnel is necessary.

Status and participation were rated second by employees and sixth by employers. Each worker should be treated as an individual and be made to feel an important, intricate part of the organization team.

Help on personal problems was rated third by employees and ninth by management. If a worker's personal life is not happy, he will not do a good job. Most large business organizations have personal counselling services for their empoyees. Complaints or problems are heard by an individual or a grievance committee, and help is given or proper action is taken. For example, credit unions and loan funds can provide financial aid when needed.

Working conditions were rated fourth by both administrators and employees. An office or work area should be comfortable with adequate equipment and facilities. The field man needs adequate time and good equipment to do the job demanded of him. Optimum work loads are necessary. Too little work may be more harmful than too much. Trouble, rumors and prejudice result in either case.

Wages and fringe benefits, ranked first by employers, were rated fifth by employees. This shows that monetary benefits are not everything to the worker. However, an adequate salary is mandatory, as are good fringe benefits. Chances to improve performance and to qualify for advancement should be made possible through company scholarships, education possibilities, educational leaves and in-service training schools. Other items, such as uniforms, low-cost housing, liberal expense accounts, vacations, vehicles, insurance and retirement provisions are also important. Equally important are fringe or social benefits for the employee's family. These promote worker satisfaction and group solidarity.

Workers must find their work interesting (rated sixth by employees, fifth by employers) because drudgery breeds dissatisfaction, and job satisfaction is extremely important. Most natural resource workers would not be in their positions unless the work were interesting and enjoyable. Salaries are low compared to most other professions, so money isn't paramount. This also points to the necessity of workers being suited to their jobs. An instance is known of a good, capable, efficient biologist who passed high on an examination and was promoted to an administrative position in the central office. In his new position the biologist wasn't happy, and as a result did not do a good job. The individual suffered, other workers suffered, the organization's image suffered, and the publics the organization served also suffered.

A rating of seventh was given by employees, third by employers, to advancement possibilities. How important this is depends a great deal upon the nature of the individual. Some workers are happy without advancement as long as permanence is assured and talents and abilities are recognized. Certain individuals are appalled at living in big cities or doing a different job with more responsibilities.

If they were unhappy, they would not do a good job and generally, should not be moved. Again, it is pointed out that each case must be judged on its own merits.

Advancement should be based on ability, performance and examinations, and not on politics or an individual administrator's likes and dislikes. Employees should know why one was chosen over another for advancement.

Loyalty of the organization to the employees was rated eighth and seventh by employees and employers, respectively. Employees need to know that if something should go amiss, the agency will do everything possible to support them.

Although still considered important, stability and security were rated last by employees and second by employers. Protection from injustice and recognition and appreciation are all that most employees ask. State and federal civil service organizations, labor unions and tenure all help to establish job stability and security. To know that action is based upon merit, and that one's job is protected, can mean much.

Retired employees or alumni groups should not be ignored as an internal public. Such a group can have a great deal of influence, good or bad, on current employees, and their knowledge and experiences can be valuable. Retirees should be kept informed and in turn can help the organization keep abreast of current employee attitudes.

New employees should be oriented as soon as possible and as completely as possible. Lahr (1953) stated that a six-month training period is necessary for all new employees. This allows a chance to become well acquainted and oriented. This type of orientation and training in all phases of the organization's operations is now being done by the Arizona Game and Fish Department (Cosper, personal communication), the Colorado Wildlife Division, many other state conservation agencies, by some branches of the U. S. Fish and Wildlife Service and by the National Park Service.

The researcher in a natural resource agency may present a special headache. He is a specialist and is trained to do a certain job. He often lacks conception of the importance of other happenings and positions. Many investigators lack patience when their findings aren't used immediately (they should not be ignored). Implementation of research results, like any other action, must be accepted by other departments within the agency, then by outside publics. Before this is done, the findings must be weighed as to how they will affect the enterprise as a whole. For example, it may be foolish to poison the fish in a lake (at a certain time) to remove undesirable species. Research may prove this feasible but public pressure may be too strong at the time that it would be unwise to carry out the operation. Or, perhaps a dense stand of pinon-juniper is to be chained to open it up and allow grass and browse to grow. This is according to research findings. On the other hand, if this stand of scrub timber is destroyed, an erosion problem may result. It would be folly to put the results of this research into practice in this area.

Researchers often do not or are not interested in getting the message to others than their own group, yet these research results are the basis for most of our game and fish legislation. Pengelly (1959) wondered why we entrust the selling to uninterested amateurs (in this case the researchers) if selling is such an important job? The job of translating research results from technical jargon to a usable, understandable message should be considered as important as the research itself, and should be a function of the Information and Education or Public Relations Department. In most instances the researcher should not be expected to make that translation. Usually he does not want to, nor is he trained to do the job.

Certainly research is important. Research in the natural resource professions has provided the modern techniques, ideas and principles in use today. There always will be need for research and researchers to provide additional knowledge plus new and better ways of getting the management job accomplished. But, all the investigations and researchers in the world will not advance management one bit beyond our effectiveness in communicating the results.

Good two-way communications within an agency are a must. An employee should be told by the organization of the benefits he has or he may not be aware of them. In turn, the agency must know how the workers feel and be aware of trouble so it can be curbed.

The extent to which all employee interests are satisfied measures the attitude of the employee to the organization. Business shares profits over and above costs as an added inducement toward compatability with its employees. Natural resource organizations are public agencies and cannot do this. Therefore, natural resource agencies *must* be above reproach and *must* do a better job of setting policies, informing their employees and in keeping their employees generally satisfied. Good employee relations are reflected in morale.

Administrators

Administrators, although an important part of the employee public, are considered separately because of the effect exerted upon those whom they supervise. Supervisors must attain and maintain the faith, loyalty and respect of the workers for whom they are responsible. The ability to accomplish this not only hinges on the technical knowledge of the individual supervisor, but also depends upon his ability to stimulate interest, to influence opinion, to control people and to "get along" with others; in short, it depends upon his ability to practice good public relations.

Clearly established policies must govern the actions of all employees, including supervisors. To illustrate, if conservation agency employees are prohibited from hunting during a certain portion of the season or from using an agency car for certain purposes, the administrators also should abide by those rules. Public relations men should be part of the management voice in policy making decisions.

Line supervisors, those directly over the majority of the employees, are generally the weakest administrators in an organization. This seems to be true in the natural resource professions too. These men are often older employees. They usually are not trained in supervision and may lack entirely the qualities needed for doing the job. The organization suffers as these men may not have the ability to advance and agencies are reluctant to move them back.

An administrator needs three types of knowledge: technical knowledge, knowledge of human nature and conceptual knowledge. All are important.

Technical knowledge of the job is a prime requisite because poor supervision puts undesired pressure on the workers, which, in turn, brings about resentments and causes low efficiencies. If a supervisor has adequate technical knowledge, he will have respect and prestige for that knowledge in the eyes of those he supervises. As Swift (1960) said, a conservation administrator should be a working conservationist first and a talking conservationist second. It certainly helps if a supervisor knows how to handle the job before he tries to handle the people working on that job for him.

Knowledge of human nature is as important as technical knowledge. Talent is needed to reprimand, adhere to policies, give orders, still attain the desired results and have the respect of those supervised. Changes often need to be introduced without provoking resistance.

Many authors stated that no individual should ever be reprimanded in front of others. This is a common error of administrators. When necessary, the worker should be reprimanded privately and the "talking to" should be accompanied by praise or a compliment. Disciplinary measures should never be taken until a complete investigation has been made as to fairness and necessity. Civil service organizations have created problems at times because a worker cannot be discharged except for "just cause." Usually this cause must be extreme and well documented before action can be taken. The presently used, and obvious solution is a transfer to "Siberia" (an undesirable location) which may be worse than being fired.

Knowledge of human nature requires that the administrator understand and like people. He must have the power to motivate.

The administrator must have the interest of his employees and his job foremost at all times. He should not let stereotypes or preconceived attitudes about others influence his judgment. Stereotypes can be difficult to erase. An example which is typical in natural resource work, held by some of the older employees, might be that all college "kids" think they know all of the answers. This isn't always, or even usually, true. Each individual and situation must be evaluated and handled on the merits present.

A good administrator must be human and a humanitarian. He needs to be a semantician and able to communicate. Actions are inherent or cultural. Some traits may be inborn, but most behavior stems from cues in the environment. All people differ in temperament, ability and stability. They react differently to praise and criticism. A good administrator must realize these differences and act accordingly.

Every organization has informal as well as formal leaders. This internal structure may be referred to as internal social organization. Informal leaders have status and power to influence, although they may not be leaders from the standpoint of position in the formal organization. An informal hierarchy is characterized by tension, cliques and dissatisfaction. Included are all relations and interrelations of people in the hierarchy that grow out of the natural tendencies to associate and behave as a group.

The health of this informal organization is as important as that of the formal organization. A proper balance of power and communications with informal groups can be of material aid to the formal organizational operation. Informal power will rise up to resist harsh and unfair management practices, such as authoritarian leadership. This informal power also is important in the struggle for leadership between two factions or individuals. Informal lines of communication, such as rumors and the "grapevine," can be extremely effective.

An organization of any size may have conflict, be it external in part, or strictly internal. Internal conflict might occur between sections within the organization, such as between conservation officers and biologists; or the conflict might be between individuals. Some degree of conflict may be "healthy" as it is a sign that things are being done and noticed. Some conflict serves to keep the agency on its toes and destroys complacency.

Conceptual knowledge is the ability to recognize the forces and pressures which impinge on an organization and which shape its destiny. A project must be judged as a whole, and its entire effect, both immediate and in the future, upon the organization must be calculated. Most operations are like a chain reaction with one reaction stimulating another. To illustrate, a proposed hunting season may have far reaching effects on landowner-sportsman attitudes in years to come. It may be better not to hold a season in a particular year. Perhaps a better public relations foundation could be constructed and the season held the next year. A good administrator must be able to evaluate the far-reaching effects of any action or operation.

Catalyst Publics

Concessionaires for the National Park Service, and dude ranchers for the Forest Service, were presented in Table 2 (page 43) as being analogous to the license agents public for a game and fish department. These groups constitute a potentially important ally or enemy of any natural resource organization. The license agents are usually business operators who sell hunting and fishing licenses as a sideline to their regular business. Concessionaires and dude ranchers sell goods, lodging, rent horses and provide other services for visitors to parks and forests. These people have been neglected as a communications link between the agency and sportsmen or visitors. These groups undoubtedly have great influence on the ultimate users of the resource. Their influence should be utilized by the natural resource agency involved.

License agents, concessionaires and dude ranchers can be likened to stockbrokers for a corporation. Cutlip and Center (1964) suggested stockbrokers should be wooed and won. Natural resource management organizations should treat their "stockbrokers" the same way. These people need to be made to feel they are closely associated with the agency and are a part of it. They need to be "courted" as other publics are. A banquet, meeting or conference to inform them of happenings would contribute to winning their confidence. The reasons behind actions and regulations should be explained clearly and simply so that accurate information can be passed on to license buyers or visitors. Explanations of happenings and regulations should be made through frequent and regular contact by the field force.

License agents, and to some extent concessionaires and dude ranchers, should be included automatically on all mailing lists and should receive all newsletters. More and better aids (posters, displays, and advertising) should be given to these people to assist them in selling the organization and its values.

Since they have direct contact with the customers, the views, feelings and attitudes of these catalyst publics often reflect those of the sportsmen or visitors. Therefore, the opinions of these groups should be polled before establishing policies. A survey of the attitudes of these publics often will reflect attitudes of the users of the natural resources.

John J. Mooty, while a graduate student at Colorado State University, investigated the place of the license agents as an internal public (Mooty, 1967). Although his study specifically was relative to a catalyst public for a wildlife management organization, his suggestions are valid for any natural resource management agency. As a result of his research, Mooty made the following suggestions:

1. A decision should be made as to the place the catalyst public (license agents, concessionaires, dude ranchers) is to occupy in the overall program. Are these people simply vendors of goods and services, or are they to be part of the organization? Assuming they are to be part of the organization, the following is recommended.

2. These publics should be composed of carefully selected, qualified, capable, interested individuals. Quality and interest are essential.

3. Successful communications within the organization and including these catalyst publics are necessary. Efficient operation and benefits for the parent organization depend upon mutual trust. These publics should be completely informed of rules and regulations and the reasons for the rules and regulations.

4. A continuing effort is necessary to make these publics feel a part of the organization. Periodic contact by agency personnel plus news releases and other materials help to achieve this unity of purpose and group.

5. Information given to these publics from the organization and its personnel should be understandable. People composing these catalyst publics are, for the most part, not professional natural resource managers. A complicated, technical message may alienate rather than inform them.

6. The duties and responsibilities involved in selling goods or services for a natural resource management agency should be kept as uncomplicated as possible. Equitable and just monetary return to the seller to pay for his time and effort is important.

Governing Boards

Most natural resource organizations operate under a commission or governing board of some type, such as the typical game and fish commission for a game and fish department. A typical governing board consists of from 4 to 10 people; theoretically, it is nonpolitical; usually it includes the governor as an administrator or an ex-officio member; and it is composed of people interested in natural resources. All members of an advisory board should be treated with courtesy and respect.

The primary duty of the governing board should be to advise or to establish policies. A policy can be a guide to conduct or a pathway to action. It can be a shelter to hide behind in case of trouble. Policies should be based on information and advice from department workers and other publics. The importance of two-way communications is obvious. If information to aid in policy formation does not come from the publics to be served, how can these policies be established to serve the best interests of all? Good public relations start with good policies.

Current public thinking, action to be taken, possible impact and reaction should be a part of planning and policy making. Therefore, a public relations specialist should be present to aid in the planning of policies and in predicting the results.

Policies should be available to workers at all times in a clear, simple, concise manual in which only essentials are included. A policy manual should not become clogged with "red tape." Shomon (1959) said that only 10 of 48 state conservation departments had written policy manuals at that time. The Wildlife Management Institute (1968) showed 39 of 50 states had a policy manual. Eleven did not.

Members of an organization should be informed of the reasons behind policies. This should be done quickly and simply so there is no doubt why a policy was established. Communications channels for informing personnel should be established at the time a policy is established. Unless this is done, the policy is not complete.

The supervisor and agency personnel are responsible for carrying out policies established by the commission or governing body. Internal strife results when the agency (department) and the governing board (commission) try to do each other's jobs. Too many commissions interfere with administration, management activities and personnel matters. Commission members should realize that their job is an avocation and not a vocation. They should leave the action program to professionals in the field (Gilbert and Hill, 1964). The authority of the director to handle personnel and operations must be accepted, respected and maintained by commission members.

After a policy has been established, it should be followed and not questioned by the director, chief, supervisor or other employees. Once the policy is firm, all individuals must close ranks and adhere to the rule, regardless of individual ideas (Cain, 1960).

Boards of directors of some businesses have labor leaders and workers' representatives present at policy-making sessions. Why should not game and fish commission meetings have representatives of conservation officers, biologists, fish managers, information and education personnel and others, present to speak in their own behalf instead of through supervisors who may not know the situation? This would be a real asset to modern wildlife management. Usually the only department officials who attend the typical game and fish commission meeting are the director and some of the division heads. A similar situation also may exist for other natural resource agencies. It also is a good idea to be aware of the policies of other agencies. This adds knowledge and strength to any position of authority.

Board members or commissioners should be aware of, and should participate in, the natural resource agency's public relations programs. They should see the position of the organization as a whole and should not be a local representative out to "get what they can" for a small area. The board members should be treated as agency members and should conduct themselves accordingly. Policies pertain to them also as they are part of the organization.

A "Short Course For Commissioners" was started at Colorado State University in 1965. Specifically designed for Game, Fish and Park Commissioners of the Western States, it has also been open to state wildlife federation members and personnel of other land use agencies such as the Bureau of Land Management, the Forest Service and the Soil Conservation Service. The three-day school is designed for the layman working in natural resource management (such as a Game, Fish and Parks Commissioner) or as a refresher course for technically trained people who have been away from school for some time.

At first some state directors thought that a little knowledge for their commission members would be dangerous; that they would think they "knew it all." However, such hasn't proved to be the case. Attendance has increased and participants and administrators alike seem to be satisfied with the offerings. Basic concepts and new ideas are stressed, and the effort is now self-supporting (Gilbert, 1967). The course has been conducted for 11 years straight as of 1976.

Legislators

Legislators at state or national levels should be considered an internal public. These elected officials often control the budget, create licenses, establish rules and fees and approve land exchanges. For some state and federal natural resource management agencies they will have more or less authority than for others.

The legislative public should be kept informed constantly. Newsletters and other published materials should be sent to them. Personal contact with legislators at critical times and on critical issues should be made only by high echelon administrators who are confident and capable.

Officials of the natural resource organization should be aware of the legislator's attitudes and past voting record. This is essential so that techniques of influence can be used to facilitate desired action at the proper time. The reason behind needed legislation, if explained properly and at the right time, will do much to obtain the desired results. Good natural resource management is good politics because so many people are interested. Therefore, good management should be sold easily to any politician. Many satisfied people mean many votes at election time.

Employees of a natural resource department should not be expected to act as servants to legislators. However, the influential position held by legislators should be recognized by all. Dealings

with this public will be presented in detail under the heading
Politics and Natural Resources on Pages 90 to 96.

External Publics

External publics are those groups of individuals with a common
interest that are not part of the organization. Important external
publics of natural resource agencies include the communities where
personnel are located, the harvesters, outdoor enthusiasts or visitors,
ranchers and farmers, schools and youth groups, personnel of other
land-use agencies, newspaper people and the operators of radio and
television stations.

It is well to re-emphasize several important points. Public relations processes are going on, good or bad, at all times. A wagon
can only coast downhill and public relations go the same way unless effort is constantly put forth to push them uphill. Also, good external public relations can only follow good internal public relations.

Communities

A community is an aggregate of many publics living in close
association. It is a social group of any size whose members live in a
specific locality. A community's members often have a comparable
culture and a common government. Our nation is composed of communities, and state and national opinions originate in communities.

Community relations can be considered the same as neighborli-
ness. Legal, political and biological organizations all can be the
reason for community formation and maintenance. Geographical
location or common environment can be responsible for a group
belonging to a community.

The trend of big businesses, large organizations and some natural resource agencies has been to decentralize authority and to
attempt to become a part of a community. In addition to increasing
operating efficiency, decentralization reduces the air of superiority
and bureaucracy which accompanies large organizations. The local
sponsorship idea is now used for the same reasons. Your automobile
dealer sponsors the news (but the automobile company pays for
the sponsorship). Most people automatically equate large organizations with manipulation and control. Thus, people tend to feel more
favorably toward smaller organizations.

An organization of any kind has personality, friendliness, a reputation and prestige, just as does an individual. These qualities, on
the positive or negative side, are the result of the agency's relations
with the community. The acceptance of an agency by a community
is based on the attitudes, actions and acceptability of the agency's
employees.

Both the community and the organization can expect fulfillment of certain conditions. The agency wants good employees, fair treatment, adequate transportation and housing, police protection, good schools and churches, hospitals, friends and a way to satisfy cultural and social needs. The community, in turn, expects and demands jobs for residents, adequate wages, taxes, patronage of local businesses, contributions to community causes, leadership, a good neighbor and participation in civic efforts.

Specific ways in which any conservation agency might participate in community affairs include free use of equipment, such as airplanes and snowmobiles when needed for emergencies; formation of a rescue team; agency personnel helping and joining service clubs, such as Lions, Rotary and P. T. A.; and personnel becoming part of community affairs, such as becoming scout leaders (Figure 23).

Figure 23.   Agency equipment can be used in rescue work, thus aiding public relations in the community.

Other businesses, such as oil companies and automobile manufacturers, often have a committee to handle public relations at the community level. The organizations use many millions of dollars a year to finance education, sponsor conferences, build facilities, bring cultural events to the community, promote safety and offer career guidance in schools. Personnel of the businesses act as chairmen of drives and campaigns for community betterment and are encouraged to hold public office. These businesses operate speakers bureaus and finance motion pictures, radio shows and television shows not necessarily dealing with their product. Community effort awards are donated by the business. Contests for community causes are funded and promoted. The agencies sponsor floats in parades and displays at community gatherings. They spend many dollars on beautification, playgrounds, parks and on pollution control. Employees are given leaves of absence at full or partial salary for education and self-betterment. These employees belong to the community.

These large companies offer help and advice to the community in many ways. The community accepts them, has faith in them and likes them. Deposits are made in the "Bank of Good Will" and can be drawn upon in time of need.

Efforts used in community relations of a business are not all applicable to a natural resource management agency, especially a government operated one. Nevertheless, most natural resource management agencies could do much more to further the cause of good public relations at the community level.

Brion (1967) gave an example of a business, in this instance a construction company, using an ingenious idea and doing a little bit extra to promote good public relations at the community level. A landmark building was torn down and the company was under severe criticism for this and for creating an unsightly hole. A fence barrier was constructed for safety while the construction was proceeding. Holes were cut in the barrier fence for people to use in observing the construction in progress. In addition, segments of the fence were portioned out to community clubs, service groups and schools for use in a company sponsored art contest. The whole idea was publicized in newspapers and good will was won instead of lost.

One instance is known in which a game and fish department had particularly poor community relations. State property was stolen, personalities clashed, private property was closed to all hunting and fishing and a general feeling of distrust existed. A capable individual moved in, and in a short time he had organized scout troops, opened and developed state lands for visitation and picnicking and joined the Lions Club in the small town. Soon he was accepted by the community. A few years later he was voted "father of the year" by the local Cow Belles, a nationwide association of stockmen's wives. In this livestock-industry dominated state this was an unprecedented event which shows what good community relations can accomplish.

Before an organization moves employees into a community, it should determine how the community will react. What are the obstacles to overcome? Will agency personnel and their families be happy there? Will religion, race or beliefs be a barrier? Are cultural and social outlets adequate? How about schools, recreation, youth opportunities and shopping facilities? These and other factors, are important and are changing constantly in an area.

Administrators must realize that the organization's presence will exert new forces in a community. The balance of a community, especially if small, may be upset by new buildings, an influx of new people and greater pressures on existing facilities. Will a higher, or lower, salaried class of people upset the present residents? The repercussions of these and other pressures must be anticipated.

There is no place in community relations for secrecy. A "closed door" policy should be avoided unless secrecy is absolutely necessary. Fear, antagonism and suspicion result when something is not understood. Cooperation is essential and an "open door" policy of clarity and understanding can promote much good will. Projects and proposals will be accepted if they are explained and understood as being for the benefit of the community.

The efforts and values of a natural resource organization to the community should be publicized to bring about better community relations. All local media should be used as equitably as possible to bring this publicity to all community sub-publics, from children to the city council. Opportunities to publicize natural resource management, such as chances to give speeches and programs, should be accepted.

A natural resource management agency should take a stand on controversies when possible. For example, should a large water impoundment be built or not? Research must put this stand within bounds of organizational policy and, if possible, in accord with the community majority. If these two stipulations cannot be met, it may be better to say nothing. Leadership often can be taken by the conservation agency in attempting to influence the community toward the thinking that is beneficial to the community, the natural resources and the natural resource management agency.

Harvesters

The harvesters of the natural resources are one of the most valuable, yet most difficult, publics of those encountered by a conservation agency. They can rise up in wrath against the natural resource agency or the agency's opponents. They think they run the organization, and in a way, they do! They are the paying customers, or the stockholders, of the natural resource agency.

Harvesters (sportsmen, visitors, users in general) must be cultivated, indoctrinated and educated. To avoid or to neglect them is folly. The importance of selling any program to sportsmen or users is as important as any of the technical research that precedes a management effort. As with all publics, the entire, long-range, land-use, water and soil aspects of conservation should be stressed with harvesters wherever possible. Disagreement should be expected, but this can be counteracted by showing and telling plain and simple facts; and, the more facts, the better. If the basis and principles of good management are understood, a harmonious solution often is well on the way.

The large lumber companies and tree farms have found it hard to convince people they aren't denuding the forest. To do so would be the end of the business! The same is true of other natural resource management agencies. If the resource is destroyed, the company or agency is out of business. It is axiomatic, then, that the organization will want to perpetuate the resource and will manage it as wisely as possible.

Many of the larger, private tree farms and lumber companies, such as Georgia-Pacific and Weyerhauser, spend large sums of money publicizing their good work. They also try to create good will for their company by cooperating with other user publics, such as campers, picnickers, hunters, fishermen and hikers. These companies welcome people on their lands in certain areas and under certain restrictions. The companies even provide some of the facilities the users require. The companies print maps and aid in emergencies. And, the companies publicize their efforts in many ways so they will get public relations credit for the work they do.

Relative to governmental agencies and public lands in natural resource management; hunters and fishermen, the harvesters of wildlife; and park visitors, the users of national and state parks, offer more of a problem than do the harvesters of timber and grass. The forest ranger usually knows the stock owners or the sawmill operators. However, the harvesters of wildlife and the users of parks are a mass of unknown, often uneducated (in good harvesting methods and courtesies) and occasionally uncaring individuals (Figure 24).

Figure 24.   An unscrupulous camper can cause a landowner to post his land against all trespassers or users.

Harvesters of the natural resources can lobby legally for laws. Employees of most of the natural resource management organizations, as public employees, cannot. State and national wildlife federations have done a great deal to bring about the recognition by legislators of wildlife management and conservation in general. The harvesters should be courted for the help they can render in bringing about desired legislation.

Harvesters or users should be treated with courtesy and respect. This is especially true in any law enforcement work. Why should the publics pay the salaries of agency personnel only to have the agency people police them? Some authorities believe that all natural resources law enforcement work should be turned over to the sheriff's office or a police force. Perhaps the best solution is preventative law enforcement through education as to why the conservation laws should not be broken. A "game warden" or conservation officer should have a college degree including courses in public relations.

Law enforcement should always be fair. Impartiality is good, but each case has its own merits. An inquiry of "may I see your license" is better than "do you have a license" because it does not imply doubt. It is possible to make either a good friend or a vicious enemy for the parent organization, depending on how borderline cases are handled. For example, unknowing violators of big game tagging regulations can be hauled into court and fined. The department probably will have made a few dollars, some enemies and certainly no friends. Or the violators, and it is a violation of the law, can have the regulation explained to them in a courteous manner. They can be told why the law exists. Then they can be made to tag their animal in the correct way. Thus, friends are made for the department (Figure 25).

Landowner-sportsmen relations offer a particularly difficult problem in wildlife management public relations work. This conflict directly influences the conservation department in many ways, and the conservation agency often acts as the "middle man" in attempting to settle differences.

Many attempts at facilitating good landowner-sportsmen relations have been described. Titus *et al.* (1939) described the Williamston plan of landowner-sportsmen cooperation started in Michigan in 1929. This appears to be the first attempt at organized sportsmen-landowner cooperation. Leopold *et al.* (1939) advocated a test which must be passed before a hunting license could be purchased. Wagar (1958) suggested that a firearms safety examination should be included. Shick (no date) suggested that rewards offered by sportsmen for apprehension of violators is an effective technique. Throckmorton (1958) found that 9 of 39 states had an organization or council to coordinate efforts between sportsmen and landowners aimed at better understanding.

Bromley (1945) explained a working approach to the land-owner-hunter problem in New York. The plan, called "The Fish and Wildlife Management Act," was simple, easy to manage, financially sound, protected the landowner and provided remuneration. Land areas were leased from private landowners for long periods and small sums were paid by the state conservation department for the leases. These areas were posted by department personnel to mark boundaries. This method, still in operation today, also allowed the lands to be used for research and demonstration.

Chalk *et al.* (1940) described a rancher-sportsmen council in Utah that helped resolve differences relating to big game manage-

Figure 25.   Courtesy and respect are especially important in law enforcement work.

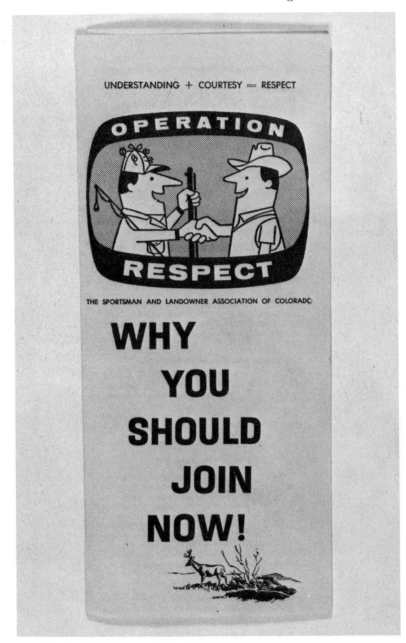

Figure 26. "Operation Respect," The Landowner-Sportsman Association in Colorado, uses the slogan "Understanding + Courtesy = Respect."

ment, specifically elk damage and control. This council was com-posed of sportsmen's representatives, delegated personnel of natural resource agencies and landowners. The writers stressed that problems must be handled on the local level, as each case is different. Proper results were achieved by discussing the problems, by judicious posting, by deputizing landowners to help control violators, by issuing booklets and other publicity and by issuance of hunting permits signed by the landowners.

The Izaak Walton League of America has advocated good hunter-landowner relations with their H A T (Hunt America Time) program. Some states have organized sportsmen groups that pledge themselves to gentlemanly conduct. A card identifies the member. This plan seems to have much merit.

Colorado's "Operation Respect" has been the pattern for similar operations in other states. The slogan, "Courtesy + Understanding = Respect" is on their stationery and cards (Figure 26). A card system is used to identify the potential hunter. The cards are left with the landowner, and a contact has been made between individuals. They have had a chance to become acquainted and to exchange ideas or rules and regulations so that understanding is achieved. The landowner knows who is on his property and he can tell them what to do and where to hunt.

The Colorado Wildlife Federation, an affiliate of the National Wildlife Federation, recently adopted the following "Sportsmen's Guarantee" against doing damage (Figure 27). Each member of the Colorado Wildlife Federation carries a card which states that the organization will pay up to $100.00 if a member damages pri-

Application for Membership
Colorado Wildlife Federation, Inc.

I wish to support the objectives and purposes of this organization.

Member's Signature

_____
Name

_____
Street

_____
City

My signature certifies that I will uphold the Laws and Regulations of Colorado and will adhere to the Sportsman's Guarantee Against Property Damage.

Application for:

Associate Membership _____

Affiliate Membership _____

_____ Membership _____

_____
Secretary of Club

From _____, 19_____

To _____, 19_____

SPORTSMAN'S GUARANTEE AGAINST PROPERTY DAMAGE

It should be understood that the Guarantee shown on this card is **not** an insurance policy. It is, when presented to a landowner, a promise to conduct yourself as a sportsman, backed up by your fellow members of the Colorado Wildlife Federation who have faith in your good sportsmanship. We do not believe we have a member who thinks so little of the friendship of his fellow members as to violate this faith. The Colorado Wildlife Federation has confidence that our member, whose name appears on the front of this card, is a gentleman and a sportsman. May we request that you allow him to hunt and fish on your property, with the understanding that if he in any way damages your property or livestock, and refuses to make settlement, we will, upon presentation of his name and proper proof of damages, pay for said damages up to the amount of $100.00.
Good only for the life of membership period shown on opposite side.

Figure 27.   The   Colorado   Wildlife   Federation's   "Sportsman's   Guarantee" against damage to private property.

vate property. The Colorado Federation has not yet been asked to pay one claim!

Nearly all plans bring forth the idea that remuneration to the landowner for producing wildlife is desirable. One wonders how fair this is? The farmer or rancher should view the game as another crop, but in many instances the game is there in spite of the landowner, not because of him. Yet, the right of controlling trespass and potential damage to private property cannot be denied.

Another problem, and a good opportunity to promote good sportsmen relations with many publics, is that of hunter safety. Brown (1959) described a hunter safety program that has been successful in Idaho. This program, as most other hunter safety programs, was under the auspices of the National Rifle Association. Hunter safety programs currently are being conducted by nearly every state. The Wildlife Management Institute (1968) reported 40 of 50 state conservation departments (80%) had a hunter safety program of some type. Many states require such instruction by law.

Figure 28. Big game seasons are presented to interested groups and individuals in Colorado before being set by the Commission.

In Idaho, the instructors were trained by department personnel. Awards were given to the instructors on the basis of numbers taught. Accidents were greatly reduced, sportsmen's maliciousness and carelessness were lessened and better cooperation resulted between landowners and sportsmen. Many landowners and natural resource management agencies agree that the nuisance problem created by sportsmen really is more important than the damage they do.

Sportsmen and landowners should have a voice in setting the seasons for harvesting wildlife. However, they must be made to realize that they do not set the seasons in a legal sense. Some states involve sportsmen by presenting the big game seasons to them for their comments before the dates are firm (Figure 28). What the sportsmen, through their federation and the landowners and stockmen, through their associations, say may not make a difference, but the groups do feel included. Cosper (1958) said that selling the program to sportsmen is as important and must be as carefully planned as the game season itself.

Small groups of sportsmen or stockmen can be used as testing groups. This is the public relations practitioner's "trial balloon" technique. One says, "We are thinking of . . ." Then watches the reaction of this small group. If accepted, the idea or season might be tried on a larger scale.

It should be realized, too, that other people and groups, the opposition in some cases, will also be in contact with the same groups the natural resource management agency is trying to influence. Therefore, the agency must keep them informed and be kept informed at all times. The good job of natural resource management that is being done should be publicized. All media should be used and every opportunity taken to show all publics that we know how to manage their resources and are doing a good job of it.

Like any other public, sportsmen should be praised when they do a good job. Colorado did this for many years by awarding a "sportsman of the week" prize (Appendix B). To win, a hunter or fisherman must have done a good deed or acted in a manner which furthered the cause of good sportsmanship. The individual had to be nominated by one of the Game and Fish Department's men. The winner then received a one-year subscription to the department magazine, *Colorado Outdoors*, and a binder for the magazines. Special honors also were given the winner on radio and in the newspapers. Recognition was provided for good sportsmanship. How effective or important this was, is not known. However, it undoubtedly did some good toward furthering the cause of good sportsmanship.

The leaders, formal or informal, of the harvester publics should be known, contacted, and sold on the item or idea desired. These leaders, be they bankers or janitors, cattlemen or beet-growers, must be used to reach their respective groups. They must be kept informed. If an agency works through the leaders of a public, the leaders will be more likely to work for the agency. They, in turn, will influence their followers. A majority of the harvester public simply does not care one way or the other about most issues. The agency, or opposition, whichever makes the first and most effective contact, has the greatest chance to succeed.

As with most publics, harvesters, including hunters and fishermen, need help to realize their potential. The power they can exert, if organized, is tremendous. In most areas, however, they are not organized. Rod and gun clubs seem to limp along, doing nothing, unless someone comes to their aid. That someone should be from the conservation agency and should sell the agency's principles and practices.

Conservation clubs must be kept from starting greedy, selfish projects or those which flout good game management principles. Some examples are promotion of bounties, artificial propagation, introduction of unsuited exotics, most artificial feeding (Figure 29) and prizes for the largest kill or catch. In many instances the so-called "kids' fish-ponds" projects, which are so popular, do more

Figure 29. Artificial feeding of game animals usually is not good game management and should be discouraged as a club project.

harm than good. The crowded conditions and prizes offered for the first, largest, or most, really do not further the cause of wise management and good sportsmanship. Too often those of the younger generation aren't particularly interested in learning how to fish, where to fish, the sport involved, or courtesy for their fellow anglers. They want fish, prizes and recognition. The sight of children scooping trout out of gutters with their hands certainly does not promote the ideals of good natural resource management. The gutters may be filled with water and the project promoted by the local rod and gun club, but it is not a good project from the standpoint of training youth and future sportsmen.

Club projects can be designed to help the club and the state agency. A few examples are the previously mentioned Hunt America Time of the Izaak Walton League and other safety programs, stream cleanup and development and sportsmen-landowner cooperation ventures (Figure 30). In some states this cooperation has been aided by signs furnished by the conservation agency or the sportsmen's group. Red signs with *STOP—NO HUNTING* mean exactly what they say. Green signs with proper wording indicate permission is not required, *GO* ahead, but act like a gentleman. Yellow signs mean *CAUTION* and permission must be asked before trespassing. One should note color orientation with traffic signals. In some instances, the signs also are put up by the conservation organization (Figure 31).

Other worthwhile projects include liability insurance for landowners, insurance for landowners which covers wildlife damage, wildlife education scholarship funds, conservation teacher workshop sponsorships and junior conservation club sponsorships. The harvester organizations can aid in fish stocking, habitat improvement, rifle range development and conservation parades and displays. Many bulletins and articles are available that list excellent projects and make suggestions for club success.

All club meetings should be attended by one or two (not an army) of department officials. Too many department people at a conservation club meeting may work in reverse when an important issue is being discussed, and a "stacked deck" appearance may result. Department officials should help with the club, but should not hold office. Clubs should be encouraged to join state and national federations and to lend their support to beneficial causes and legislation on a larger scale.

Businessmen

Businessmen in the community constitute an important external public. These people need to be told how important natural resource agencies and resulting operations are to the businesses in the vicinity. Many economic studies have been conducted and all point out that natural resources in the community area mean much to the prosperous condition of that community.

Figure 30. The best solution to landowner-sportsmen conflicts is courtesy and cooperation.

To use an extreme example, what are the natural resources of Yellowstone National Park worth to the businessmen of West Yellowstone, or Gardiner, Montana? A little more realistic perhaps, what is the deer season worth to the residents of northern Michigan? Dollars and cents figures may not be available, but many of these businessmen go south for the rest of the winter after the short hunting season is over. If you have tried to get service in a restaurant during the rush hours of the opening day of deer season, there would be no doubt regarding the importance of sportsmen to the business. Nor is it necessarily as sporadic as are the fall seasons. Many states have year-round fishing seasons. The sports of hiking,

Figure 31.   Sign furnished and put up by the state agency to bring about good
landowner-sportsmen cooperation.

bird watching, skiing and others make the out-of-doors areas year-round playgrounds.

The good that is being done and the importance of natural resources to the community should be publicized and businessmen should be made aware of this importance. This publicity can be done in many ways. One of the most effective is for personnel of natural resource agencies to join and become active in businessmen's and community organizations. Nearly every town of any size will have Junior and Senior Chamber of Commerce groups as well as Lions, Rotary, Kiwanis or other service clubs. The major reason more conservation organization personnel do not belong to these clubs is because they do not choose to spend the time required.

The agency personnel should take advantage of opportunities to give talks and programs where businessmen congregate. Newspapers, magazines, radio and television outlets in the community should be used to explain the job and the organization and the importance of both.

Natural resource agency personnel should try to patronize local business operations whenever possible. This not only promotes good will, but also gives an opportunity to exchange ideas and information. Some of the businessmen also hold high elected positions in the city, community or state. Their influence on others can be great.

Outdoor Enthusiasts

The outdoor enthusiasts include the general conservationists, the bird watchers, the members of garden clubs and the photographers; in other words, the people who use and appreciate the outdoors without "harvesting." This is the primary public of the National Park Service.

Some of these publics may not be particularly interested in natural resources. Others are vitally interested. All can exert a great influence when aroused for or against a cause. Dr. Ira N. Gabrielson, former President of the Wildlife Management Institute, once made the statement that he would rather have one woman's group behind him than ten sportsmen's clubs. Over 85 per cent of the nation's buying is done by women (Cutlip and Center, 1964). Is it any wonder that they have such influence (Figure 32)?

Figure 32.   Outdoor enthusiasts, such as women's groups, can constitute an important public of any natural resource agency.

These publics also need someone to introduce and coordinate conservation efforts. Department personnel should do this. A little effort on the part of conservation officials can win support of some very influential groups which, among other ways, have been especially helpful in backing desired legislation.

Landowners

The natural resources managed by the U. S. Departments of Agriculture and Interior are found on, and include, lands that are publicly owned. However, ranchers and farmers own much of the land that supports wildlife. In the West, private landowners control access to much public property. They also have great influence in legislative matters. As with other publics or sub-publics, work with landowners should be done through the leaders of groups such as stockmen's associations, the Grange and landowner cooperatives. Stockmen's associations are very influential groups. If the president is convinced, the others are often much less formidable. Informal leaders should be identified and treated similarly to the formal leaders. Two-way communications between the department and the landowners are essential. Money and good will can be saved with proper action at the right time. Complete honesty and frankness are necessary (Figure 33).

Figure 33. Landowners support much of the wildlife harvested by private citizens. They should be kept informed and should be assisted with good wildlife management projects.

Landowners too, should be considered when seasons are being set. They cannot set the seasons but good relations will be engendered if they have a voice in the process. As stated earlier, Colorado Division personnel present the seasons to the stockmen's groups for their comments before the final regulations are passed by the Commission.

It is an everlasting job trying to keep peace between sportsmen and landowners since nearly 80 per cent of the total game shot annually in the United States by hunters is taken from private land (Shea, 1948). Trespass and access are constant problems (Figure 34). A continuous, adult education program which explains the pros and cons of both sides of the problem seems to be the only sound approach to a permanent solution. Anything to get the participants

Figure 34.   An array of signs, all with the same meaning and an indication of poor public relations.

Figure 35.   Damage to private property by game animals is a difficult situation that takes delicate handling to keep from resulting in poor public relations.

on common ground, such as a sportsmen-landowner banquet, furnished by the sportsmen, may help to break down the barrier.

Damage to private property by game animals constitutes a particularly knotty problem between landowners and a game and fish department (Figure 35). Some states are required to reimburse the landowner for damage that is caused by game animals. Other states try to ignore this damage. Many claims are just, others are falsified. This problem can be greatly reduced by good public relations. It is one that must be handled delicately, yet firmly and fairly. The greatest asset a game and fish department can have under these conditions is a man who can speak the rancher's or farmer's language and can gain their respect and trust.

Schools and Youth Groups

Schools and youth groups constitute other publics of importance because they not only use the resources immediately, but the young people today will be the sportsmen, landowners and businessmen of tomorrow. Too often an information and education officer or a wildlife conservation officer, will spend either all, or none, of his time working with these young people. There is no doubt about their importance, but work with them should not be done at the expense of the other publics.

Often the quickest and most effective way to reach a public, composed of older people such as sportsmen or landowners, is through their youngsters. A presentation may be given at the local school and then the message is taken home to the landowner or sportsman parent. This has proven to be very effective in efforts at protection, law enforcement and proper land use.

A simple appreciation for things of nature may be the most important subject matter taught to young people (Figure 36). Good conservation principles and the long range approach through ecology should be stressed with youth. Professional natural resource managers agree that if we treat land properly, the grass, shrubs and trees will be present, and if the vegetation is utilized reasonably, wildlife will be present.

Teachers are school leaders. Therefore, teacher training is an important approach to the youth public. The chief bottleneck in conservation education in schools is a lack of interest by the natural resource management agencies, not the teachers, although conservation department sponsored workshops and fellowships to those workshops are fairly common.

Weaver's (1957) study showed that only six states required, by law, that conservation education be taught in the schools. Throckmorton (1958) said that 90 per cent of the states have a teacher training program of some kind regarding conservation matters, and that training was mandatory in eight states. Lively (1958) stated

Figure 36. A simple appreciation for nature may be the most important subject taught to young people.

that conservation courses of some type were being offered by 86 per
cent of the nation's largest universities and colleges, Fifty-five per
cent of the small colleges offered such courses, as did 89 per cent of
teacher's colleges. But, the proportion of the students enrolled in
conservation courses is very small when compared to courses such as

mathematics, English and chemistry. Many believe that at least one course in conservation of natural resources should be included in all curricula of all schools, colleges and universities. In 1968, 41 of 50 state conservation departments (82%) had a "youth education" effort of some kind (Wildlife Management Institute, 1968).

It has been said that it is important to stress the basic principles of biology and ecology in conservation work with youth. It is logical that the same is true with teachers. Experience in teaching high school biology teachers shows that many know the anatomy of the human, the paramecium and the frog, but many know little or nothing about the environment and ecology. Interest in conservation of natural resources is naturally present from the elementary grades through college (Figure 37). Excellent conservation classes can be

Figure 37. Conservation and natural resource management classes can be conducted for all ages.

conducted at all levels. Natural resource management agencies should help where possible and should furnish personnel and materials of many kinds.

Figure 38. Youth groups are constantly searching for worthwhile projects. Habitat improvement for fish and game usually is constructive effort.

Youth groups other than those directly associated with schools, such as 4-H, Future Farmers of America, Boy Scouts and Girl Scouts of America and church groups, want work projects. Many can be in the area of natural resource appreciation and management. Their interests must be channeled in the right direction. Projects should further appreciation and learning of conservation principles. Examples that have been successful are checklists and identification charts, a study of soil factors and their influence on living organisms, a comparison of used and unused wildlife habitats, track and scat identification and counts, surveys, mapping, habitat improvement and many others (Figure 38). Hjelte (no date) in his publication, *Tools for Teaching Conservation,* suggested many projects. Material sources, references and texts for each age category are included. Hockstrasser (1957) described a junior conservation club in Colorado that won national recognition. Reavley's (1957) National Wildlife Federation Bulletin, *Conservation Clubs for Juniors,* gave many worthwhile suggestions for the formation and operation of a successful youth conservation club.

There is an inherent interest in nature and natural resource conservation. With a little encouragement in the right direction by the natural resource management officials, another natural resource management effort is started. Where will it stop? No one knows. These young people will contact others, and it will go on. Perhaps some of them even will become professional natural resource managers.

Land-Use Agencies

Land-use agencies which are involved in natural resource management must give each other cooperation and respect. All should have a voice in management practices that affect other land-use agencies. For example, all should be allowed a voice in setting seasons for the game animals which use the lands under their management. Colorado does this by having Forest Rangers, Park Rangers, Soil Conservation Service personnel, and Bureau of Land Management officials present with Wildlife Division officials when the initial season recommendations are made. Supervisory personnel of these organizations also are present at the final meeting before the seasons are firmly set by the Commission.

In the same way, grazing cuts or increases, vegetation management changes or any operation planned by one agency should be made known to, and cleared by, all agencies that may be affected directly or indirectly by the operation. In some western states, however, situations still exist where there is no cooperation. Programs of browse spraying by one land-use agency may directly oppose the desires of another. Acres of deer food are destroyed at the expense of having more grass (Figures 39 and 40). Another example, organizational disagreements which have resulted

Figure 39.   Large areas of sagebrush have been destroyed in the West by one land-use agency, often without consulting others. This has resulted in animosity and poor public relations.

from some of the large water impoundments are common knowledge. And still a third example, the controversy that exists regarding hunting in national parks and ownership of wildlife in national parks originated, and has grown, because of a lack of coöperation and understanding.

There should be no place in natural resource agency public relations matters for individual pettiness and dislikes. Too often one

Figure 40. Many of the areas where sagebrush has been destroyed were valuable deer winter ranges.

person, perhaps a high administrator, has "an axe to grind" over some specific issue. When this happens, cooperation and mutual trust between the agencies suffer and a barrier of distrust and poor public relations is erected.

Especially with these publics, communications lag and cause many conflicts. These land-use agencies should inform and be kept informed of happenings of interest to other organizations. Newsletters and magazines should be exchanged regularly. A "natural resources club" of all land management agencies in a community has served the same purposes of contact and idea exchange as a service club. A chance to help one agency should never be turned down by another agency. For example, in many western states, U. S. Forest Service personnel and game and fish department employees cooperate in solving mutual problems. They work together in analyzing big game-range plots (Figure 41). They used to argue about range conditions and do nothing toward arriving at a mutual agreement, but this has changed.

Media Operators

It should be stressed that good public relations with personnel of communications media are mutually advantageous. The media operators want news and information of interest to their viewing, listening and reading audiences. The natural resource agency needs publicity. Free time or space usually will be provided if programs

Figure 41. Personnel from different natural resource management agencies should work together to solve mutual problems instead of arguing about them.

or articles are of interest to enough people and are well presented. All goes smoothly until one side or the other does not keep its share of the bargain.

Too much effort at contact with the people responsible for communications media operations may work in reverse. After the initial effort is made, and the media personnel know of the possibilities, they should come to the natural resource agency as often as the agency contacts them. Most media operators realize that natural resource management and conservation in general is interesting to people, and a place will be made for information to be presented about natural resources.

Organization personnel must know and abide by the rules set by media standards. Deadlines or program schedules should be met, and the ultimate in quality always should be sought. The unvarnished facts should be given quickly, correctly and in the detail necessary for clear understanding. Agency policies must be adhered to. Yet, it is a mistake to try to educate a public too much. The education "pill" can be sugarcoated. Much entertainment and interest are needed to accompany a little education, or the program will be turned off or the article not read.

The Public in General

There are many additional points of good public relations that a natural resource organization should strive for. These points pertain to any public or the public in general.

People believe that they are financially supporting the conservation agency. They usually are, directly or indirectly, through license purchases and taxes. Therefore, a simple, accurate, understandable, financial statement should be made available to those who are interested. If this is required by law, as it is for some organizations, the conservation agency should go beyond the legal requirements and publish the statement wherever possible. Smooth business operations with an efficient accounting system make this easy and prevent dishonesty.

A regularly published, attractive, simple and complete annual report is an aid to good customer and stockholder relations in any public. The annual report should be sent to all individuals of internal publics and be available to interested individuals of external publics on request. There is no reason to assume that such a report is not equally as important for all natural resource management agencies.

Waste and the appearance of waste must be avoided. Frugal management develops confidence in the conservation organization by its publics, including those who allocate the budget, that the organization is well run. For example, high officials should drive economy cars instead of the high-priced models. Wise and honest use of airplanes, expense accounts, time and equipment can keep the confidence which lawmakers, governing board members and other publics have in the organization so that embarrassing investigations can be avoided.

Examples have been known where an official hired his wife (with department funds) as secretary to do some office work in his home. There may have been no dishonesty, but the supposition was too easy to make. Another instance, one department official used organization owned cameras and company time to illustrate, write and sell stories for personal gain. In both cases, criticism was just and severe.

A public agency must be impartial at all times and should not sell goods or yield to pressure groups. All factors should be weighed before a policy is made or a season is set. But, once the decision is made, the department should not change that decision.

It is not wise for the natural resource management agency to compete with private business or individuals for anything of material value. In this regard, private business should be allowed, or created if necessary, to sell licenses and other materials, such as game meat, camping and boating permits and confiscated items. As an alternative, materials can be donated to charity or given away on a first-come, first-served basis. The burden of success or failure should be put upon the individual not the natural resource organization. If a drawing is necessary for a limited number of licenses or validations of licenses, the drawing should be open to all and should be strictly honest.

All natural resource agencies, including both state and federal organizations, have been criticized severely for buying land and taking it from tax rolls, thus reducing the tax base of the community. If not prohibited by law, it seems reasonable that recompense should be made to the counties in lieu of taxes. Many conservation agencies do this. Others do not. Natural resource organizations also should be required to pay for fire and police protection in a community as does any other business. If these are paid for, the people of the community should be told about it so they will appreciate the efforts of the organization.

Tact in all contact should be insisted upon by administrators and developed by all employees. An air of friendliness, whether personal, in a letter or over the telephone, can do much to bring about desired results.

One should realize that all agencies have public relations problems. Public relations is important and necessary at all levels of the organization and must be a coordinated effort designed to influence the particular public. Yet, it is necessary to shift with changes in ideas and feelings of a public. If in doubt, the item or idea should be tested on a small scale to see what happens.

It is necessary to be a good neighbor to organizations and individuals alike. An opportunity to be of assistance to any agency or a person should never be ignored by a natural resource agency. Discourtesies and nonchalance by officials in times of stress can be drastic. No group ever should be slighted.

The agency should try to sell natural resource management and wise conservation ideas on a permanent basis so they will not soon have to turn around and unsell ideas. For example, it is better to sell a deer season on range conditions than on population numbers or increased kill (Jones, 1960). This may be harder to do, but in the long run, results will be better. Both long and short range items often need to be used to have the proposal accepted.

An image of awareness and appreciation of the organization should be developed in the minds of the publics. The department should sell itself as a capable friend of the people and of wise natural resource management. An emblem or slogan associated with the workers and the job can help. A good illustration is the Smoky Bear image of the U. S. Forest Service. This image, or "gimmick" reminds people of forest fire prevention. Just how many millions of dollars of timber Smoky has kept from going up in smoke never will be known. The wildlife manager may even say that Smoky has done too good a job.

THE SOCIOLOGY OF PUBLIC RELATIONS

The pressures of our era are forcing public relations practitioners to discard, or at least re-examine, outdated concepts of persuasion. New efforts involve fields such as social psychology, group dynamics, cultural anthropology, linguistics and computer programming for testing purposes. The full potential of public relations will not be realized until professionals begin to incorporate the knowledge of the social sciences. Lane (1965) stated that the lack of application of material from the social sciences is greatly curtailing the effectiveness of public relations efforts. This statement is equally true today.

Group Organization

Every group, formal or informal, has standards for membership. These include restrictions on qualifications, procedures to follow, costs of joining and participating and rules concerning actions. The individual must meet and conform to these standards in order to belong to the group. It usually is beneficial if the rules and standards are established by the members.

The factors which curtail participation in a group include fear (perhaps of ridicule), insecurity, lack of knowledge about the group, lack of time or a lack of vested interest. Perhaps the individual doesn't fish or hunt; therefore, he doesn't see why he should join a conservation club or attend meetings.

Groups are structured horizontally, vertically or in some combination of the two. A horizontal structure has several people of equal rank but with different jobs or roles. This is the typical structure of an organization that functions with committees and subgroups and is common with the staff organization of most conservation departments and federal agencies such as the Forest Service. A vertical structure has a leader with subordinate individuals in positions under him. Each decreasing position has less authority, as in the line organization of the military services.

Each society or group has its own class structure based upon rank, beliefs, sex, age and occupation. These social classes stem from wealth, power, respect and other characteristics, and result in organization. Each person in the structure has status and a role, or roles. Every person has some degree of prestige and is rated according to many factors in the eyes of his fellow men. Each individual must be handled differently in the process of attempting to change opinion.

The social organization has leaders and followers, and these must be known in order to facilitate changes in the thinking of the social class.

Any member of a class or group has attitudes, opinions and beliefs typical of that class. These mental conditions are the result cf culture and of current socialization with others in the same group. In many areas of Europe, for example, it is generally accepted that only the upper social classes and the landowners can hunt. In a typical American town too, classes can easily be discerned. The terms "upper-class," "lower-class" and "middle-class" are common. This categorization usually results from wealth and home locality, with their attendant ways of life.

Groups or classes, can be either formal or informal (Pfiffner, 1951). A formal group has definite and known lines of authority as in a typical president, vice-president, secretary chain of command. Informal groups are those cliques which result from ritual and sentiment. Informal groups, too, can have rigid structure, with leaders, spokesmen and followers, based on prestige or position in the "peck order."

Individuals feel a definite need to belong to a group. This is necessary for status which is a basic emotional drive. Once a part of the group, the individual has status and a role in that group. He conforms to tradition or is ejected. If cast out, he may start another group as leader.

Groups consist of individuals. Therefore, we try to predict group action by sampling a number of individual intentions. Statistics have reduced much of the guesswork, but it still must be realized that all individuals are different. Michigan sportsmen are different from Colorado sportsmen. A deer hunter is different from a duck hunter. A buck hunter is different from a doe hunter; yet, all belong to the sportsmen category. To attempt to predict what deer hunters in Colorado will do on the basis of the opinions and actions of Michigan deer hunters would be folly.

Motivation

Motivation is an urge to fulfill a need and is the result of a stimulus. This desire for fulfillment causes a person to think, believe or act in a certain way toward a specific goal or incentive which must be present for motivation. The stronger the drive, desire, want, frustration or urge, the greater will be the impetus of the individual to gain the desired goal.

The sources for motivation, according to Morgan (1956), stem from the basic urges which also are responsible for group or class participation. The physiological, biological or hereditary urges are those which satisfy a basic bodily need. A few examples are self-preservation, warmth, sex, cold, thirst, security and hunger. Instrumental or environmental drives, on the other hand, are those behaviors resulting from nonphysical needs. These needs are common, to some degree, to all members in a social system. Some examples are learning, enjoyment, status, recognition, morality, thrills, adventure, security and spiritual needs.

Molders of public opinion try to determine which need is strongest. The practitioner then tries to direct motivation toward fulfilling that need. Public relations practitioners attempt to motivate by stressing the need for their idea or project to the individual in the light of his basic urges.

Another type of motivation is when adjustment is made because of response to frustration. This also is reaction to a stimulus. Aggression is a common reaction. The individual wants to strike back. He refuses to join or accept because his idea was not accepted or he was not elected. Or, an adjustment may be made in compensation. He wasn't elected president of the conservation club, so he takes the social chairman position.

In rationalization, the person makes himself believe he didn't want the job anyway. Perhaps it would have taken too much time (in his mind, after he wasn't elected), and he is better off. Projection means that the blame for failure is placed on other people or on nonexisting factors. Displacement occurs when feelings are transferred elsewhere. He wasn't elected president of the club, so he kicks the dog or starts a family argument.

Conversion is an adjustment to frustration where anticipated failure is turned into a real physical complaint. He has a headache and can't make a speech or perhaps is ill and can't attend enough meetings. Or the person may react through idealization. He thinks that he really was the best man for the job, even if he was not elected.

Action, or the results of motivation, is measured in three ways. Breadth of participation refers to how many members took part. The intensity of motivation can be reflected in how much actually was done. The pattern of motivation would show in interactions, such as who were the leaders and the chain of events that took place.

Social Action and the Diffusion Process

Adoption or rejection of an idea or proposal takes place in a series of complex steps which occur in definite sequence. The farther along the chain of acceptance the group or individual is, the more difficult it becomes to change the group's or person's way of thinking and acting.

Social action doesn't "just happen." Programs involving people must take place within a social system or a group and start with convergence of similar interests. Two or more people agree that a problem or situation exists. The social system to which these people belong then becomes the medium for social action. These two or more people with the original idea are the initiators and are necessary for any social action to begin (Case and Hoffman, 1960). They agree that something should be done about a situation and try to motivate others to act toward the desired end.

Some writers disagree with the exact sequence of steps toward rejection or acceptance of an idea, but the following seems most logical. An example is given to illustrate stages in the adoption (or rejection) sequence (Figure 42).

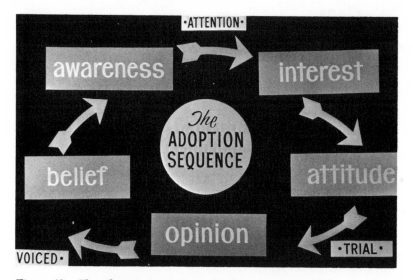

Figure 42.   The adoption or rejection sequence incorporates sequential change toward acceptance or rejection of an idea.

The first stage toward acceptance of a proposal or change of an idea is the state of *Awareness*. Prior to this time components of the public do not know or care that the proposal exists. Their attention must be gained and they must be made aware that a proposal or problem is present. For example, people are told that deer are too numerous in a certain area. Something must be done or a heavy winter loss may result. An either-sex season is recommended by the agency. Information at this stage may be obtained from mass media.

Next, *Interest* is developed by the public. People become interested enough to want to know more about the proposal. They are intrigued. What are the possible solutions to the deer problem? Mass media methods of communications still are best for the average venture during the interest stage (Iowa Agricultural Extension Service, 1955).

After interest has been generated, an *Attitude* is developed. The individual in the public starts to react positively or negatively. Relative merits of the proposal are weighed and evaluated by a person on the basis of his own situation, experience, knowledge, influence or money, and if possible, in accord with group thinking. During this phase, more information usually is wanted by the public. There is a resultant feeling by the public for or against the proposal. The proposed either-sex season for deer should, or should not, take place.

Good public relations methods can create favorable attitudes or eliminate those considered unfavorable to the proposal. Attitude changes are either congruent or incongruent. A congruent change is toward the same side of the issue as was the original inclination. An increase in the degree of negativity of a negative attitude toward an issue or an increase in positivity of a positive attitude are both congruent changes. For example, a mild preservationist may change to a strong preservationist. This is a congruent change. An incongruent change, on the other hand, is a change in the opposite direction; from positive to negative or vice-versa.

Change may be difficult to achieve. The degree of difficulty is based upon many factors. These include strength of conviction or extremeness, complexity and multiplicity of the factors, consistency of impressions and mutual support, among many others.

Opinions are stronger convictions than attitudes and result from attitude evaluations. For people to form an opinion, however, a controversy must exist. The individual may still have some doubts, but one side of the controversy definitely has been taken. Verbal expressions usually are given at the opinion stage of a proposal. It has been decided by the public that there are too many deer, and something should be done. Some people think that the proposed either-sex season is the answer; others in the public may not agree.

Opinions are more difficult to change than attitudes. Consent often is given by the public at this point to try the idea on a small scale. The Iowa Agricultural Extension Service (1955) stated that personal contact through neighbors and friends is the most effective method of motivation to use after opinions are formed.

A *Belief* is the last stage in the adoption sequence and is definite. The idea has been accepted or rejected, and the individual and the public act accordingly. There is no more doubt. Beliefs are very hard to change because many stem from culture, customs or traditions. A public has a great tendency to want to preserve its beliefs. Beliefs acquired through culture and as a child are stronger than those acquired as an adult from authoritative opinion or from personal reasoning. For example, feelings toward church, school and the home usually are more firmly entrenched than those about natural resource matters.

Klapper (1960) stated that firmness of beliefs results in predispositions. Predispositions include selected exposure, selective perception and selective retention. People only expose themselves to that to which they wish to be exposed (selective exposure). They simply do not attend the lectures or read the articles on the deer problem. People tend to emphasize facts that already fit existing attitudes, opinions and beliefs. They tend to de-emphasize those facts which are contrary to their preconceived ideas (selective perception). The publics believe only what they want to believe about the deer problem. People remember what they want to remember and forget what they wish to forget (selective retention). The audience soon forgets the points made about the deer problem which are contrary to their ideas.

So, the either-sex deer season does not take place. There never has been a doe season there before, and nothing too drastic happened. A good enough job of influencing public opinion was not done. Perhaps the belief is just too well rooted to change. "My old pappy and his pappy never shot does, and I ain't either." Officials can wait until next year and try again. Of course, the deer population then is too low to have an either-sex season because of winter starvation losses. Perhaps the next time the die-off is imminent, the job can be done.

An idea spreads, is diffused and may or may not be adopted. Adoption or rejection takes time and cannot be rushed beyond certain limits. The rate depends upon the stage in the sequence the public now occupies, the complexity of the program and the cost of the program. The more involved and expensive the proposal, the longer the adoption process will take. The rate of adoption for sportsmen, ranchers and timber cutters, all harvesters of the natural resources, should parallel that given for farmers (Iowa Agricultural Extension Service, 1955; Bohlen and Beal, 1956; Anderson, 1957). The rate of adoption for ranchers, deer hunters and timber cutters is given in Table 4.

All social action takes place in a social system, but all people in this social system do not adopt the proposal simultaneously. In this process there are leaders, followers and others. The following categories were suggested by the Iowa Agricultural Extension Service (1955).

The *Innovators* (initiators) are the first to accept an idea. These are the information seekers. They have money, prestige and already have "arrived." The innovators usually are influential in an area larger than a community. Their activities and position may extend to county or state influence. Their main sources of information are the agencies or departments where the idea originated or they may originate the idea themselves. The innovators are few in number and can afford to take risks (Figure 43).

The *Early Adopters*, or *Influentials*, are often community leaders. They may be elected officials of a formal group or leaders of an informal group. They usually are young, active, well educated and well informed. Their main source of contact and motivation is through the communications media. The early adopters accept for the community and usually are financially secure.

Table 4. Rates of Adoption for Three Publics Based upon Complexity and Cost of Proposal.

Rating (1-Fast, 4-Slow)	Operation, Ranked According to Complexity and Cost	Rancher	Deer Hunter	Timber Cutter
1	Material and equipment changes	Cattle food supplement	Caliber regulation	Crosscut to chain saw
2	Improved practice	Pasture to feedlot	Tagging regulation	Change in D.B.H. restrictions
3	Innovation	Black Angus to Hereford	Increased license cost	Different sawmill set-up
4	Enterprise	Cattle to sheep	Either-sex or closed season	Saw log to pulp operation

The *Early Majority* are the local leaders. These people usually are informal leaders who operate within cliques and small social groups. They are older than the early adopters, have average education and cannot afford financial setbacks. They have good judgment but generally are slower in making decisions than the innovators or early adopters. Their main sources of communications are the media, neighbors and friends. These local leaders often are not recognized as being leaders by the rest of the public.

The *Group Majority* may be discussed along with the *Late Adopters*. These are the masses, the "hangers on" or the followers. They often are less well established in the community, have less education and are older. They have fewer social aspirations and participate less in public or community affairs. They have a "wait and see" approach and can afford few risks. Change for them is difficult and the best method of contact is through neighbors and friends.

In any group there are the *Non-adopters*. This group may go along with the idea, but not willingly. The non-adopters are never completely won over. They do not participate very much in community affairs. The non-adopters often are older and have the least amount of education (Iowa Agricultural Extension Service, 1955).

Case and Hoffman (1960) pointed out that each public has its own *Legitimizers*. These individuals are constantly evaluating ideas

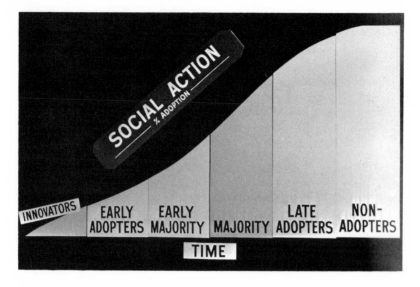

Figure 43.   All people in a group do not accept or reject an idea
simultaneously.

and reporting the results to the leaders. The legitimizers are part
of either a formal group or an informal group and even may be the
leaders. It is hard to determine how they reach this status of prestige. They may rule negatively or positively at any stage of the
process.

In molding public opinion it is necessary to find the stage in
the adoption sequence occupied by a majority of the individuals
composing the public. The innovators and early adopters, the people who are leaders, should be known early in the process. Thus,
after being won over, they can be used to influence the others in
the public. After the operation is under way, concentration can
change to the early majority and late adopters.

Politics and Natural Resources

It is often stated that natural resource management should be
taken out of politics. This is highly debatable because the natural
resources belong to the people and politics is, or should be, the
voice of the people. Politics gives form to public desires and our
very freedoms are in the hands of the elected officials (or politicians).

Politics is people management. So, in a certain sense, politics is
one type of public relations. The dictionaries define politics as "the
science of government." A politician is "one skilled in the science of
government." Government implies rules and regulations governing
people; therefore, it can be deduced that politics is the science of
establishing rules and regulations which govern people.

We are dependent upon political decisions in most of our natural resource operations. The laws governing use of the resources and the dollars allocated to pay the cost of managing the resources are made or given as a result of political decisions. In a primitive economy, decisions were made at the market place. Now the voice of the people is transmitted through the ballot box. The natural resource manager must work with, and convince, the legislator, at organization, state and national levels. This is necessary so that the resource manager will be able to work within the policies and laws and have adequate budgets and personnel to do the job.

It is likely that natural resource management will never be taken out of politics, and perhaps it shouldn't be done. Some controls are needed, and these controls should reflect the will of the people within the framework of what is good natural resource management. Most states have a commission form of policy-making board. The U. S. Forest Service and Bureau of Land Management have advisory boards that are less powerful. Nevertheless, these governing boards, in some cases, actually make policy. The members of these boards usually are politically appointed. A board usually is bipartisan, but politics still is very much in evidence. In states with a politically appointed director or commissioner, political influence is even greater.

Any operation that depends partly upon tax money, as most of our natural resource management agencies do, never will be free of politics. Federal and state laws governing natural resource management operations, such as license fees, violations and the penalties for violations, establishment of licenses, delineation of which species may be harvested, boundaries, rules of operation and many other regulations governing natural resource management are established by constitutional right, federal law, state law or commission regulation.

As stated previously, wildlife on public lands belongs to the people. The professional resource manager must convince the people of the soundness of his management programs. The kind, number, distribution and condition of natural resources depends largely upon the decisions of these owners as expressed through the political process. These decisions are complicated by the fact that, although owned by the people, fish and wildlife live on privately owned lands, sometimes against the wishes of the landowner. When wildlife exists on federal lands, there is the problem of coordination with the federal agency involved, with state conservation departments and other users of the lands.

The market and price system does not regulate most kinds of natural resource production. The market system is the great regulatory and control system in the United States, but it is almost totally inoperative as concerns fish, wildlife and recreation. When market controls do not operate, we turn to government for controls and regulatory devices, through politics.

In addition there is a problem of increasing demand as a result of increased population, increased leisure time, increased mobility and increased income. In many cases the increased demand confronts a diminishing supply brought on by the competition of other land uses, excessive use or harvest, water pollution, drainage, improper highway or other construction and general ecological disturbance.

The natural resource manager has fallen heir to a multiude of traditions and attitudes. Some of them are opposed to progress. Unfortunately, even positive attitudes may be difficult to handle because of the intense emotions involved. Natural resource management operates in a highly charged political milieu, and the managers are extraordinarily dependent upon the efforts of sympathetic interest groups. This dependency requires public relations skills to maintain support without becoming the captive of the supporters. This adds to the complexity and importance of actions in the political arena.

Elected officials may be divided into two groups: (1) those who have a strong ideological commitment to some values which impinge on a problem, and (2) those who do not (Foss, 1960). The actions of politicians in the first category can be predicted with reasonable accuracy if it is assumed that they understand the problem. They often do not understand the problem unless the natural resource manager has seen to it that they do. Nevertheless, this first group of politicians can be expected to act in terms of their ideological commitments.

Some politicians do not have any real ideological position but are committed to a few values. It is generally assumed that every political decision maker has a definite opinion on every issue. This cannot be true because there are too many issues. The politician must, however, maintain a pretense of interest and knowledge on every issue that concerns his constituency. He dare not go around implying that he "could not care less." He must ask questions and obtain information to maintain a superficial knowledge. The natural resource manager must supply this information in sufficient quantity, accurately and at the right time.

The politician without strong commitments of his own wants to know many things about the issue at hand and the feeling of the people, his voters, relative to that issue. First, he may try to find out who is behind the policy or proposal and how intense is their commitment. In other words, how hard will they fight or how much will they spend? How much influence does the group backing the issue have with other persons and groups? How will various alternatives be accepted by the sponsoring group and by constituents? How will the anticipated effects on his constituents and the public affect their voting behavior? The natural resource manager must ascertain that proponents, assuming the issue is favorable to natural resource management, or opponents, if the point of contention is unfavorable, make their voice heard in sufficient quantity and at the right time to sway the outcome in the right direction.

This is the essence of democracy. In effect, the above questions are "What is the will of the people and how intense is that will?" Therefore, the true will of the people must be relayed to the political decision maker. The natural resource manager must inform the people so that their will is for the good of the natural resource.

Once a decision is made, it will most likely be explained or rationalized in technical terms. The elected person can't say "I did it to get votes." So reasons and rationale are often not the same, and cannot be because of cultural antipathies.

Political and democratic considerations tend to expand the limits of rationality. Technological considerations alone do not always provide rational choices. Thus, in planning the route of a highway, if cost, safety, and speed of movement alone are considered, the resulting route may be totally unacceptable to the people for reasons of noise, lack of amenities, effect on natural resources or some intangibles.

Politicians are likely to be extremely sensitive to the demands of natural resource management groups because of the strong emotional appeal of the values represented by these groups. Politicians are also likely to be wary and possibly somewhat resentful of natural resource management programs because of their almost religious tone and the strong backing possible if the supporters of the natural resource management program can be organized. Some politicians also resent the fact that, due to bipartisan governing boards, in some states natural resource management is about as free of politics as possible. The commission, or governing board, is put beyond the direct control of the legislature. Funds for the operation of the activity may be derived from specific licenses or fees, the proceeds of which cannot be appropriated by the legislature for other purposes. These facts add fuel to the fire and make the resource manager's position in dealing with politicians a bit more difficult.

Conflict causes legislation. If there were no controversies, laws would not be necessary. It is fair to assume that with increasing demands on natural resources by more people, laws are going to increase in number and restrictions are going to become greater.

The natural resource manager can operate in two ways. First by influencing and informing the lawmaker so he will understand the issues at hand; second by informing and motivating the publics so they in turn will make their wants known to the lawmaker.

Public relations with the politician should not be postponed until the legislative body is in session. A crash program often will cause suspicion of the natural resource manager, his organization and of the proposal. More harm than good may result. The politician should be contacted continuously as important matters arise. He should be informed and convinced by the one most authoritative on the issue, the professional natural resource manager. The politician should not be fawned over or given special privileges, but he should be informed about the issues and hopefully convinced along the lines of good natural resource management. With especially important issues, and in current critical times, it is best that only the most knowledgeable individual of the organization provide information to the political officials. Conflicting views from inside the organization can be disastrous.

The natural resource manager also should inform the various publics of desired legislation well in advance and long before the legislature is in session. The politician will be in contact with the people. The people should be thinking along the lines of good natural resource management when this contact is made. Politicians understand votes, and votes come from the people. Telegrams and letters from the people will produce results if the elected officials are sufficiently motivated.

Several references have been made to the importance of timing. Background information is stored in the minds and notes of the legislator, so constant reminders are necessary. But, one time may be more opportune than others in influencing legislation.

Bills are introduced in either the House or Senate, usually within the first few days of the legislative session. The legislator who proposes the bill will usually write a rough draft of it himself, but it will generally be put in final form by a special committee of the legislature.

After the bill has been drafted and assigned a number, it will be read by title on the floor of that branch of the legislature where it was introduced. It then will be assigned to a committee, printed and indexed. Titles can be misleading. Often a bill contains provisions not specified in either the title or the general description. If in doubt, the full text of the bill in question should be read. The sponsoring legislator usually will be glad to furnish a copy of the bill. One can write for a copy of any legislative proposal.

The time to influence the passing or rejecting of a bill, once it has been introduced, is in committee. Once the bill reaches the floor of the legislature there is little chance of influencing its eventual outcome. For this reason it is vital that the better part of the campaign be directed at the committee of the legislature which will decide whether the bill should be put to the entire body for a vote. Usually the committee's release of a bill for a vote is a recommendation that it be passed. As few legislators can take the time to digest the entire contents of all bills introduced, many are inclined to vote favorably on any bill that comes out of committee.

It is not necessary that personal contact be made with each member of the committee. A polite, factual, well reasoned letter or telegram to the committee chairman or specific legislator will generally be sufficient. If the legislators making up the committee hear from enough natural resource managers and other people interested in the issue, the resultant action should be in accord with good natural resource management.

A lobbyist makes personal contact with lawmakers during legislative activities. In some instances, opposition to natural resource management issues will have paid lobbyists. Most states require they be registered as such. Groups interested in promoting good natural resource management usually cannot afford a paid lobbyist. In a broader sense, almost everyone is a lobbyist of some kind or another when he tries to influence the outcome of legislative action. State laws should be checked concerning definitions of a lobbyist and lobbying activities if there are doubts. Lobbying activities in behalf of wise natural resources management often are done by local, state or national clubs and federations.

On important issues with much controversy, the committee may decide that a hearing should be held. These may be scheduled on short notice. Instead of written evidence for or against the issue, people have a chance to voice opinions. The most factual, concise, accurate testimony will carry the most weight. The committee, the press and the public will appreciate copies of presentations and any other documents to be included in the record.

Hearings are handled in many different ways. Some states automatically hold hearings on all bills, others do so only on request. In the U. S. Congress and in some states, different committees of the two legislative branches hold separate hearings on bills, and presentations should be made before the committees of both bodies. Other states have joint committees and only one hearing is held.

If the bill gets a favorable report from committee, it will be sent to the branch of the legislature where it originated for a vote. If passed, it will be sent to the other branch. As with hearings, votes on the floor are usually scheduled on short notice and are quickly completed. Thus, any campaign to write letters or send telegrams to legislators should be well under way before the bill comes out of committee.

Passage of a bill through one branch of the legislature does not necessarily insure passage in the other, so efforts should not be stopped until the bill reaches the governor or president and is signed into law. Since few bills ever live again after being vetoed by the governor or president, he also should be considered.

When the outcome of a bill is clear, the legislators should be contacted and thanked for their help. Politicians seldom get thanks, and good will can accrue in preparation for the next political issue, when it comes.

At the end of every legislative season it is a matter of practical politics that a legislator return home to take the pulse of his constituents. Not only is he trying to find out how the people who elected him feel about how well he did his job in the last session, he is also trying to get some idea how they feel about measures that will come up in the next session. While the lawmaker's time is greatly in demand during the legislative season, he is usually available and ready to listen at home.

Because this is also the time when he is beginning to think about votes for the next election, he is usually eager to contact people and will speak before groups of all kinds, particularly those that have an interest in pending legislation. This is the time to start the influencing, the explaining and the understanding that is necessary for legislation to be passed at the next session.

Public relations certainly is a part of politics. The politician uses public relations methods to become elected. The natural resource manager uses public relations with politicians to get some laws passed and others stopped. He uses public relations with people in hopes that they in turn will influence politicians and political action in the proper direction. Right or wrong, good or bad, politics and politicians will have a great influence on natural resource management for years to come. The results of this influence will depend directly upon public relations and their effectiveness.

PRINCIPLES OF COMMUNICATIONS

Good communications are not synonymous with good public relations, but most authorities agree that good communications are a necessary, basic element and a vital part of good public relations. Communications with all publics involve a source, a message, a channel and a receiver (Figure 44). Conflict and misunderstanding occur when any part is lacking.

Figure 44. Communications should be a two-way interchange of thoughts, ideas and opinions. The sender becomes the receiver and the receiver the sender.

Definitions and Methods

Cutlip and Center (1964) gave the following definition. "Communications involves the interchange of thought or opinions by words, letters, or symbols where there is an effort to move the audience by the message given through the right channels to a desired goal." Seigworth (1960) of the Forest Service, said that "Communications provide the thread that binds an aggregation together by insuring common understanding." Other definitions include the following:

> "The essential feature of communication is that one
> person infers from the behavior of another . . . what

idea or feeling the other person is trying to convey. He then reacts, not to the behavior as such but to the inferred idea or feeling" (Davis, 1949).

"The use of symbols to achieve common or shared information about an object" (Krech, Crutchfield and Ballachey, 1962).

"The establishment of a social unit from individuals, by the use of language or signs. The sharing of a common set of rules for various goal-seeking activities" (Cherry, 1957).

One word stands out in the meaning of all of these definitions. That word is *understanding*.

Methods used in communications can be classified into four categories. The first category is the printed word and includes newspapers, magazines, bulletins, house publications, stickers, posters, manuals, bulletin boards, inserts and enclosures, handbooks and written suggestions.

The second category, the spoken word, includes communications by use of meetings, rumors, speeches, press conferences, training sessions, the "grapevine," contacts with friends and neighbors, speaker's bureaus, public address systems and radio.

Images, the third category of methods, include television slides, motion pictures, models, photographs, drawings and exhibits or displays. A picture or facsimile of the real object or situation is used to aid in understanding.

The fourth category of communications involves action. Examples are a pat on the back, a nod of the head, a glance with meaning or a handshake. A stand on a controversy may be shown by a deed. Events, tours, field trips and open houses are other examples of this method of contact.

There are many combinations of the foregoing communications methods. All can be used singly or with other methods to any degree. Regardless of the method used, the end product of communications is understanding and involvement which will result in participation, support and acceptance or rejection of an idea by a public.

Requirements for Good Communications

The flow of information must be bi-directional to be adequate and effective. The sender must receive information from the person(s) being contacted. The response from those receiving the message tells the person responsible for the communication whether he is successful and suggests changes that need be made.

Reynolds (1966) stated that two-way effort was necessary in that we put information into the minds of our audience and extract information from them. He also said that "we need down to earth communications, that which comes from the ground up." Thoreau wrote that "It takes two to tell the truth." This also implies the two-way, circular response in communications. There is no beginning or end to a good communications operation.

Channels of communication must be clearly defined and followed for maximum effectiveness. Communications channels for a typical conservation agency are listed in Appendix C. If a link is missed in the process of communications, the message may bridge the gap, but perhaps with a loss or change of meaning. Informal methods of communications, such as rumors and the "grapevine," may take over when channels are not provided for the process. Dissemination of accurate information is the best method of rumor control.

No communications effort is better than the ability of the communicator or the interest of the person or persons being communicated with. Research, planning and effort are necessary.

Selection of a Communications Method

The communications method should be carefully chosen for the specific public and used at the proper time for the best results. To illustrate, a 2:00 p.m. radio broadcast may be the best method to reach many housewives, a 5:30 p.m. television program may contact the most youth and a late edition newspaper article may be the most effective means to reach businessmen. Especially critical issues, such as landowner conflicts and disagreements, may need to be handled by direct, individual contact or by small meetings.

To stress a point, *contact does not mean communication*. Mass media messages reach many people, but often few are motivated enough to act or even to think. The effectiveness of a message should be measured in results or impact, not by the size of the audience or the time involved in the effort.

Research must be done to select the best method of communications for each public. The method must be designed to fit the culture, situation, time, place and mental set of the specific audience. Empathy increases the chance for success because the communicator puts himself in the position of the public which he is trying to influence. In other words, he views the situation through the eyes of the people he is trying to communicate with. The situation or idea then can be analyzed as it appears to the people who are to be influenced. Thus, obstacles and beliefs that are present to the audience can, in theory, be detected and clarified by the communicator.

Three factors are involved in selecting a communications method. The effort needed for preparation and presentation must be considered. The number of people that can be reached by the method certainly is important. Last, the impact effect, or the result of the "input:output ratio" must be judged. To illustrate, a personal interview with one or two people takes much time per person contacted, but the impact is great. On the other hand, a large audience may be contacted with a television program, but how many of these people will really get the message and be motivated to act? The input per person contacted (effort) is small, but the output (results) is also small. Murphy (1967) stressed that the medium is not the message. It is not how much information is made available, but what is the context of that information and how well it is understood that are important.

All factors pertaining to the message and the public must be considered in selecting a method. For example, if the audience consists of landowners who are firm in their opinions or beliefs, a personal interview with each person may be the only solution to a problem. If the message is of general importance regarding a season and the desire is to reach as many sportsmen as possible, a mass medium might be the best method of contact. The greatest impact or output ratio from the least effort or input that will get the job done is usually the best guide in choosing a communications method. As Klapper (1960) pointed out, mass communications methods are better for obtaining attitude change or support than for opinion change or conversion.

The Communications Process

Regardless of the communications method to be used, certain realizations and procedures are suggested for success. The process may be thought of as a trip. Like a trip to a nearby town, certain steps are necessary and certain questions are asked. What are the goals, obstacles and destination? What route should be followed, and is this trip really necessary?

Planning

Assuming the effort is necessary, communications requires planning. The moral and physical correctness of the idea must be ascertained. All possibilities of being wrong should be uncovered and analyzed. Weak and strong points of the proposal should be determined. The weak points can be bolstered by facts and figures. The strong points can be stressed.

Goals need to be established in relation to the money and time available. All information should be assembled and evaluated and a written plan of attack should be developed. An educated guess then can be made as to the probable outcome of the effort. More data and facts should be gathered to insure that possible, undesired results do not occur. Alternate plans should be developed in case the first one does not produce the desired results after the process is under way.

The final plan that is chosen should be completely clear. This written plan should include all the facts, the situation, the problems, the obstacles to be overcome, the message, the specific public to be influenced, the timing, the detailed methods to be used and a system of evaluation to be continued at the end of the communications effort.

Preparation

Preparation comes after planning. The materials that are to be used should be assembled and the people who are to participate should be alerted. All props and individuals must be made ready for their part in the operation.

A promotional venture may be in order to alert the audience. This can be advertising or publicity of many types. It is usually a good idea to have as large a representation of the public as possible present or available to be exposed to the communications efforts.

The communications attempt should be well coordinated and timed. It helps to work from an organizational calendar of events (Appendix A). The calendar should be prepared ahead of time so each subject can be coordinated with other events that are to happen and with the proper dates. For example, a field trip to see deer range may be necessary in order to show overbrowsing of the shrubs and to promote a liberal season to reduce the deer population. This trip should be made when it will not interfere with hunters, will do the greatest good, will attract the largest audience and will provide an opportunity for the participants to see the most. Timing of community activities also must be considered in arranging events.

A climate of opinion or emotion which is favorable to the cause should be created. A common ground with ease of understanding should be established. The opening statements should be so obviously true and clear that it is impossible to have disagreement or misunderstanding. These opening statements must catch and hold the attention of the public long enough for the main message to be developed. An idea cannot be sold if the audience is not listening. An example of a good opening statement for a surplus deer problem might be, "The deer will starve if we have a hard winter." This statement has impact and no one should be able to disagree with it as pertaining to an overbrowsed area.

Transmission

There is no doubt that contact is an important, necessary part of communications, but it is only one step in the process. Understanding also is required. Something that does not penetrate the "life sphere" or the inner consciousness of the person or public receiving the message is not being understood. As Mapes (1966) said, the audience must be in "sharp focus." The person receiving the message must identify himself with it for adequate communications to exist.

This step involves the actual transmision of the message. It may be more effective to present both sides of the issue, but to present your side of the issue last. The audience gets the impression that the speaker is fair and broadminded, but they tend to retain the ideas given last. However, Klapper (1960) pointed out the danger of the two-sided presentation in the light of predispositions. He suggested the two-sided technique is better for an educated public, but the one-sided approach may be better for a non-educated audience.

The objective of the third step of the communications operation, transmission, is to influence the audience, to lead them without forcing them. They should be given what they think they want and what the speaker thinks they should have. The public should be shown why a liberal deer season is needed in this area and that such a season makes sense. Perhaps the audience can be made to remember past situations where winter loss did occur. Statements must be backed with facts and figures.

Barriers to Communications

There are many barriers to effective communications that must be recognized and planned for. Anything that distorts the message, prevents understanding or prevents a conscious thought process or action should be anticipated and handled accordingly. When understanding is lacking, pseudo-communications will result. Other meanings than the true ones are held valid and the effort goes astray.

Semantics and Language

One of the greatest barriers to effective communications is semantics and language. If the subject matter is not clear and if points are not understood, failure will result. Words used by the sender may be too technical to be understood by the receiver. The dialect spoken may not be familiar. Research should have determined the vernacular in the area and the educational level of the audience (Figure 45).

Clarity is necessary. Many words mean different things to different people. To illustrate, the word "cat" can mean a tractor, a lion, a domestic feline pet, a "hep" music lover, a malicious woman, a prostitute or a bobcat. An example more suited to natural resource

Figure 45. When trying to educate or influence, the person should converse in language understood by the audience.

management, an area is known where sage grouse commonly are called "sage chickens" by the local people. To use any other term in promoting a hunting season for sage grouse would immediately brand the individual as an outsider and a barrier would be raised.

There are times when another word or a new word must be used to increase clarity. One such word used to replace palatability (a word with many meanings) is "eatability." It is not in the dictionary, but no one should confuse the meaning, "Popullution" recently was coined to indicate the pollution effects of population. "Ego-plexus" is a coined word to illustrate a vulnerable target of the inner person.

Words also wear out. For example, the word "conservation" has been used so often, in so many different ways, that its true meaning is vague. Conservation of what? Nearly everything can be conserved to some extent. Many also confuse the meaning with preservation or exploitation.

It is possible to aim the message at a certain level to approximate the average intelligence of the individuals in the public being contacted. Most authorities on communications agree that this level is about the eighth or ninth grade for the average adult audience. A person should not talk or write below the intelligence level of the audience. However, making something too simple can be as fatal as making it too difficult. Flexibility and adjustment to the specific audience is the key to success.

Research has proven that the more senses involved in a communications operation, the greater are the chances that understanding will result. Many researchers have proven sight is the most effective single sense in achieving understanding. Other senses in decreasing order of effectiveness are sound, smell, touch and taste. A combination of several senses in the learning and retention of an idea is more effective than a single sense (Figure 46).

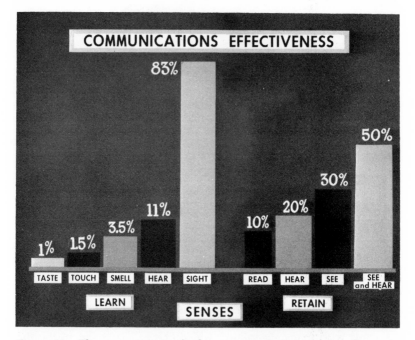

Figure 46.   The more senses involved in a communications attempt, the greater is the possibility of understanding. Retention also will be greater.

Social Barriers

Social barriers are difficult to overcome. These include such things as background, political affiliation, monetary situation, social status and age categories and differences. All are extremely important and should be determined for a public by research prior to any communications effort. Many of these social differences take a long time and hard work to overcome. The more acceptance and trust placed by the public in the communicator, the more likely the message will be received correctly.

Bias and distortion may be inherent with the medium in the individual's mind. Perhaps the individuals composing the public do not like television. Or maybe the group doesn't like the only newspaper that is available. This barrier often is due to some obscure event that occurred in the past.

The internal public of the organization must be in accord on the subject of the communications effort. One internal dissenter, speaking at the wrong time, can do much to erase the good that has been done. To illustrate, a public might say "They (the natural resource department personnel) cannot agree on this proposal themselves, so it must be a poor idea." This too often has been the story of many proposed ideas in natural resource management. The administration and every worker, from top to bottom, should have been convinced at the very beginning. Those who do not agree must at least be made to keep quiet.

Predispositions also can be barriers to the reception of an idea or proposal. These prejudices are the beliefs growing out of past experiences and can be extremely hard to overcome. What happened when the last either-sex deer season took place? Good or bad, these experiences should also be made known by research. If good, they should be used as supporting evidence for the currently desired season. If bad, facts should be gathered to explain where things went wrong and how they will be different this time.

Even a "captive audience," such as a class of students, can be present but be oblivious to the message. Students can look a professor right in the eye, then "tune him out." The lecture must be so interesting, so vital, that their inner consciousness, their life sphere, is reached. They associate themselves with the idea or issue, and then they learn! There is no such thing as a captive audience; captive bodies perhaps, but not captive minds. People may have to be present but they do not have to listen. But they must learn for good communications to exist.

Apathy, or "not caring enough to do something about it" often is a barrier to communications. If a person is uninterested, he will not receive the communique.

People want to preserve their beliefs and will usually act defensively against change. This is a barrier that should be detected through early research. Details are covered in the section of this book on the Sociology of Public Relations (pages 83 to 96).

Physical Barriers

Physical barriers are important. These barriers to communications include the availability of the medium to the public, the accessibility of the public and the personal characteristics of the public of a non-psychological nature. For example, rural folks may not have television sets or may not get the publication. Or, they may not have the modern modes of transportation easily available and necessary to attend the meeting. The public may be too large to reach with one effort or the message may not be repeated often enough.

Errors by media personnel are common and can drastically change the intended meaning of a message. The natural resource manager can write or tell the story himself, or he can have someone associated with the medium do it. A combination may be the best approach. The facts can be given to the medium personnel by the expert. The personnel associated with the medium then prepare the story or program. The story or program then is checked by the professional natural resource manager before it is released. Each situation should be considered separately and judged on the merits of the individuals and the message involved.

The speed at which the message is presented can be an important barrier. A person should not try to present too much, too fast. Once confused, most people have the tendency to shrug their shoulders and let the rest of the message go by. The message also should be designed so that if someone comes in during the middle of the presentation, the person will not be completely lost.

Competition for people's time is very keen. It is necessary to entice the public into a position where they will be exposed to the message. Their interest then must be retained so the message can be communicated. Few publics *have to* read, look at or listen to anything, unless they wish to. People naturally prefer to be exposed to something they enjoy. Therefore, the pill (message) must be sugarcoated and served with cake and ice cream (interest and entertainment) to compete for available time. Why should the people in the public go to a meeting on deer management when their favorite program is on television? The best solution to this barrier is to convince the public that the issue vitally concerns them. Their recreation, income, homes, families or prestige may be affected unless the deer are managed properly.

The what, why and how of a subject must be given and must make sense. Rote mechanical learning is not retained as long as learning which appears to be logical and has practical value. The more interesting the learning or communications process is, the more easily the subject will be learned, the better the job of communications will be and the longer the retention will be. The more complex a subject is, the harder it is to understand and the harder it is to achieve communications.

All of these barriers should be known from the preparatory research at the start of communications. To disregard the beliefs, habits, emotions and customs of a public is detrimental to any attempt at communications with that public. When vital information about a public is known, then proper steps can be planned to combat the barriers and to influence the public's thinking. A fact file, concerning the specific audience and compiled before the active communications operation starts, is suggested.

Evaluation

Evaluation should be a constant thing while the communications process is taking place. This can be done with sample opinions, polls or tests anytime during the operation. If these samples show that failure seems imminent or progress is unsatisfactory, an alternate plan may need to be instituted.

The last process in communications is a final analysis of the efforts of the completed operation and a "follow-up" in order to see if the desired results were attained. Did the actions that were taken by the public proceed according to the communications plan? If not successful, why not? Where did the plan fail? Was the message too complicated? Did the message reach too few? Was motivation lacking? Was propaganda too obvious? What should have been done? What should be done now? All answers and results should be incorporated in a fact file to help with further operations.

Comparative Use and Effectiveness of Communications Methods

Data were gathered from state conservation agencies. Many of the state conservation organizations include forest, range or parks functions and divisions. Characteristics of state organizations and the degree to which they use various communications methods are given so that comparisons can be made with other state and federal natural resource management agencies.

The purpose of communications is to inform and influence. Understanding is necessary. The ideal result is motivation toward the desired objective or goal.

State conservation agencies were asked to rank the most frequently used methods of communicating with their user publics. These methods include personal appearance programs, radio, television, magazines and pamphlets, newspapers and field contacts (Table 5).

Table 5. Comparative Use of Communications Methods Rated by State Conservation Organizations, 44 States (Gilbert, 1962).

Communications Method	Use Rating (1-High, 6-Low)
Publications (magazines & pamphlets)	2.4
Newspaper articles	2.5
Personal appearance programs, including slides and motion pictures	2.9
Television programs	3.6
Field contacts	4.2
Radio programs	4.6

The conservation magazine is the most popular method of communications used by a state conservation department. Approximately 20 per cent of the information and education budget is spent to make a regularly scheduled, departmental publication available. Perhaps federal natural resource management agencies should follow the state lead and publish a popular or semi-popular version of their activities. The U. S. Bureau of Land Management publication, "Our Public Lands," is the only, periodic, semi-popular publication on natural resources that is made available by a federal natural resource management agency.

The other methods of communication, with the exception of radio and television, were used spontaneously or as the need dictated. Both radio and television were regularly scheduled efforts but were far behind written, field and personal methods of contact in popularity. Some states indicated radio and television operations were very ineffective and used them little. Other states put much faith in radio and television. Less than five per cent of the information and education budget was spent on radio and television efforts. The remainder of the budget allocated for information and education work was spent on salaries, equipment (including projectors and motion pictures), supplies and travel.

Regarding effectiveness of communications, the data obtained were very hard to analyze. Many individuals confused the most popular or most used with the most effective. Effectiveness is very difficult to measure and must be calibrated in results rather than in numbers contacted or hours spent in the effort. State information and education personnel that attempted to rate the effectiveness of communications methods used listed them in the following order: field contacts and field trips; personal appearance programs, including the use of slides and motion pictures; television programs; newspaper articles; magazines and pamphlets; and radio programs.

PERSONAL APPEARANCE PROGRAMS

The big advantage of personal appearance programs as a contact method is the directness, the air of reality and the questions which can be asked and answered immediately, resulting in two-way communications. A responsive outburst is possible and everyone can have a chance to voice opinions. No other medium or method can replace direct contact when clarity, understanding and impact are needed.

Attempts to influence a public should not be too obvious. If it is possible to entertain as well as educate and motivate, the desired goal will be attained more easily. Many people attend a conservation meeting or talk to be entertained, to see a series of slides or a motion picture. They must be educated and motivated along with the entertainment.

Evaluation of personal appearance programs is difficult. Most audiences want to leave when a program is over rather than to be bothered with an evaluation of the presentation they have heard. The best method of evaluating the average talk on natural resources management is informal observation of audience reaction during and after the program. Congratulations and positive comments may mean success. Argumentation and discord may reflect the opposite, unless the subject was very controversial.

All categories of conservation department personnel, excluding office help, are asked at some time to give personal appearance programs. The main advantage of this type of contact is the directness of face-to-face communications which allows immediate interchange of thoughts. The three most used types of personal appearance programs used in the natural resource professions are compared in Table 6.

The state conservation departments averaged 13.7 speeches or straight lectures per week (Table 6). Administrators used this method more than other types of communication. They also gave 24 per cent of all lectures given by natural resource management agency personnel. Perhaps this is because administrators often are called upon to give extemporaneous presentations concerning the agency and its operations. Administrators also comprise the category of personnel that most often is involved in the "banquet circuit."

An average of 7.2 slide talks was given each week by state natural resource management personnel. Information and Education employees used slides in 37 per cent of all their programs. They also gave more slide illustrated lectures than other categories of conservation agency personnel (Table 6). This is because these people are most skillful in giving accompanying commentary. Information and education work is their main duty.

Table 6. Popularity and Use of Straight Lectures, Slide Talks and Motion Pictures, 44 State Conservation Agencies (Gilbert, 1962).

Comparison	Lectures	Slide Talks	Motion Pictures
Average number per week	13.7	7.2	15.7
Per cent given by Information and Education personnel	30	37	32
Per cent given by Conservation Officers	26	27	39
Per cent given by Administrators	24	13	14
Per cent given by Biologists	15	14	10
Per cent given by other categories of wildlife agency personnel	5	9	5
Totals	100	100	100

State conservation agencies averaged 15.7 motion pictures shown per week. Conservation officers presented more motion pictures (39% of the total) than other categories of conservation agency personnel. Motion picture showings constituted the main type of personal appearance programs given by conservation officers. This may be attributed to a lack of experience and training in public speaking for this category of workers.

Biologists were low in all phases of personal appearance presentations given by conservation agency employees. This may be because many state biologists are federal-aid employees, and as such are prohibited from giving public programs during working hours.

Another reason may be that most conservation agencies employ fewer biologists than other categories of personnel. Or, perhaps the biologist or research worker, is least interested in doing this type of work.

Information and education personnel are hired to give programs and to use all methods possible in order to inform the publics. It only is logical that they should do the majority of this work. The basic field men, in this instance the conservation officers, are second only to information and education personnel in the number of presentations and the time spent on this activity.

The direct contact methods of communications, such as personal appearance programs, where straight lectures or slide talks are given or where motion pictures are shown, are unsurpassed for impact on an audience. The air of intimacy, brought about by person-to-person contact, is not available with radio, television or the printed media.

Public Speaking

Every professional in a conservation organization is called upon at some time to disseminate information to a public through personal appearance. Responsibilities as a speaker will continue to increase with responsibilities in the profession. Many courses are offered in public speaking. Therefore, only those points will be presented here which have been found to be especially important to natural resource management personnel.

Zelko (1970) listed the steps in giving a speech as planning, organizing, developing, practicing and presenting. Perhaps purpose should be added as a first step. Definite objectives should be decided upon before the other steps can follow. Planning implies the thought processes necessary to organize points into a logical presentation. The actual organization effort should result in a written outline of important topics and sub-topics. In the developing process, details are added as necessary and visual aids are procured. Development also incorporates activities of compiling supporting statistics, analogies, anecdotes, testimony, humor and logic. It also seems that two additional steps, should be included after practice and presentation. These are evaluation in light of success or failure of the presentation and for future reference, and filing of materials and ideas for future efforts that will be forthcoming.

After an appointment to speak is made, every effort must be put forth to fulfill that appointment. A promise has been given and must be kept. Desire to do the job and to do a good job are the first requirements toward a successful end.

Advance notice should be insisted upon. If last minute appointments to speak are accepted, procuring groups will start thinking of that person or organization as an always available, second choice.

A person should become "speech conscious." This implies he should try to speak more distinctly and correct any faults relative to volume and nervousness. Reading about how to give a speech is like reading about flying an airplane. It is only a start. One must do it, and experience is the key to success. A degree of nervousness is normal and if this nervous energy is harnessed, it can be an asset. When a person is not nervous to some extent before a speech, he probably should not be giving the talk.

Casualness and calmness are important attributes of a speaker. A helpful method used by some to retain confidence is to remind ones-self that he must know something about the subject or he would be listening rather than talking. A good solution for the individual desiring more confidence and speaking ability is to practice. One way this can be done is to join a Toastmaster's Club. This club can be composed of organization personnel as a worthwhile evening or noon hour's diversion. Toastmaster's Clubs also may be found within most communities of any size. In these clubs, constructive criticism is offered by friends for each speech given. The quickest way to become proficient at speaking is to do it often and to try constantly for improvement.

Cockiness and overconfidence lead to disaster. A cocky approach creates a barrier in the minds of the audience and they look, and hope, for the show-off to fail. An overconfident person is courting trouble because he tends toward less preparation.

There is no such thing as a captive audience. Captive bodies may be present, but captive minds do not exist. One should attempt to establish a receptive audience attitude at the beginning of the talk. A mind is like the will-o-the-wisp and wanders. The audience should be "grabbed" in the first three minutes of a talk or it is lost. This can be done by establishing rapport with a significantly interesting, irrefutable statement or idea. A bad joke is a poor introductory method and a presentation should *never* start with an apology. If the speaker is ill-prepared, the audience will know about it soon enough without being told. After the air of friendliness and compatibility is achieved, the next task is to maintain it.

The speaker should not drag, roam from the subject or explode in personalities. The speech should be given slowly (about 200 words per minute is a good average) and in a strong, clear, lively voice. A monotone may indicate lack of interest by the speaker and lack of interest also may be the reaction of the audience. Specific situations about real people add to clarity and idea formulation.

If the presentation is long or complicated, it is a good idea to talk from an outline or note cards. A speech should never be memorized. Memories fail under stress. It usually is best not to read a speech but upon occasion a speech must be read. For example, it may be someone else's talk or may be too involved or complicated to deliver from an outline. Many people feel more secure if a type-written copy is available just in case they need it. They do not use it, but the secure feeling resulting from a written copy being present helps greatly.

A written copy of an oral presentation should be triple spaced. This allows for notes and additions to be made and makes the copy easier to follow at a glance. Segment or topic headings should be used freely and underlining in red will designate the more important points. Pauses also can be shown on the manuscript. Still, for most, the key to success is practice.

Informality and friendliness are important. A memorized or read speech usually does not have these qualities. Visual aids help to increase clarity, decrease formality, and also take the place of an outline.

It is not good to talk "down" or "up" to a group relative to intelligence levels. The degree of complexity should be pitched to easy understanding by the majority of the audience. If people don't understand, they soon will lose interest. Or, if the presentation is too basic or simple, they also will lose interest. For audiences composed of lay people, an average of 8th or 9th grade levels of comprehension is suggested.

Repetition of important points is essential. A good speaker tells something, explains what he said, then summarizes what he talked about. Repetition especially is needed for figures and statistics. These should be as simple as possible and should be kept at a minimum.

Gestures, expressions and emphasis are important, but they can be overdone. A jittery, running delivery can be as bad as a stoic, deadpan lecture. The audience will concentrate on the characteristics or actions of the speaker and not on what is being said. Relief devices while speaking, or reading a speech, such as looking up for eye contact, a pause for effect or asking a question, break monotony and aid the speaker in retaining the interest of the audience.

One should do everything possible to end the speech on time, even if forced to start late. If another speaker follows, both the chairman and the next speaker will appreciate it if the first speaker stays on the schedule or returns to it. This is a particularly difficult situation, because most people tend to give their entire speech, regardless of how long it takes or what time it is. Of course, other factors may be involved, such as audience fatigue, but it usually is best to stay on schedule.

At the end of a speech attention should be focused on main points with a concise summarization. This can be done with an appeal, question, challenge, quotation or a restatement of the problem. The summary should be short and forceful.

A speaker's bureau, so common in large business, can do much for an organization. Capable individuals with certain abilities and specialties are scheduled by someone else in the organization to give presentations. Requests are funneled to the person handling the scheduling. However, there are very few speaker's bureaus in natural resource agencies.

Forums

Interest seems to be increasing in natural resource management forums. These incorporate the use of slides, straight lectures and motion pictures in a series of programs which complement each other. This type of communications in natural resource management was pioneered by Montana in 1949 and since then has been adopted by many states (Severy and Pengelly, 1956).

A program sequence is suggested. These talks often start with basic land management and ecological relationships of soil, water, plants and animals. The registrants can be taken through natural resource agency administration problems and principles of natural resource management and research as applied to local situations. The average program consists of an hour lecture and one hour of informal discussion. Guest speakers are used as needed.

Forums often are sponsored by a local public, such as a sportsmen's club or service club. Publicity and arrangements of place and time are made by the sponsor at the discretion of the person or persons responsible for giving the programs. In this way good attendance virtually is assured.

Severy and Pengelly (1956) suggested that the forum instructor not be an employee of the conservation agency. They believe that a well-informed, apparent outsider, such as an extension specialist, will be more acceptable to most audiences. However, Brown (no date) indicated forums are very effective even if conducted by natural resource agency officials.

Visual Aids

All communications should be designed to create understanding. Investigators agree that learning and understanding are increased in proportion to the number of senses employed in the communications effort. The process of learning, as determined by psychologists, generally is about 83 per cent dependent upon sight, 11 per cent on sound, three per cent on smell, two per cent on touch and one per cent on taste (see Figure 46, page 104). It seems logical, therefore, to use as much sight as possible in trying to influence public opinion.

A visual aid is an object which incorporates the sense of sight and perhaps uses movement in the teaching process. Thus, the clarity of the presentation should be helped. Visual aids are just what the name implies, an "aid." They are no panacea but if used correctly they will increase understanding.

Visual aids, if used properly, can accomplish several objectives. First, they create and retain interest. Second, clarity is increased greatly. Third, retention is increased because more than one sense is used. Fourth, there is greater chance for motivation and action by the audience from something they understand. Fifth, the presence of visual aids, if publicized, may increase attendance. And sixth, and perhaps as important as any reason, visual aids can be a great help to the speaker. They take the place of notes and are a reminder of what should be said next. It must be stressed, however, that visual aids should augment a speaker, not replace him (Figure 47).

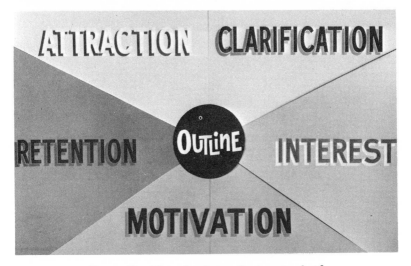

Figure 47.   The advantages of using visual aids.

Too many visual aids can complicate and confuse rather than clarify, and may be worse than none at all. Only those which are necessary and which will help the presentation should be used.

In preparing to use visual aids, an outline of the talk should be constructed to determine the major points to be stressed. Visual aids then should be developed or acquired to stress those points (Figure 48). If a choice is possible, the visual aid that has movement and will employ the greatest number of the senses should be used. To illustrate, an "active" graphic, one that is built up or torn down as the talk progresses, usually is better than a "static" graphic if quality is comparable.

A visual aid should have appeal as well as being technically correct. Cartoons and caricatures can add humor and increase interest (Figure 49). Bright colors and a brief message in simple words make understanding easier. One style of letters should be used for one effort, and a simple, bold style is suggested.

All parts and letters should be of relative size and large enough for the audience to see them easily. If the visual aid cannot be

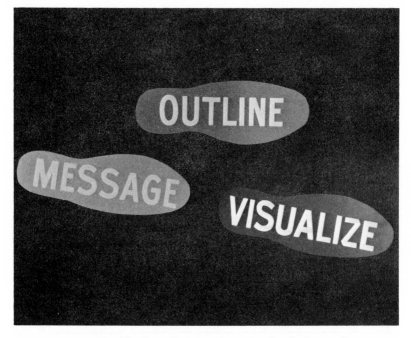

Figure 48.   The "steps" in preparing visual aids for a talk.

seen, it should not be used. Too often the first comment concerning a photograph, chart, or slide used in a lecture is, "You can't see this, but . . ." Why show it if it can't be seen?

An object or letter 1/4 inch high is visible for about 8 feet. An object or letter 1/2 inch high can be seen for approximately 16 feet; one inch for from 30 to 35 feet; and a three-inch object or letter should be visible up to 110 feet. Line spacing should be about 1 1/2 times letter size. Letters should be from 1/4 to 1/7 wide as high, depending upon the boldness desired.

It generally is better to have materials too large than too small. If time is available, and to be sure, before the talk the speaker should go back to the farthest seat and see how the sign or object appears from that distance.

Color harmony can help a visual aid. Cool colors, such as green, blue and gray, are good for backgrounds. Warm colors (red, orange and yellow) add emphasis. Good combinations are black on yellow, green on white, black on gray, white on blue or blue on white. Black on white may be too contrasty and formal.

Legibility, too, is the result of wise color choice, but glare of artificial lights can destroy color harmony and legibility. Light colors make objects appear larger, while dark colors make letters and materials seem smaller and narrower. Dark colors and heavy lines should be at the bottom of a chart so the end product will not appear top heavy.

Wildlife Willie   by Charles Hjelte

Figure 49.   Cartoons and caricatures add humor and increase interest.

Visual aids should not be seen or examined by anyone in the audience before they are to be used. For example, if a handout is given to the class at the start of a period and before the subject is discussed, the students will be attempting to interpret the handout material instead of listening to the lecturer. Models, charts and other visual aids should not be seen until they are to be used.

A visual aid should be explained as it is being shown. The speaker should read a graph and simultaneously point to the important points. Care must be taken so the speaker does not block the view with his body and he should talk to the audience and not the chart or screen (Figure 50).

Selection of which visual aid to use depends on many factors. First, what is the nature of the presentation and the point to be developed? What talent is available for developing the visual aid

Figure 50. The visual aid should be used "in addition to," not "instead of" the speaker. The speaker should talk to the audience, not the visual aid.

and in using it? Are good visual aids of one kind or another already available? What is the size of the audience and the room where the presentation is to be given? How much money is available? The prime question is which visual aid will do the best job of illustrating the points in the presentation.

Actual objects often are the best kind of visual aids to use. For example, if a wildlife conservation officer is explaining how to tell the age of deer from the teeth, nothing can help the presentation as much as having a collection of deer jaws available for the audience to see, feel, hear about and smell. The "air" of reality is important. But the actual object may be too large, too small or not present in sufficient amounts for all to see. Other visual aids then may be better.

Models can be helpful. They allow control of size if an object, either too large or too small for actual use, is duplicated in facsimile and used in the talk. Models can be made so they can be dismantled, and they offer possibilities for central dimension in that they can be constructed so parts can be removed and the inside be visible. They can be animated to show working or component parts. An elk trap is too large and bulky for the classroom or studio (Figure 51). A model will show the trap almost as well as the actual trap (Figure 52). Excellent plastic models of some biological objects are available commercially (Figure 53).

Figure 51. It may be impossible to take the actual object into the classroom or television studio.

Figure 52. A model of an elk trap can be used for instruction purposes.

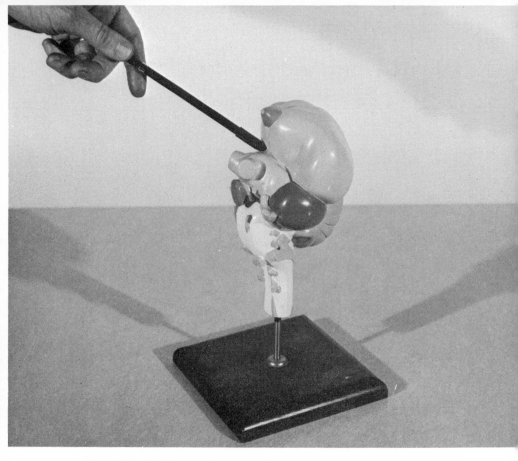

Figure 53. Models can be animated and size can be controlled. Excellent
models of biological subjects are available.

Active graphics are visual aids which can be put together
or taken apart, step by step, as the talk progresses. The key is movement and building up to the climax or completed illustration. Examples are use of chalk boards on which objects are drawn as the
talk progresses, magnet boards, flannel boards, hook or velcro
boards and charts or graphs with movable parts.

Flannel boards, hook and loop boards, or velcro boards can be
used successfully to show various, preworked equations illustrated
with caricatures (Figure 54). The ferriergraph is the opposite of
the "slap" boards where objects are stuck on as the talk progresses.
The ferriergraph is comparable to a "strip-tease" in that material
is uncovered as the presentation continues.

The chalk board is used widely, sometimes well, sometimes
badly, in teaching and in lecturing. Neatness, size and speed of
writing are important in obtaining effectiveness. Colored chalk and
art ability help. Dr. Sam Knight, Professor Emeritus of Geology at
the University of Wyoming, had an extraordinary ability to use the
chalk board. He would draw in three dimensions with colored chalk.
Erasing would indicate erosion and presentations regarding such
subjects as formation of the Rocky Mountains were outstanding!

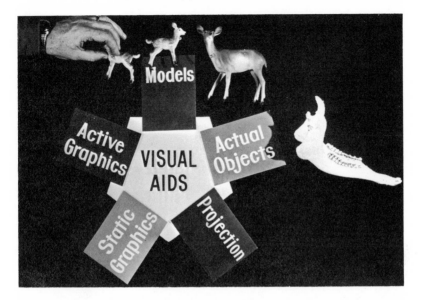

Figure 54. With an active graphic, the visual aid is put together or uncovered as the talk progresses.

Static graphics include still photographs, charts, graphs, maps and posters. These should be kept uncluttered and simple. Anything to increase clarity and interest is good. Bright colors, pictures and cartoons are better to use than black and white colors and too many words (Figure 55).

Projected visual aids are very popular. These save space and are convenient to use. In addition, they are versatile, generally are comparatively reasonable in cost and can be very effective. Included are opaque projection, overhead projection, motion pictures and transparent slides.

With an opaque projector, the item to be shown does not need to be transparent. For example, pages from a book can be projected on a screen. This is accomplished with a series of mirrors and requires a completely darkened room. If the room is not completely dark, the quality of the image will be inferior. An added person is needed to operate the projector if the speaker wants to face the audience and talk from in front of the room. An opaque projector is large, heavy and clumsy, but does project an exact duplicate.

An overhead projector allows the operator to draw with a waxed pencil or to lay transparent materials on a glass area for projection onto a screen. With this type of projection, the speaker faces the audience and the quality of the image is excellent. The room need not be darkened. The projector is placed close to the front of the room and is operated by the speaker (Figure 56). An image of adequate size usually is no problem, but strongly upward angles will cause "keystoning" of the image unless the screen is tilted outward

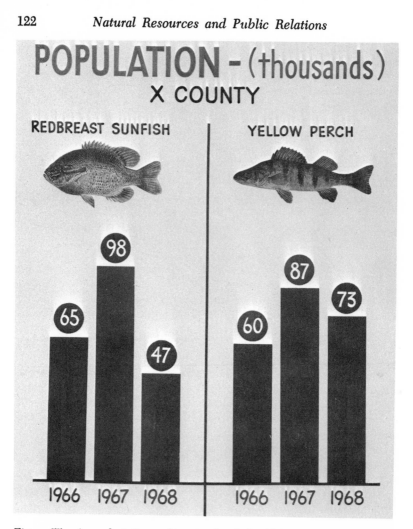

Figure 55.   A good static graphic visual aid should be large enough, simple and colorful.

at the top to compensate for the projector angle. That is, if the screen is vertical and the projector is tilted upward, an image which should be rectangular will be wider at the top than at the bottom.

Rolls of acetate or plastic material are now available to take the place of single 10 x 10 inch sheets and allow much more information to be prepared ahead of time without fear of loss or disarrangement. The rolls holding the plastic material are mounted on the sides of the overhead projector. Cardboard frames for single sheets provide a place for penciled notes and stabilize each transparency.

Colored acetate sheets and tapes are available, as are colored wax pencils and inks for drawing on clear sheets. Several overlays, superimposed, can give the projected images advantage of added colors and of active graphics in that the visual aid is added to as

Figure 56.   An overhead projector allows the speaker to face the audience in a room that is not darkened.

the talk progresses. A piece of paper over part of the overlay sheet to be projected can be moved to uncover each point, segment or step. Thus, the ferriergraph is duplicated.

A tremendous illusion of continuance can be achieved by using the "strip-tease" technique with an overhead projector. The desired illustration may be to show the progress of a canal being dug or the construction of a telephone line, fence or similar item. The entire picture can be drawn on a sheet of acetate. This can be complete with colors, dates, cartoons and other techniques to add interest and increase clarity. When projected, most of the transparency is covered. The illustration then is uncovered as time and progress proceed.

High quality, colored, transparencies are commercially available for many biological, geological and natural resource management subjects. Pages or opaque materials can be duplicated with a rapid, dry photographic method (Thermofax, Xerox, etc.) on acetate material. These can then be used with an overhead projector.

Slides and motion pictures are used universally to illustrate messages. They incorporate sight, sound and often color. Any object or scene can be brought to the present from the distant or past. Authenticity is present because "I saw it myself." Size of item or area is no problem. Reductions or enlargements are simple and cost is relatively low. Both slide talks and motion pictures are discussed in detail in later sections.

Meetings

Each meeting should have definite, clear objectives for a specific audience. Decisions as to audience size and background need be made before speakers and facilities are arranged. If these objectives and decisions are not clear or cannot be made, the meeting probably should not be held.

Personnel of natural resource management agencies frequently are responsible for a meeting. If such is the case, the person in charge of a program should select speakers with care. All courtesies possible should be extended to them. Their abilities should be known, and it should be determined that speakers will accentuate the subject matter desired. If a proposal is being promoted, speakers should be in accord.

Facilities should be clean and neat with comfortable chairs, good ventilation, adequate lighting, good acoustics and ample room. An uncomfortable person will not be able to concentrate on what is being said and anything that detracts from presentations will detract from the overall effectiveness of the meeting or conference.

Advance publicity of a coming meeting is essential. Success depends upon attendance. Therefore, it is good business to reach as many people as possible. This can be done in many ways, including the use of posters and brochures. News stories should be released at least one or two months before the meeting or conference. Details relative to date, time, place and purpose can be given. Additional news stories can then follow the first release at two- to three-week intervals. Publicity costs generally are absorbed by the sponsoring group. If this is not done, and the meeting is quite important from the viewpoint of the individual or the natural resource management agency, there is nothing wrong with the speaker or the agency publicizing it.

Radio and television also should be used for publicity purposes. These programs can be interview of personalities involved or short, forceful, spot announcements.

Maps of the general area and room locations may be needed. These can be included in the printed brochures along with a detailed agenda.

Materials should be checked and double checked to be sure that equipment, including projectors, extension cords, screens, lecturns and other materials needed by the speakers are available. This equipment should be in good working order with spare parts, such as projector bulbs, immediately available. Accidents relative to equipment should be anticipated and planned for. Water should be easily available to the speaker because a dry throat or cough will detract from a talk.

In a very large and important meeting, someone should be assigned to the specific tasks of equipment procurement, care and operation. Another approach, a person may be assigned to each speaker to see that the speaker's equipment needs and operation of that equipment are taken care of.

Stretch breaks and coffee breaks allow for informal discussion and offer a chance to relax. These should be included in the planned schedule. A tired, bored, sleepy, or uncomfortable audience is not receptive.

Introducing a speaker is an art. Tact, sincerity and enthusiasm aid an introduction. A good introduction will relieve tensions and establish topics. The audience will want to know about the speaker and what his subject will be. They should be stimulated by the person giving the introduction so they want to hear what is to be said.

The person making the introduction should not embarrass the speaker or the audience. The introduction should be short, factual and to the point. The following points are suggested for an introduction:

1. Who the speaker is (twice, once at start and once at end).
2. Where the speaker is from.
3. Why or how the speaker is qualified to give this presentation.
4. Why this presentation is important to the audience.
5. Do not give personal views, apologize for anything, or use trite phrases, such as "needs no introduction."
6. Do not be too elaborate.

The person making the introduction should stand as the speaker comes forward. After the talk, a sincere thanks should be given to the speaker and the audience. If a summarization is given, it should be done by the speaker, not the chairman or the person that introduced the speaker. Nor should they take issue or add to the presentation.

I shall never forget one introduction given me while working for the Colorado Game and Fish Department. I was to make a slide presentation. The introduction was, "Some guy from the Forest Service is here to show us a film about something." I am sure the resulting program suffered, perhaps not on purpose, but my heart wasn't in the presentation!

The person responsible for a meeting or acting as program chairman must be sure the time schedule is maintained. Speakers should know how long they have and should not be allowed to exceed that time limit. One speaker going over his allotted time will cause others to start late, and the entire conference will be out of phase. Someone will be cut short at the end, and good will is not the result.

One approach to keeping speakers on schedule is to use a belled timer or alarm clock. This is effective, but is not too delicate. With some speakers, it may be too much regimentation. Some may become confused and perhaps insulted, so this method of control should be used with care. A slip of paper given to the speaker five minutes before his time is up may be quite inobtrusive but effective. Another technique is to have a closed circuit with a blinker light at the podium. The chairman flashes the light when time is up. No one sees the signal but the speaker.

A follow-up publicity venture after the meeting is as important as advanced publicity. Photographs of speakers add human interest. Results and highlights of presentations are publicized for those who could not attend. This late publicity also sets the stage for the next effort at another time.

A guide to planned meetings was published in a Wildlife Society Newsletter (Anonymous, 1965). It is presented in Appendix D. A checklist approach, such as this, insures that nothing will be omitted.

Slide Talks

A script is the first step in developing a slide series. This especially is important if the photographer doing the shooting does not have necessary technical knowledge of the subject being photographed. The script will describe the desired scenes and stress the points that should be illustrated. A script also will be very helpful in editing additional slides to fit the talk. However, a photographer should be opportunistic at all times.

One technique in organizing thoughts and developing a script for a slide series is to use the "story board." Cards (4 x 6 inches) are used for a segment of the script and to depict the slide that best will illustrate that script segment (Figure 57). These cards are changed and moved about as a new subject or order in the presentation are experimented with. The result is a logical script from which the photographer will know what pictures are wanted. One or more slides can be used for each card, idea or point in the script (Figure 58).

Signs and lettering in slides often are a problem. All lettering must be large enough to be seen easily. A size of ¼-inch letters on a standard 8½ x 11-inch sheet of paper is about minimum for photographing letters to be used in a slide. Image size is adjusted with the distance from projector to screen but it also depends on how large the object was when the slide was taken. If a choice is available, an object, such as a deer, a trap or a person, should fill about one-half of the slide frame. A more detailed discussion relative to size of projected materials is presented in the previous section on visual aids (Pages 114 to 124).

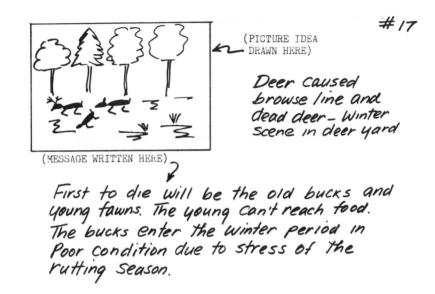

#17

(PICTURE IDEA DRAWN HERE)

Deer caused browse line and dead deer - Winter scene in deer yard

(MESSAGE WRITTEN HERE)

First to die will be the old bucks and young fawns. The young can't reach food. The bucks enter the winter period in poor condition due to stress of the rutting season.

Figure 57.　Each idea for a slide in the talk is depicted on a card. The cards are rearranged, added to, or subtracted from as ideas change.

Figure 58.　The cards on the "story board" are rearranged as the shooting script is developed.

Each slide talk should be developed with one central theme in mind. It is better to tell one story completely than to tell several half-way. As difficult as it may be to do, the proposed number of slides to be included usually should be reduced because an impression of hurriedness in a talk distracts greatly. A few good slides are better than many mediocre ones. A timing of one slide for every 30 seconds is a good rule of thumb for an average presentation to an average audience.

The sequence should be edited and arranged with care. Some truly excellent pictures at the start act as "attention grabbers" and are extremely important to catch and hold interest at the beginning of the presentation. Anecdotes, poems, quotations or a challenging statement also create attention and interest. Lighter commentary and pictures interspersed occasionally will help the speaker to attain and retain attention and interest. But, the "fun stuff" shouldn't be overdone. It is possible to detract too much from the main message of the talk. Care need be taken to be sure that "off-beat" slides will not offend someone in the audience.

To protect them, slides should be mounted in glass. This protects the film from dirt, scratches and fingerprints, and does away with the necessity of very frequent focusing caused by a slide popping out of focus due to heat changes. A standard mount should be used for all slides because each time a differently bound slide is shown, the focus will have to be changed. The type of mount depends upon individual preference. An alternative to glass mounts is to show only duplicates and not original slides.

Time taken before the presentation will insure that the slides are in the proper order and will not be shown on the screen upside down or backwards. There is no excuse for pictures not being projected correctly. An aid is to put a mark or a paper dot in the upper right-hand corner of the frame of the picture as it goes into the projector. This allows the speaker or operator to tell with a quick glance if all pictures are in correctly. Another hint is to remember that emulsion goes toward emulsion. The emulsion side of the slide, or the dull side, always goes toward the screen. Some of the newer projectors have a small, built-in, preview screen which allows the operator to see the next slide before it is shown on the screen.

All slides should be labeled in case they are loaned or lost, or for easy sorting. A complete label contains the place, date and photographer, and perhaps the owner if different from the photographer. Some people also add a number if their slides are catalogued.

A catalogue and filing system depend upon individual preference and the number of slides in the collection. Most filing is done by subject matter. An outline of subjects included in the slides is a good starting point.

Sorting slides for a presentation also depends upon many factors, including the number of slides, type of filing or catalogue system, time and individual ability. A light table as used for drafting, or a light frame, allows one to view many slides simultaneously and choose and sort at the same time. Some of the more elaborate filing cabinets are constructed so many slides can be seen at once (Figure 59).

Figure 59. Some of the more elaborate filing cabinets for 35 mm. slides allow many slides to be viewed at once.

Room organization is important in any presentation where projected visual aids are used. Mechanics of "setting up" should be taken care of before the time of presentation.

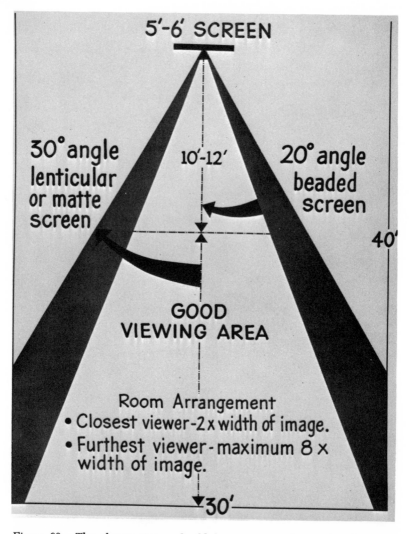

Figure 60. The closest viewer should be no nearer than twice the image width. The maximum for the farthest viewer is eight times the image width. The ideal viewing cone varies with screen type.

Characteristics of the projection room should be examined and compensated for if necessary. One big fault of many rooms is inadequate darkening facilities. A slight illumination, but not on the screen, is good because it creates a social or friendly atmosphere. But this light must be dim in order that quality of slides is not reduced.

Electric outlets and switches should be located ahead of time. Ventilation and acoustics also are important. If a room echoes when empty, the same may not be true when seats are occupied. Outside noises, such as jackhammers and motor vehicles, will detract from the talk and annoy the speaker.

Table 7. Suggested Bulb Wattage, Approximate Projection Distance, and Image Width Based upon Focal Length of Lens, 35mm. Projectors.

Projector Distance in Feet	Focal Length of Lens							Suggested Minimum Bulb Wattage
	90.0 (mm.) 3.5 (in.)	100 4.0	120 4.75	150 6.0	175 7.0	200 8.0	250 10.0	
			Image Width in Feet					
5	1.75							
10	3.75	3.50						
13	5.00	4.50	3.75					500
16	6.25	5.50	4.50	3.75				Watt
18	7.00	6.00	5.25	4.25	3.25			(To 25
20	7.75	7.00	5.75	4.50	3.75	3.50		feet)
23	8.75	8.00	6.50	5.25	4.25	4.00	3.25	
26	10.00	9.00	7.50	6.00	5.00	4.50	3.50	
30	11.75	10.25	8.75	7.00	5.75	5.25	4.50	
33	12.75	11.50	9.50	7.50	6.00	5.75	4.75	750
36		12.50	10.25	8.25	6.75	6.50	5.25	Watt
40		14.00	11.50	9.25	7.50	7.00	5.75	(To 50
43			12.50	10.00	8.50	7.50	6.00	feet)
46			13.00	10.75	9.00	8.25	6.50	
49				11.25	9.50	9.00	7.00	
52				12.00	10.25	9.50	7.50	
56					11.00	10.00	8.00	
59						10.75	8.25	1000
62						11.25	9.00	Watt
65						11.50	9.50	(Over
69						12.50	10.00	50
72						12.75	10.25	feet)
75						13.50	10.75	
85							12.25	
95							13.50	
110							15.00	
150							20.00	

Distances from projector to screen also can be computed with the following equations (Eastman Kodak Co., 1967). All estimates or measurements must be in inches or the results will be confusing.

1. $\dfrac{\text{Desired Projection Distance}}{\text{Image Width}} = \text{Factor}$

2. (Factor x Image Width) + Lens Focal Length = Projection Distance

3. $\dfrac{(\text{Projection Distance} - \text{Lens Focal Length})}{\text{Factor}} = \text{Image Width}$

The screen can be the weakest link in the chain of a good presentation. Old, discolored, spotty, dirty screens make for less than a desirable program. A beaded screen is the most popular and is adequate for small groups and for long rooms that have a narrow viewing cone. With a beaded screen the viewing angle should be no greater than 20 degrees from a line mentally drawn from the center of the screen and at right angles to it. Viewers should sit in this 40-degree viewing cone (two 20-degree angles, one on either side of the imaginary line) but should sit no closer than two times the width of the screen. The most distant viewer should be no farther back than eight times the width of the screen (Figure 60).

Lenticular and matte screens have metallic surfaces and diffuse an equal amount of light in all directions. Thus, the image has equal brightness at any angle. These screens are better for a room that cannot be darkened to the extent that it should be. The allowable viewing angle is 30 degrees from the center line with a lenticular or matte screen, and the allowable seating cone is an angle of 60 degrees. Maximum, allowable distances for the closest viewer (2W) and the farthest viewer (8W) are the same regardless of screen type.

The projector should be far enough back so the picture almost fills the screen with no overlap on the sides. A square screen is advantageous because both horizontal and vertical slides can be shown from the same distance without having part of the picture miss the screen.

The focal length of the projector lens dictates the extremes of distance that can be tolerated with a certain size of screen and a corresponding size of image (Table 7). Some "zoom" lenses are available for projectors. These allow the projectionist to fill the screen from a range of distances.

Screen location depends upon the room dimensions. Generally, the screen should be in the darkest portion. This must be compatible with room arrangement and the number of people in the audience. If the room is square, a screen placed in a corner will allow more people to be seated in the good-viewing cone than if the screen were placed along one side of the room.

In addition to the type of screen, brightness depends upon other factors such as wattage of bulb, projector design, cleanliness of optics and nature or denseness of the material to be shown. Very seldom is a projected image too bright. However, it can be too light or "washed out" due to the picture being overexposed.

Most projectors take a certain size (wattage) bulb. A projector with a 500-watt bulb is adequate for short distances and correspondingly small groups (Table 7). A 750- or 1000-watt lamp and projector are suggested for long projection distances and large audiences. For extra dark, dense and underexposed slides, the projector can be moved closer to the screen, but this produces a smaller image. A projector moved to one-half the original distance will project an image four times the original brightness.

It would be nice if all equipment could be the best and would work, if the room were closely surveyed and compensated for if necessary, if errors in projection and screen distances were measured and corrected and if every one in the audience were seated in the best viewing areas. But such usually isn't the case. Generally, it is a situation of not knowing characteristics of facilities or the audience. Good projection equipment, plus spare parts and a knowledge of the subject matter are the best aids one can have. A third asset is the ability to handle the mechanics of a slide presentation in a professional, efficient manner.

When possible, the equipment should be set up before the scheduled time of the talk. This includes the first slide in the projector, properly focused, for instant projection. Lack of this preparation results in an embarrassing lull and a less than auspicious start. Although a smooth beginning may not be appreciated by the audience, a disorganized start is readily apparent.

It is better for the speaker to have complete responsibility for changing slides. With modern projectors, this is done easily with a remote control cord. The speaker can address the audience, change slides and focus the slide from the front of the room. This is better than talking from the rear of the room near the projector. If the speaker is in front, someone should be near the projector at all times to change cartridges or to take care of minor mechanical situations that may arise.

Some projectors are not constructed to allow focusing with a remote cord. If this is the case, the person at the projector also will have to focus each slide.

If it is necessary to have someone project the slides the individual should be capable. The whole presentation can be negated by sloppy projection and mechanical errors.

If a projector operator is used, the best signal for slide changes is a small, closed circuit light that flashes near the projector. This light is activated by a remote push button held by the speaker. Other signals for a slide change, such as a clicker, a tap with a stick, a wave of the hand, a light beam, or voice deflection all detract from the speech. Voice deflection signals are good if the speaker and projectionist can work well with each other, but signals are easily missed. A small spot of light from a flashlight, held by the speaker and shown in the upper right-hand corner of the screen, is a fairly unobtrusive signal, but also may be missed by the projectionist.

Pointing can be done rather unsuccessfully from the projector, or it can be done from up in front. The hand, a yardstick, or something similar may be used as a pointer. An old automobile radio aerial is not bad, and a similar, telescoping pointer can be purchased commercially. However, the best pointer is a small spot of light. An adapter can be purchased to concentrate the beam of any flashlight. This has the advantage of being operable from a distance and allows the speaker to point anywhere on the screen with ease.

A smooth commentary is essential to a good slide presentation. Triteness and redundancy must be avoided. Common errors include many "uhs," "this slide is of," "as you can see here," "this is a view of," or "look closely and you will see." The audience can see what the slide depicts and what is on the screen.

One can be so familiar with the sequence that he remembers which slide is next, but, memories fail and slides do get mixed up. A better method to insure smooth commentary is to let the talk slightly follow the change of slides. In this way, one can be saying the last words about the preceding picture when the next one is flashed on the screen. The speaker will know what slide is next, and the flow of words will be smooth. Slides should supplement the talk rather than compete with it.

In ending the talk, a closing slide will avoid a short, choppy, stop. The words "THE END," scratched in the sand and photographed can result in a good ending slide. More elaborate, and perhaps humorous, possibilities take little imagination. The much too frequently used sunset certainly can be improved upon. The glare of no slide at all at the start or end of a talk can be avoided with a piece of cardboard cut to fit the projector.

A score card to evaluate a slide presentation is given in Appendix E. This was used to grade students giving slide presentations and could be used to grade oneself. It also acts as a reminder ahead of a talk to be sure all is in order and nothing is forgotten.

Slides generally are considered better than motion pictures for most educational purposes. Points of stress can be repeated until understood. Slides have a more personal contact, because a living, talking individual is doing the narration. The person in charge must know his subject better than he needs to if he is showing motion pictures, because the entire program is his responsibility instead of only the introduction and discussion at the end.

A few slides of nearby scenes can be included with any sequence and will give a local flavor to the presentation that most motion pictures do not have. This is important in winning an audience. Slides do not have the entertainment connotation that motion pictures have. People come to see a motion picture to be entertained, not educated and this can be a block to the educational effort.

There is more flexibility in a slide presentation than with motion pictures. For example, the same slides can be used in more than one lecture and in different sequences. The length of the presentation also can be varied as needed. A specific presentation can be designed for a specific public without great cost or permanence.

Slide shows are much less expensive than motion pictures. An average cost of $100.00 to $500.00, depending on equipment and time involved, for a 30-minute slide show compares favorably with a conservative cost of from $5,000 to over $15,000 for a quality, sound, 30-minute, color motion picture. Slide projection equipment costs less and is easier to operate than motion picture projection equipment.

Various comments from natural resource management agency personnel regarding slide talks stressed that the value of slide talks depends directly upon the ability of the speaker. Some agencies do not use slide talks at all due to the limitations of amateur commentary. Other organizations have as many as 50 slide talks given per week by their staff. Some natural resource management agencies are starting to distribute slide packets and accompanying written lectures or voice tapes on specific subjects just as they distribute motion pictures.

Motion Pictures

One of the most used visual aids, in terms of the number of people contacted, is the motion picture. Graham (1960) stated that at that time the *New York Times* estimated more than 3,000 companies and trade associations were sponsoring one or more 16 mm. films. He stated that the reason for the popularity of films was their closeness to presenting reality. Through the use of a motion picture, the audience is able to project itself into the situation portrayed on the screen. Hosie and Mayer (1963) stressed that excitement and anticipation can be created with a good motion picture and that attention and interest are a natural result.

Commercial theatres use 35 mm. motion pictures. Films in most libraries, including natural resource management motion pictures, are on 16 mm. film. A film size of 8 mm. is satisfactory for home showings but generally is not considered suitable for public presentations. However, possibilities for 8 mm. and "super-8" motion pictures are increasing with better equipment. Most television studios use 16 mm. film. A discussion on the use of motion pictures in television is presented in the section of this book on television (Pages 177 to 187).

Motion picture production needs more careful planning than does a slide series. This primarily is due to greater cost. The purpose of the film should be definitely established and kept in mind throughout the production.

Many films are made for a certain public, and the public or audience should be well defined. What is the reaction desired from that public? All efforts then are pointed toward bringing that reaction about.

Details of the motion picture should be worked out completely before photography starts. Is the story or message a good one?

Where will this film be photographed? How long will it be? One thousand feet will take about 30 minutes to show at sound speed, or 24 frames per second. Will this film be in color or black and white? Is it to be serious, or humorous, or a combination? What are the time schedules that must be adhered to? How about music, sound and narration?

The answers to these questions, and others, often depend on the budget and cost can be high. Dunn (1961) gave an average of 18 business films for 10 minutes of screen time as $12,000. Badler (1961) used a figure of $1,000 per minute for a quality, sound-color motion picture. Costs have increased since these studies. All details of finance should be solved before the cameras start. Too many natural resource films are the result of splicing haphazard photographic efforts of amateurs. The reception of the public reflects this, and what money is spent largely is wasted. It is far better to spend the money that is necessary to do a top-quality job and to have the desired message reach the chosen public.

After the preliminary planning of a motion picture, the next step is to develop the story. This is the narration which will accompany the pictures. The narration should arrange sequences and define points to be stressed.

The shooting script usually is composed from the narration. A paragraph is taken from the story and the scene is visualized which will best illustrate that paragraph. This process requires much cutting and fitting because the pictures must exemplify exactly what the words convey.

After the shooting script has been developed carefully, the scenes are then photographed. The film stock will be the cheapest part of the venture, so it is best to be sure that each scene is obtained. From 5 to 20 times as much film generally will be exposed as is used in the final copy.

All editing should be done from a black and white work print which is made from the original film. This is regardless of whether the film is in color or not. The original film negative should be carefully protected. After this first editing, there undoubtedly will be changes necessary in both photography and narration.

The last step in motion picture production is to synchronize the sound with the pictures. This operation requires professional equipment and knowledge. Actually, it may be better and cheaper to have a professional studio do all the technical work, including photography. Few natural resource agencies have either the knowledge or the materials to produce the professional motion picture that is desired. Of course, a technician from the organization is necessary to insure that all information is biologically correct.

If a motion picture is to be used as a visual aid, it is essential to preview the film before the actual showing. This especially is true if others show the same print. The film may not be rewound or it may be broken. Adjustments during a presentation can be extremely difficult. When one is working under pressure, things often seem to go wrong. This appears to be especially true if the audience is not receptive (Figure 61).

Figure 61. Repairs and adjustments are difficult to make under pressures of a viewing audience.

Another reason for an early examination or a preview is to make necessary repairs when time is available. Many film libraries ask that their films not be rewound before returning them. This gives a chance to examine the film during the rewinding process.

A broken film should be permanently repaired in the laboratory or office by someone who knows how. It is a simple operation with the right equipment. If the film breaks during the showing, an extra lap of film can be advanced around the take-up reel. This should be made taut, and the show can proceed. Plastic tape splices may not be repaired before the next showing and can cause no end of trouble.

A person should become familiar with the mechanics of motion picture projector operation before trying to use one with a viewing audience. Most projectors are relatively simple to operate—after the first time. A person should be sure that spare parts, including bulbs and fuses, always are available. He should know what might go wrong and how the fault can be remedied. Lenses and tracks also can be cleaned in this preview operation.

Many minor repairs can be fixed immediately and the show can go on. A "trouble-shooting" chart can be taped to the inside of the projector case so it will always be available. Such a chart is presented in Appendix F.

All the mechanics of setting up the projector and room organization as discussed in the section on slides (pages 126 to 135) should be taken care of well in advance of the actual showing. This includes positioning, threading the film, focusing and warming up the sound.

Sound will be best synchronized and most audible to the entire audience if the speaker is placed near the screen and is high enough to be seen by all. A low-positioned speaker causes loss of quality for all except those seated in the extreme front of the room. If the acoustics of the room leave much to be desired, a corner or part way back location for the speaker may improve the sound. Poor acoustics also can be improved by having the sound tone set at maximum treble. Crisp speech will reduce reverberation. Extra speakers should be aimed toward the back of the room.

There are several tricks that can add much to the "showmanship" of a motion picture. These include advancing the film to the title before the audience has arrived, adjusting the sound volume control to the right level ahead of time and at the end fade out the sound while "The End" is on the screen. A film should not be rewound during the program. Some extra take-up reels make this unnecessary. A step by step checklist for motion picture projection is given in Appendix G.

No motion picture should be shown without being introduced properly and discussed at the end. Far too many motion pictures of natural resource management operations or general conservation are "just shown" without any introduction or discussion. A question and answer session should be a part of the program after the film presentation. It is well to remember that a motion picture is an aid; it should not be considered the complete program. Hjelte (1957) wrote that a motion picture is justified only if the contact creates a lasting impression or where a special attitude is important, and that a motion picture must be augmented by further contact.

If the film is borrowed, it should be returned promptly. If not done, someone else's program will suffer.

Motion picture programs have some definite advantages over slide illustrated programs. Once the film has been completed, it virtually is impossible to disarrange it. A box of slides can be dropped, some may be added, others may be taken out. Even if they are numbered, time will be needed to rearrange them.

The commentary that accompanies slide presentations often is amateurish. The voice in a quality motion picture usually is that of a professional announcer.

Motion pictures seem to have a connotation of entertainment; thus, they have greater attraction for most people. A slide talk simply is less appealing to the average person.

Gestures, expressions, actions, natural sounds and mood music can all be incorporated into a motion picture. All of these are valuable aids in creating a mental image. The speaker in a slide presentation only can use voice inflection, amateur mimicry, repetition or he can synchronize taped sounds.

Excellent motion pictures about natural resources management can be purchased or borrowed from other agencies. The cost of purchase usually is less than that of production, but the film is not unique. There are many 16-millimeter film libraries in the United States. Many catalogues and indices of conservation films are available. One of the most popular and complete is compiled yearly by the Audio-Visual Department of the Conservation Foundation. Samson (1965) published a bulletin listing films and filmstrips on forestry. It is fairly difficult to buy satisfactory sets of slides depicting natural resource management, although suitable, individual slide duplicates or small packets of slides and film strips can be bought commercially.

Ninety-five per cent of the state conservation agencies had their own motion picture libraries (Gilbert, 1962). Only two states indicated they did not have a motion picture collection. The film libraries of state conservation agencies averaged 38.7 different titles. Kilgore (1953) gave an average of 28.5 titles per library. One state, in 1962, had 80 different motion pictures in its library. Others had from 75 down to 3. Thus, it appears that film libraries are increasing in size.

Miscellaneous comments of the state conservation agencies indicated that motion pictures are much in demand by the publics. Motion pictures are used widely because they are self-contained and do not require that a state official be present. They often are used to ease pressures when commitments cannot be met by personal appearances. It was pointed out that motion pictures are especially good for schools. However, most knowledgeable people state that motion pictures are far from a good communications method when used alone.

In-Service Training Schools

An in-service training school is one of the most valuable techniques available for reaching the internal publics of an organization. With an in-service school the employees are given a sense of recognition and the important feeling of participation. Workers have a chance to better themselves, to gain knowledge of new techniques and to become acquainted or reacquainted with others in the organization. These attributes all are important in bringing about good morale and internal harmony so necessary for a successful operation. However, an in-service training school must be more than an agency "get-together." It must be an essential organizational activity that is well planned and scheduled.

Most of the techniques already discussed under public speaking and group meetings are applicable to in-service training schools. For example, the school should be held in comfortable, uncrowded, clean, airy quarters. All techniques of good delivery, including use of visual aids, should be used to communicate effectively with the participants.

Each natural resource agency or region should employ a full-time training officer whose main responsibility is to inaugurate, coordinate and evaluate the effectiveness of in-service training schools. Too often this seems to be a "tack-on" duty in addition to other jobs.

Each in-service school should have only one theme. It is better to concentrate on one subject than to try to cover the whole natural resource management profession. This one subject should be chosen after research has shown the area of greatest need within the organization. The chosen topic can involve law enforcement, research, public relations, any phase of management or other problems that include efforts of all the people who will be attending the school.

Employees should be notified of the school and their part in it well in advance of the meetings. All individuals in the organization should be required to help with the school if asked. Dates must be arranged so they do not interfere with other important departmental activities, if possible, but the school must not become subordinate to individual whims or less important departmental functions.

Most agree that employees should participate in conducting the school, and if possible, participation should include all categories of workers. Not every individual can take part in each school, but each grade of employees should be represented to give the feeling of inclusion to the workers in that category. This will help to reduce internal friction because all employees participate together. But it is also a good idea to have outside specialists from other agencies for guest lecturers and leaders. Outside specialists lend authority to presentations and keep the school from becoming introverted.

Every courtesy possible should be shown to the speakers. Speakers from within the organization should be treated with the same respect given to those from outside the agency. This includes proper introduction and free facilities, such as board and room. Speakers should be made to feel important. The less experienced speakers should be helped in any way possible, but assistance should not be forced upon them. Similarly, all participants attending the school, regardless of rank, should be treated identically.

The sessions of an in-service training school should be brief with frequent breaks. Field men find it especially difficult to sit for long periods. I have wondered about a correspondence, in-service school, but this would defeat the personal nature of the event. Perhaps the correspondence method could be used in alternate years. This would lend variety and be better than no school at all.

One should aim at variety in the presentations. For example, two motion pictures should not be scheduled with one following the other. Lectures should be intermingled with laboratory work, field trips and demonstrations. The ability of the speakers and the nature of their presentations should be known. Novice speakers should be alternated with capable ones and lighter moments can be included to relieve boredom.

All participants and speakers must be told at the start of the school that schedules will be adhered to. All sessions and speakers should start and stop on time. An overzealous speaker may not appreciate being stopped before he is done, but the audience will be grateful.

Discussion should be stimulated as much as possible. "Buzz" sessions or small group discussions are an excellent way to facilitate participation. These give all employees a chance to take part and keep the program from dragging. Ample time allowed for questions and answers following each presentation, plus scheduled debates and opposing panels, all help to bring this about.

An examination often is given at the end of the school to all who attended. This examination increases concentration and attention during the school as well as giving a record of an employee's knowledge. The results of the exam may only be discarded, but an examination generally should be given.

Most state conservation departments (68%) had an in-service training school of some type (Gilbert, 1962). There was much variation in the way these schools were conducted. The most popular frequency was one per year. Some conservation department in-service training schools were regional, while others were state-wide. Most (46%) were one week long. Others varied from six weeks to one or two days. Some states indicated that attendance was voluntary; other conservation department in-service schools were required only for administrators; only conservation officers attended some; and still others were only for new personnel.

Some state conservation departments require as long as six months training for all new employees. Arizona and Colorado, for example, insist that all new employees finish an indoctrination course that introduces them to a variety of work within the organization. New employees must do everything from feeding the fish at the hatchery and law enforcement to television programs and office work. This gives the new man an appreciation of the group effort and work and problems of all divisions. He sees the necessity of coordination and an overall, unified approach.

Federal natural resource management agencies (U. S. Forest Service, National Park Service, Soil Conservation Service, Bureau of Land Management, and the Fish and Wildlife Service) are having increasingly more and better in-service training programs. Some of these agencies have permanent installations or training centers

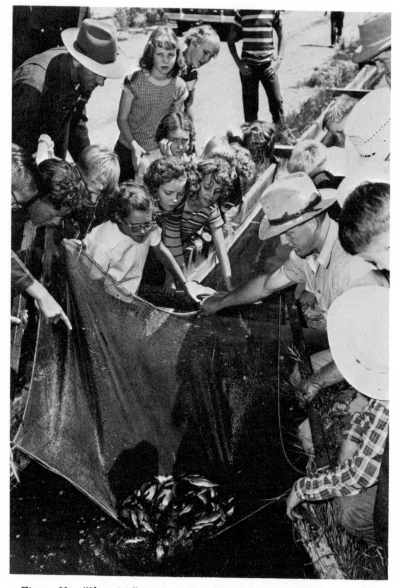

Figure 62.   "Show-Me" trips can be adapted for any group of any size.

where a class is nearly always present. Both the Forest Service and the Park Service use this approach. These organizations also contract for university facilities and operations.

In other instances, some organizations are paying salaries of employees who wish to return to college for a year. Universities are developing non-research, graduate programs where an individual can earn a Master's Degree in 12 months of academic time.

Public Field Trips

Public field trips are especially applicable to natural resource management use. This method of direct contact affords the opportunity to take the leaders of the various publics and others who are interested into the field and show them why such an item, proposal or facility is necessary. These "show me" trips are equally adaptable to adult clubs or youth groups. The "conservation caravans" can be used to inform teacher groups as well as nearly every other public (Figure 62). It is possible to clarify many points and to promote many good conservation and natural resource management principles while in the field. Examples can be made vivid and pointed. All senses, including sight, sound, touch, taste and even smell, can be used. People are interested and are easily influenced when reasons are explained and shown to them right in the field.

For example, the "show me" trip approach can be used to "sell" deer seasons to fellow workers, legislators, sportsmen's clubs and other influential persons in the community. By taking them to the overused deer range, pointing out browse "hi-lines" where food is gone as high as deer can reach, explaining how overuse affects soil and erosion and showing them carcasses of starved animals, it is possible to explain why a liberal, either-sex season is needed. An added inducement to agreement is to perform a necropsy on an animal. Parasites nearly always are present, and some of the more common ones, such as bot flies, can be elaborated upon by finding large quantities in certain age classes and conditions of deer (Figure 63).

Figure 63. Public field trips are especially useful because the public can be shown conditions as they actually are.

An important hint, it is much better if the animal to be necropsied is killed before the group arrives. This is a precaution against the deer being wounded in full sight of everyone. When trying to influence a group that more deer should be harvested, it certainly is not a good idea to give the group an opportunity to feel more sorry for the animals.

Public field trips must be *adequately and carefully* planned. They should click like clockwork. They can be equally as effective in creating disfavor for the agency or proposal if something goes awry. Arrangements should be made for enough transportation, for rest stops, for lunch, for hot drinks on cold days and cold drinks on hot days. People should be briefed before the trip starts. A written itinerary aids in reviewing background and concentrating attention where desired. Every stop must be coordinated with distances timed and roads known. Enough time should be alloted to do the job, but events must not be allowed to drag. Minor things, such as rough roads or too much dust, can put accent on the hardship rather than on the trip or the idea being presented.

One common problem with field trips, people often cannot see what is going on or hear what is being said. Small groups and a loudspeaker will help to alleviate these obstacles.

A group analysis and discussion at the end of the trip serve to bring all parts together with a common agreement and understanding. Additional questions can be asked and answers given. If done while events still are fresh in the participants' minds, a general summation can have a lasting effect.

A self-guided nature trail or field trip approach has been used by many natural resource management agencies. The secret of success is clarity with all signs and directions. An attractive brochure, readily available at the starting point, is an absolute necessity (Figure 64). This should contain a map (Figure 65) and complete descriptions of each stop (Figure 66).

All state conservation agencies used public field trips or "show me" trips to some extent (Gilbert, 1962). Other comments from state conservation organizations concerning public field trips were conflicting. The value of this type of contact increases with diversity of the audience. However, there seems to be a great tendency for the same people to attend each field trip.

This type of communications is especially valuable where there is a need to show and influence people in high positions or with authority. Public field trips are well adapted for use with teachers, school children and other youth groups. Several states commented upon the necessity for organization and smooth operation for public field trips.

Figure 64. An attractive brochure is necessary for a successful, self-guided, field tour.

Figure 65. The brochure should contain a map of the area to be covered on the field trip.

TRESTLE CAMPGROUND

Trestle Campground has been constructed on the Arapaho National Forest for your enjoyment. It is one of the many picnic and camping grounds on the Arapaho and the Roosevelt National Forests. Why not stop here, have lunch and enjoy the spectacular summer view of the high country? Imagine what it must have been like to ride a train across this alpine terrain during a winter snowstorm!

MILES FROM EAST STARTING POINT	MILES FROM WEST STARTING POINT
23.5	10.8

LOOP TRESTLE AND TUNNEL 33

Figure 66. Each stop on the tour should be definitely located and carefully described.

MASS MEDIA

Mass media (mainly radio, television, magazines and newspapers) provide the means by which large numbers of people can be contacted with a minimum of effort. Contact, however, does not necessarily, or even frequently, produce good communications or understanding. Mass media are most effectively used when a public is just being made aware of something and no one really is trying to influence members of that public. Most people subject themselves to mass media contact to be entertained or informed and not educated.

Patronage, advertising and interest of any public agency must be distributed fairly to all media. One medium should not be used to the exclusion of others in the interest of fairness and because enemies made among the personnel of any medium can be harmful at a later time when they may be needed.

Media personnel are generally very cooperative. People are interested in natural resource endeavors, and most media personnel realize this. The people responsible for the medium operation want to give the people the information and material in which they are interested. That the media are not used more by natural resource management personnel is generally the fault of the resource personnel, not of the media personnel.

Magazines and pamphlets were rated 2.4 in importance in natural resource management communications work (Table 5, page 107). This was the highest rating given by state conservation agencies for any communications method (Gilbert, 1962).

In 1965, only 4 state conservation departments of 44 did not have a department magazine. This nine per cent compared favorably with Thompson's (1958) figure of 15 per cent and Shomon's (1959) figure of 11 per cent. Of those states with a conservation magazine, 17 (43%) published their magazine every month, 14 states (35%) every two months, six states (15%) every three months, and three states (7%) published an issue every six months. A 1968 study done by the Wildlife Management Institute showed that 45 of 50 (90%) state conservation departments published a magazine of some type.

In 1965, 33 of 39 state conservation agencies (85%) did not sell their conservation magazine by the issue or at news stands. Twenty of 40 states (50%) distributed their publication free and an equal number charged for subscriptions. Of the 20 states that charged for their conservation magazine, three states (15%) charged one-half dollar per year, 10 states (50%) charged one dollar, three states (15%) charged one and one-half dollars, and four states (20%)

charged two dollars for the yearly subscription. According to Mehaffey (1952), only one or two states at that time had conservation magazines that were financially self-supporting.

Field information and education personnel wrote more articles (26%) for state conservation department magazines than did other agency personnel. Administrators contributed 24 per cent, biologists wrote 21 per cent, and wildlife conservation officers submitted only seven per cent of the articles written by conservation agency personnel (Gilbert, 1962). Twenty-two per cent of all articles were contributed by personnel in miscellaneous job categories. Some difficulty was encountered in interpreting the positions of the individuals because their titles are extremely varied.

Thirty-six state conservation agencies published an average of 14 education pamphlets or bulletins each year. Three states published as many as 50 per year. It was pointed out by many that pamphlets are used for education and not for molding or influencing public opinion.

Newspaper articles, in comparison with other communication methods, were rated second in importance by state conservation agencies (Table 5, page 107). Ninety-one per cent of the state conservation agencies (38 of 42) had a regular news release that originated from department headquarters and was sent to various media for publication or other use. Fifty-one per cent of these state conservation department releases were made to media on a regular weekly basis. Eighteen per cent sent them out every month, and 32 per cent sent out news releases only when news was important enough to warrant a special effort. The Wildlife Management Institute (1968) showed that all states used newspaper articles to some degree.

Twenty-four (57%) of 42 states did not have *regularly* scheduled columns in newspapers in 1965. Eighteen states (43%) did have people writing regularly scheduled columns for newspapers. Fifty-eight per cent of the information and education officers wrote columns for newspapers but 98 per cent of their columns were irregular in appearance. Forty-nine per cent of the wildlife conservation officers wrote for newspaper distribution and 67 per cent of their columns were irregular in scheduling.

General comments about writing emphasize the fact that many workers in natural resource management professions are not able to write on the level of the consuming public. Too much writing is keyed for the professional and not for the average consumer or interested individual. Another comment made by many is that the basic field man, in this particular instance the conservation officer, ranger or warden, should make more of an attempt to write, especially for local newspapers. A number of people believe that more information should be made available for journalists, outdoor witers or editors to compose. This should be in addition to attempts by agency personnel to write articles themselves.

Television programming rated fourth in comparison to other media in importance and effectiveness in natural resource management public relations work. (Table 5, page 107). Thus, television ranked below all writing efforts and personal appearance programs but ahead of radio.

In 1965, the 34 state conservation agencies doing wildlife television programs averaged 2.9 television programs per week. Two states produced as many as 15 shows each week. Seventy per cent of all programs were the sole responsibility of the individual doing the show. The conservation agency that employed the individual suggested topics for 30 per cent of all programs. In 1968, 44 of 50 states (88%) used television programs to some degree (Wildlife Management Institute, 1968).

Seventy-four per cent (29 of 39) of the state conservation agencies had no problems with scheduling television programs in 1965. Twenty-six per cent (10 states) had difficulties. The main problem was the pre-empting of public service time donated for a natural resource management program by a sponsored show. Also mentioned as a problem was having less than desirable telecast time. Because a majority of time is donated, the constant change that accompanies a sustaining program makes it difficult to establish a regular viewing audience. No state conservation agency using television indicated that it had sanctioning problems from other media.

Seventy-seven per cent of the state conservation organizations used public service donated time for television programs. Only one state purchased part of its air time with department funds. Twenty-six per cent (11 states) had an outside sponsor who paid for time used. Many indicated a definite trend in interest toward educational television where the accent is on quality rather than quantity. With educational television, time is free for the asking and there are no commercial programs to pre-empt time used regularly. Some commented upon the comparatively small viewing audience of educational channels. Others stressed that the educational connotation may be a detriment and much entertainment and interest must be included to compete with commercial programs.

Thirty-two per cent (12 of 39) of the state conservation departments with television programs had 30-minute shows, 40 per cent (15 states) had 15-minute programs, 16 per cent (6 states) had 5-minute programs, and 16 per cent (6 states) depended primarily upon spot announcements for their television efforts.

All of the state conservation agencies recognized the importance of visual aids in television work. The most popular visual aid used in television was motion pictures. Forty-nine per cent of all conservation agency television programs used motion picture films to some extent. Eleven per cent of the programs included use of slides as visual aids; 19 per cent of the programs featured live animals;

and eight per cent incorporated other visual aids, such as posters, black and white photographs, and drawings. Only three per cent of all state conservation programs were either kinescopes or videotapes. The cost to the station probably was the prohibiting factor which resulted in their restricted use. Decreasing costs of videotape production have caused a recent increase in their use.

Radio rated last in importance as a public information disseminating medium by 44 state conservation organizations (Table 5, Page 142). However, all of the states used radio to some extent. The Wildlife Management Institute (1968) listed 48 states of 50 (96%) as using radio.

In 1965, 46 per cent of the radio broadcasts on natural resource management were the responsibility of information and education personnel, 21 per cent were conducted by administrators, 16 per cent by conservation officers, nine per cent by biologists or researchers, and eight per cent by personnel of other categories. Great difficulty was encountered in categorizing state workers by titles.

Forty-four state conservation agencies averaged 14 radio broadcasts per week. This figure is probably erroneous, however, as some states indicated that one program may be used by many stations. Three states indicated that as many as 80, 65, and 60 weekly radio broadcasts are aired over separate stations. The same program can be taped and used in several locations.

Interviews made up 48 per cent of all radio programs done by conservation agencies. News programs comprised 23 per cent; round table or controversy, 12 per cent; human interest or straight talk, nine per cent; and on the spot, remote broadcasts made up eight per cent. However, there was mixing of program types in many broadcasts.

The average state conservation organization furnished topic suggestions for 46 per cent of all radio programs. The individual responsible for the broadcast provided his own topic material for 18 per cent of the programs. For 36 per cent of the total broadcasts, a combination of individual and agency furnished materials was used. These figures indicated the close liaison necessary between employees doing public relations work and the conservation agency.

Eighty-one per cent of the states (35 of 40) did not have scheduling problems with natural resource management related radio broadcasts. Nineteen per cent (five states) reported some scheduling difficulty. Their comments indicated that the major problems were: first, the agency has no control over the broadcast time because most programs are sustaining; second, the stations use only part of the materials given to them; and third, the program may not be used at all. In any case, a regular listening audience cannot be developed.

Eighty-six per cent of all agency originated radio programs on conservation or natural resource management utilized free time. Thirteen per cent of the programs were paid for by a commercial sponsor and only one state conservation department bought time for radio broadcasts. Conservation agencies could allocate money to purchase time or they could expend effort to interest a sponsor. Either of these solutions would help alleviate scheduling problems and, therefore, would be preferable to using free time.

Only one state reported any sanctioning difficulties due to sponsorship. Several states indicated they meet this problem by announcing at the end of each broadcast that the natural resource management agency does not necessarily endorse the service or products advertised.

Thirty-seven per cent of the state conservation agencies (16 of 44) believed the 15-minute radio program to be the most effective. Thirty per cent (13 states) thought spot announcements most effective, 27 per cent (12 states) preferred five-minute programs, and six per cent (three states) indicated that one-half hour programs are the best.

The 15-minute broadcast was the most popular length radio program used by state conservation agencies in 1965. Forty-seven per cent of all natural resource management programs were 15 minutes long. Twenty-eight per cent were five minutes long, and 25 per cent were spot announcements. State conservation agencies were not using 30-minute broadcasts except on special occasions. Since 1965 the trend has been more toward 5-minute programs and spot announcements.

Miscellaneous comments from natural resource management agencies concerning the use and effectiveness of radio were highly conflicting. Some state conservation organizations thought radio very effective. Others believed it is overlooked and should be used more. Still other state natural resource management agencies believed it is the least effective medium and essentially a waste of time and effort. The interest and enthusiasm for radio seemed to be greater in the more sparsely settled states of the West than in the more densely settled East. This is logical, as the heavily populated eastern states depend more on television and the press for contact.

Printed Materials

Printed messages, as a communications method, are but a little younger than public speaking. Writing by aborigines on cave walls attest to the early beginning of the written idea or message. The importance of printed material has continued to increase even with the advent of newer mass media methods which incorporate sound and movement.

Printed words can be considered the foundation of other contact methods. Speeches, radio programs and television efforts usually are composed upon paper before being produced in the final way.

Also, written advertisements or notices often are used to publicize the efforts of the other media.

A message on paper seems to be authoritative. "It must be true, or it would not have been printed," is the common reaction. The public's confidence is enlisted.

A big advantage of written communications is that reading is habit-forming. Also, the printed message, in the newspaper, magazine or other source, is there to be used by the reader at his convenience, while a five o'clock newscast, once missed, is usually gone forever. Printed messages can be read any time after being published and can be saved for a permanent record. Leisure hours and availability of written material can be coordinated at the discretion of the reader.

Much thought is necessary for the average author to put what is wanted into words. This time-consuming labor forces accuracy of major items so that errors of magnitude should be less abundant in written messages than in verbal ones. Minor errors may be more noticeable in print but probably are less abundant in a written article than an oral address.

It is easy to channel a written message to a specific audience. This is aided by the nature of the publication. To illustrate, outdoor news for sportsmen and other interested people is found on the outdoor page of the newspaper. A hunting and fishing magazine can be written or purchased with fair assurance of the general type of articles and readers involved. Natural resource management professionals can read the journal of their profession. The printed message is presented for the target public to read but other publics may find it also. The message can be made intimate or encompassing, localized or widespread and still be valuable and of interest to many, especially the specific target group.

The public reached by written material can be large. Many surveys emphasize that printed material is the main source of contact for news and publicity. When one thinks of the magazines, pamphlets, bulletins, letters, newspapers and other types of written material available, the magnitude of audiences becomes obvious. In addition, newspapers can be divided into dailies, weeklies, organization papers, college papers and religious papers, among others. Similar divisions can be made for other types of written material.

Research relating to management of the natural resources isn't complete until the results are published. Actually, research can be published in at least four places, each with a different target public. First, the technical journal of the particular profession will carry the final, scientifically written article for the professionals. Second, a semi-popular magazine, such as a state conservation publication, can reach the more interested layman. Third, a popular magazine will make the material available to those who are reading primarily for entertainment. And last, the material should be published in the newspapers while progress is going on or as the results make news.

But written messages are not the complete answer to all communication needs. Many of the items listed as assets of the medium also are detriments. For example, a mistake made in an article is equally as definite to an audience as is the article. The error is there to bother and give false information as long as one copy remains.

The time required to develop written communication must be considered a disadvantage. However, the time varies with the abilities of an individual and the nature of the article. A written message usually takes longer from conception to public reception than other forms of communication. The lapse from sender to receiver in radio or television may be seconds. With the written word, the time from sender to receiver may be hours, days or even weeks. Many things can happen during the interim to change or refute the original story.

Sight is the only sense used in receiving a written message. There is no sound, movement or music to make the message more appealing and understandable. Illustrative materials, such as drawings, photographs, cartoons and graphs, increase clarity, but still, only one sense is used in reception. Therefore, assimilation of material is slower and more difficult.

Writing should be in simple language that relates clear thoughts and definite ideas. Most people do not understand words and phrases such as multiple use, sustained yield, management concepts or juxtaposition. Technical jargon is understandable by those in the profession but not by the average layman. This principle was stressed by John O'Hayre (1966) in his Bureau of Land Management publication, *"Gobbledygook Has Gotta Go."*

Simplicity is the key to understanding a written message. Little words, such as trees, grass, cows, deer and soil have "picture value" in that they easily can be mentally visualized by most readers. Personal pronouns, conversationalism, short sentences and short paragraphs aid "readability." The message should be positive, not negative; active, not passive; clear, crisp and concise. As Reynolds (1966) stated, the author should write to his reader in language that is familiar.

Several individuals have published reading ease formulas. Two of the most popular are Flesch's (1949) reading ease index and Gunning's (1952) fog index formula. Briefly, both of these attempts measure "readability" by computing the average sentence length and the number of syllables per word (Table 8).

With the Gunning "fog index" as a yardstick, two important factors are combined. First, the average number of words per sentence and/or between major punctuation breaks is used. Second the percentage of words with three or more syllables is determined. Capitalized words, short word combinations and multiple-syllable verb forms are excluded. Finally, the two numbers are totaled and

Table 8. Reading Ease Scores and the Average Level of Difficulty (Flesch, 1949, Gunning, 1952).

Score	Syllables per 100 Words	Average Sentence Length	Description	Educational Equivalent	Per cent of Total Population Able to Understand Material
0-30	192	29	very difficult	college graduate	5
30-50	169	25	difficult	some college	33
50-60	155	21	fairly difficult	high school	54
60-70	147	17	standard	grade school	83
70-80	139	14	fairly easy	seventh	88

multipled by four. The resulting figure is the "fog index" and compares with the reading ability of the respective grades in school. Thus, a fog index of 13 (college freshman) or above is difficult reading. The educated person can figure it out, but he will do so only under compulsion. The fog index of most popular magazines is well under 12, and many of these have their share of "educated readers."

Much written material is not read by the target public or any other public of consequence. Too many people never seem to get past the headlines, the sports page or the comics of a newspaper and many magazines are only partially read.

Many written messages are aimed at "the public" in general instead of at a specific public. Or it may be the other way, with the target public being too small and specific. Such is the case for most technical material which is published only in journals and read only by professionals in the field.

Most people do not show much interest in routine conservation affairs. Their interest is not in statistics, budgets, erosion, diminishing water, annual increments or sustained yields. People are not motivated until shown that they should be vitally concerned, that their existence is threatened. The written conservation story and associated problems must be told so that the stories live, that feelings are stirred and actions produced. Failure or success in writing is often a matter of language, and nothing more. Poor writing is wasted effort. The results are misinterpretation or a lack of understanding, if the material is read at all.

Natural resource management stories and pictures must hit the larger, popular "big slick" magazines, the covers, the front pages and command a place of respect on the sports page of the newspaper. Frequently, a hunting, forestry or conservation story is cut to make room for horse racing, bowling or some other competitive sport. Yet the money spent on hunting, fishing, camping and enjoying the natural resources in the United States in one year exceeds many billions of dollars.

Newspapers

Newspapers are the oldest of the mass media. Julius Caesar is given credit for publishing the first newspaper in 60 B.C. The first daily newspaper in the United States was published in 1833. Newspapers still are considered by most writers to be the leader in the race between newspapers, radio and television for numbers of people contacted. They also lead all media in money spent for advertising. Over one hundred million Americans over 12 years old read newspapers every day. There are over 2,000 dailies, 9,000 weeklies and 1,000 Sunday only newspapers in existence. In addition, there are many more agency newspapers, trade journals, campus newspapers and other smaller efforts that make news available for people to read.

Although a very important medium, newspapers should not be used to the exclusion of other media. However, press personnel are an important public that must be won over to the agency side of natural resource management. Newspaper people can be prodigious friends or formidable enemies when they agree or disagree on an issue. As an unknown writer once stated, "newspapers comfort the unduly afflicted and afflict the unduly comforted."

Basically, there are two kinds of newspaper articles. The feature story is similar to a magazine article and requires a different style than does a news story. Although correlation with current happenings is necessary, it is not a news story as such and the extreme urgency regarding timeliness is not present. This type of writing is closely related to magazine writing and is discussed in that section.

The question immediately arises, who in a natural resource agency should write for newspapers? Should the natural resource agency personnel write the newspaper article or story themselves, or should this be done by an employee of the newspaper? A categorical answer cannot be given. Individuals and situations vary. Perhaps as much talent is needed to successfully contact an editor or outdoor writer responsible for the actual writing as is needed to write an article.

Generally it is the responsibility of one or several information and education men to work with newspapers. But there is no reason why others should not try as long as efforts are within the bounds of policy. A logical, first approach by the neophyte is to have someone else in the organization who is more capable to "ghost" the first one or two efforts. This also can be done by a person on the staff of the newspaper.

It is unquestionably a good idea for the potential news writer to get acquainted with the editor and other important newspaper workers before the first story is submitted. This should be in the nature of a courtesy call. The visit should be brief with no business transacted. The press needs to know that the conservation agency and personnel want to work with them and will help in any way possible. Conservation agency employees must learn where articles should be directed and what individuals are to be contacted when news is available.

If a regular column or feature is proposed, deadlines should be set and met. Editors often depend on conservation material and even will hold a place for it if previous arrangements have been made. Daily newspapers should receive copy by noon of the day before the article will be printed. Material for Sunday papers must be in by noon on Friday and weeklies like the copy as early in the week as possible.

Newspaper articles should be correlated with an organizational calendar (Appendix A). It is best to look forward to seasons and events that will be happening rather than looking back to those that have passed, even though results, too, can be news. It is well never to forget that news is a perishable commodity. Old news is no longer news, it is history.

Newspapers want news. They are not interested in giving publicity unless it is paid for as advertising. Natural resource agencies have news, because many people are interested in the out-of-doors. But news must be current, timely and must be of consequence to readers (Figure 67). Generally any event, discovery, controversy or result that pertains to the public's natural resources or those who manage the resources is news.

The item or idea to be included in a news story must be newsworthy. The keys to a good news story, according to Reynolds (1966), are human interest, timeliness, proximity, prominence and consequence. All, or at least most, of these characteristics need be filled. The news elements which attract attention and create interest, as listed by the same author, are appeal, sympathy, unusualness, progress, combat, suspense, age and youth, sex and animals.

It is not necessary to have one of the ten commandments broken to make news, but an importance and an interest to the public must be present or the effort will end up in the wastebasket. An article must be sound enough and good enough to carry its own weight, and it must have wide enough potential appeal to interest a large enough audience.

The ABC's and a D of good news writing night be listed as Accuracy, Brevity, Clarity, and Directness. Opinions and conclusions have no place in a news story. They belong in the feature, the editorial column or letters to the editor.

Figure 67.   The news story must be immediate and of interest.

A story needs to be well written and edited if it is to be used. Newspaper editors will be much more cooperative if the rewrite job does not necessitate complete revamping. The article must be understandable, complete, accurate and grammatically correct. The writer's name, address and telephone number are put in the upper right hand corner of the first page. A brief title should be located approximately 1/3 way down the first page. All copies should be typed, double-spaced, on only one side of the paper, with adequate room in the margins for editorial notes and printing directions. Each paragraph should end on the same sheet and the word "more" is written at the bottom of the page if more pages follow. Paragraphs in a news story should be short; 20 to 60 words are suggested. An attractive, well-written news story is the first step toward publication and is the best public relations tool that exists for the newspaper medium public.

Duplicated copies can be instant death to a news story except with the one newspaper that gets the original. Therefore, Xeroxed copies should be used with discretion. The story can be reworded, a different photograph included and another original copy can be typed and sent. All copies then will have the appearance of an exclusive. But, exclusives are just that, and an awareness of their uniqueness should be presented to the newspaper concerned.

All newspaper articles, except feature stories, start with the "lead." This must be interesting since it really is the climax and consists of a first paragraph or two that tell who, what, when, where, why and how. The most interesting of these six factors is listed first, but every word is vital. The opening of a story must be so clear, sparkling and interesting that the reader wants to know what follows (Figure 68).

Wired For Living Sound

Game Animals Bugged For Better Research

FORT COLLINS - Electronics is going to play a major role in wildlife research, it was revealed here last week during a day-long conference of some 30 biologists.

The master gimmick will be a tiny radio transmitter used to locate and track game birds and animals as part of a continuous study of wildlife habits.

The possibilities of animals wired for living sound were investigated by biologists, wildlife managers and electronic specialists who met at the Colorado Game, Fish and Parks Department Research Center here. Highlights of the conference included discussions on developing radio telemetry systems, best frequencies to use, latest advancements in transmitting and receiving equipment and techniques used in attaching the small transmitters to game animals.

The first question, of course, is will it work? It already has. Small radios have been attached to a number of animals captured in the wild. When released, the biologist can follow the movements of the animal with a radio receiver as it picks up signals sent out by the transmitter.

Such techniques have been used in tracking Ruffed grouse in Minnesota. Similar networks have beamed in information on space travel effects on mice and monkeys during the nation's initial space probes.

The chief concern here is to improve techniques in locating and following the movements of game animals during research studies.

Colorado doesn't have a space ape to televise, but research teams continually encounter difficulties in determining wintering areas, breeding areas, seasonal movements, survival of young and other types of information. The data is urgently needed to improve management of such animals as ducks, geese, elk, deer, antelope, wild turkeys, Sage grouse, Ringneck pheasants and scaled quail.

In our own state, immediate use of the beast-to-biologist hookup will be used to study wild turkey movement and behavior on the Uncompahgre Plateau in western Colorado. The miniature mike will be lashed to some of the elk used in research work and the Colorado Cooperative Wildlife Research Unit has developed plans to tap the mule deer herds for bonus information.

Scientists point out that the possibilities of radio telemetry are unlimited. But it sure will be a nasty shock to a poacher who bags a bugged deer and lands in a live-wired pokey after a radar-controlled robot game warden taps him on the shoulder with a heavy metal hand - delicately wired for lie-detecting impulses, of course.

Keep Our Campgrounds Clean!

Break that Match! Douse that Cig!

Figure 68. An example of a well written news story.

Pictures and other illustrations aid a newspaper story. They make the article more interesting and understandable. Photographs should be at least 5 by 7 inches with a glossy finish for reproduction. Quality is important, as most photographs lose definition in newspaper printing. Composition also is important because most photographs will be reduced in size or cropped to fit a one or two column cut.

Photographs must depict their own story and must be able to "stand alone" or be self-explanatory (Figure 69). The caption to any print should be typed on a piece of paper and included with the photo. If there are people in the picture, written clearance for

Figure 69. Each photograph should tell its own story without the need for much explanation. This picture illustrates the precariousness of a natural resource photographers job.

use must be obtained from them. This always may not be necessary but is a sound precaution against possible legal action. Names of people are indicated in the order of first, middle and last name, and the people should be identified from left to right. The personal flavor introduced by pictures of the people involved in any story is an asset. Photographs usually will not be returned, as they will be marked up with editorial instructions.

Small newspapers especially want photographs with their copy. However, the cost of printing a picture may be prohibitive. A solution to this problem is to distribute cardboard "mats" along with photographic prints to small newspapers (Figure 70). These mats are the result of an important step that requires expensive equipment in the printing process. Mats can be produced in quantity by a larger newspaper and distributed free of charge to smaller ones. This almost insures that the photographs and the articles will be used.

Local newspapers want stories that are localized and humanized if possible. A local story should be written for the individual reader. People like to read about themselves, their neighbors and their community. Short personal pronouns, such as "I," "you," "he," "folks," and "people," increase "humaness." But, if a story is of more than local importance, it should be released simultaneously through a wire service to all newspapers and other media. This release procedure must be in accord with organization policy. Most natural re-

Figure 70. A cardboard "mat" used by most newspapers in publishing pictures.

source agencies do not like to have an important, state-wide, region-wide or nation-wide story released first in a local paper. For example, the elk season in Wyoming draws many non-resident hunters and any drastic changes in the season or other news of importance pertaining to the season is worthy of a wire service release. Important stories easily can be rewritten or shortened to give local emphasis.

All sides of an issue must be told fairly in a newspaper story. Facts should not be hidden, nor should there be an attempt to conceal obvious points. If one tries to editorialize too strongly, the re-write man will have to make it less obvious. The more people that work on an article, the greater is the chance that the original meaning or intent will be changed or some part will be left out.

People writing newspaper stories for a conservation agency must avoid intra-departmental controversy. This includes disagreement resulting from conflicts with commission or board members or legislators and arguments or controversy over policy. If discord exists in the agency, it will be known soon enough outside of the organization without it being publicized. If there is some doubt whether a story ought to be released or not, it always should be discussed beforehand with superiors.

One needs to avoid giving information about projects and individuals not directly concerned with his division or work unless the story is cleared completely. Perhaps others who are more closely connected with the operation plan to write the story. This mistake is made frequently and it is easy to see that it might be quite upsetting to those doing the work who planned to write the story.

A person should not become angry if his story is not published. The writer simply needs to try to do a better job next time. It is all right to ask why the story was not used, if this can be done in a constructive way, but editors must never be pressured, threatened or argued with. They are responsible for every word printed and the reasons for rejection usually will be clear once they are pointed out.

If the story is published, the writer must not become perturbed at changes and cuts that were made. Accuracy can be insisted upon, but most articles need to be lengthened or shortened to fit existing space and this requires changes. Cuts usually are made at the ends of the articles. It is well to remember this and to arrange the story so the meaning will not be affected.

A writer should not ask the newspaper for copies or clippings of articles. If a clipping is desired, a newspaper can be purchased for that purpose.

A follow-up story generally is routine. Nearly every bit of news is worth at least two stories. First, the headline story is written. This is the exclusive, the hot-off-the-press type or the prediction kind. In a day or so, after the event or season is over, a summary or "results" story is in order. People like to read about something they have seen or participated in.

Newspapers do not like to have news stories held from them. If *very* important, a personal appeal to the editor is the best way to keep a story out of the newspapers. Secrecy often will result in erroneous information and bad publicity; plus the enmity of the editor. Also, a frequent and sincere word of thanks to an editor never is bad public relations.

Most state conservation departments and some of the other natural resource management agencies have weekly press releases or newsletters. These are routine attempts at providing news from headquarters on a regular basis. These releases seem to be expected, but they have the stigma of handouts, of mass production and of not being news. Many are considered with a negative attitude by newspapers and are not used unless as filler because of lack of interest or the complete lack of uniqueness to any one paper.

An accurate, up-to-date mailing list for a newsletter saves money and effort. All mass media should receive these newsletters. They must be attractive and well written with all of the characteristics of good news writing incorporated. Color increases attractiveness and headings and sub-headings permit rapid scanning by the potential users. The newsletter should have a neat, indicative title with a well designed emblem (Figure 71). Margins must be wide and only one side of the paper should be used.

Why are there no press conferences by conservation organizations? This is an often used and valuable technique of big business and government for good press relations. In a press conference, a big story is explained and released simultaneously to all newsmen who are present. Accurate information is obtained directly from the people responsible for the news. Breth (1948) said that one state conservation department had a press conference some years ago. It was a huge success, but it was the first and last. He stated that this technique increases compatibility with press officials, as they then are in on the making of news.

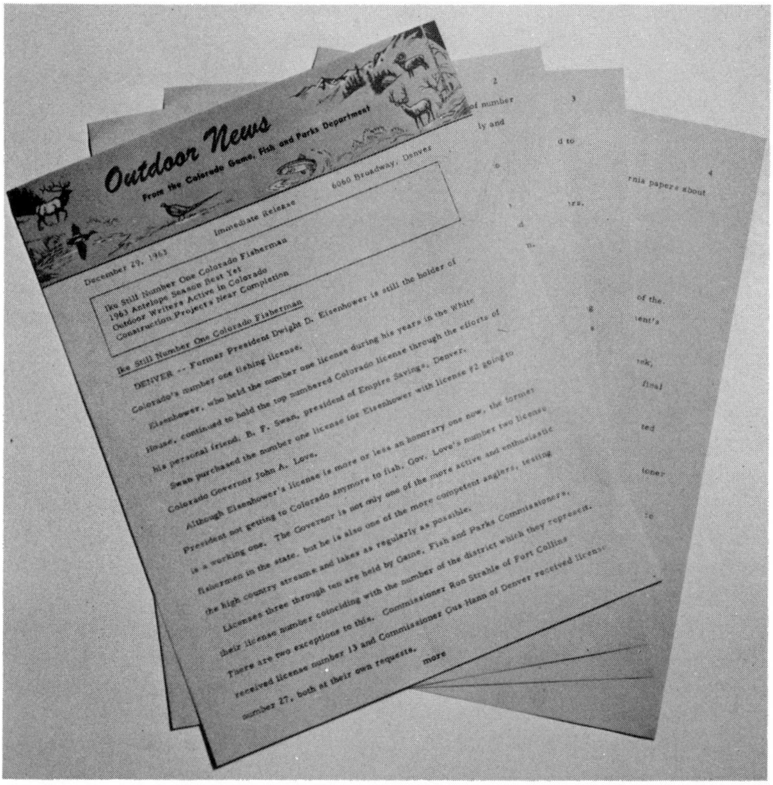
Outdoor News
From the Colorado Game, Fish and Parks Department
6060 Broadway, Denver

December 29, 1963 Immediate Release

Ike Still Number One Colorado Fisherman
1963 Antelope Season Best Yet
Outdoor Writers Active in Colorado
Construction Projects Near Completion

Ike Still Number One Colorado Fisherman

DENVER -- Former President Dwight D. Eisenhower is still the holder of Colorado's number one fishing license.

Eisenhower, who held the number one license during his years in the White House, continued to hold the top numbered Colorado license through the efforts of his personal friend, B. F. Swan, president of Empire Savings, Denver.

Swan purchased the number one license for Eisenhower with license #2 going to Colorado Governor John A. Love.

Although Eisenhower's license is more or less an honorary one now, the former President not getting to Colorado anymore to fish, Gov. Love's number two license is a working one. The Governor is not only one of the more active and enthusiastic fishermen in the state, but he is also one of the more competent anglers, testing the high country streams and lakes as regularly as possible.

Licenses three through ten are held by Game, Fish and Parks Commissioners, their license number coinciding with the number of the district which they represent. There are two exceptions to this. Commissioner Ron Strahle of Fort Collins received license number 13 and Commissioner Gus Hann of Denver received license number 27, both at their own requests.

more

Figure 71. Weekly news releases are used by most natural resource agencies. They should be attractive and well written.

House Organs

A house organ is the internal newspaper of an organization. It contains news of the company and its employees and special issues may have certain objectives. All characteristics of good newspaper writing pertain with writing for a house organ. Frequency depends on organization size. For most natural resource management agencies a once-a-month publication is suggested.

The house organ constitutes a service to the employees and the employers. To be successful, it must be accepted, read and contributed to by both workers and management. All groups and ranks of workers in the agency should be represented, including the top level administrators. Corporate viewpoints can be expressed as well as recognition for effort above and beyond the normal. The house organ is an opportunity for internal communications and to increase organization solidarity or "oneness."

Some of the bad news ought to be told along with the good news. A fair and honest viewpoint and appraisal is the best approach.

Analysis of feedback will tell whether the efforts are successful or not. Constantly done, this can be determined by listening or by an occasional questionnaire insert.

Publication and distribution of a house organ are major jobs, if done correctly. Time needs to be allocated for the tasks if quality is a goal. The best reporters, representing all categories, usually are the people who are interested in the effort. The coordinator, or editor, must have a first hand knowledge of the organization, its workings and its personnel.

Distribution for the most part is internal to the agency. However, there generally is nothing wrong with sending the house organ to other agencies and individuals who request it.

Magazines

Many of the principles of good newspaper writing also pertain to good magazine writing. Magazine coverage equally is impressive, if not quite as timely as newspaper coverage. Money spent for magazine advertising is less than that spent for either newspaper or television advertising, but is greater than the amount spent for radio advertising. There currently are over 10,000 major magazines in the United States and seven out of every 10 people over 15 years old read some magazines regularly.

Most research done in natural resources management is reported only for scientific consumption, if at all. Publication should be the last step of every research project. Publication in a popular or semi-popular magazine is as important to the profession and to the scientist as is publication in a scientific journal. Many findings are made known to non-professional publics only when the resulting management methods are used or an attempt is made to use them. Besides making the results known to the outside publics, an added incentive for magazine writing is possible pay for many publications other than the organization's own.

Readers must be able to understand the written message without undue effort. The National Wildlife Federation hired a children's writer to "bring down" articles to the desired level of comprehension. Their many publications are excellent examples of technical knowledge reduced to a level that the layman can easily understand. The National Wildlife Federation's magazine, *National Wildlife,* is aimed at an interested but non-professional audience. *Ranger Rick* is the counterpart for younger audiences. Articles are written in an easily understood manner but contain much scientific information. There is much more to these articles than the "how to harvest," or the "blood-thirsty predator" type of story often found in a strictly popular magazine.

Figure 72. Conservation magazines should be as attractive as possible.

In the past, many popular or semi-popular articles about natural resources dealt only with harvest rather than with management. For example, many wildlife stories were the "how I got a full bag limit" type, or the "vicious killer meets death" kind. These should be minimized and replaced by the good sportsman, the good management or the good research project kind. This is not the fault of the magazine publishers. The blame is on the nautral resource manager for not writing stories. The manager should provide material which will be accurate and which will impress public and editor favorably.

A magazine article can be considered about the same as a feature story in a newspaper. Instead of the climax or "lead" being in the first one or two paragraphs, as in a news story, the reader is taken along a gradual, building-up process to the climax and the end of the article. Regardless of the order of presentation, there still is need for clear, sparkling, short sentences that tell the story so it can be understood and appreciated (Figure 72). A rating sheet for conservation magazines is presented in Appendix H.

A writer must know the style of the journal or magazine for which his article is destined, and he should write in that style. Style includes such elements as length; use of illustrations; method of citation, if any; level of education of the reading audience; and general appearance, including use of subheadings. Good grammar is necessary; many failures are caused by mechanics rather than content. The immediate goal is to get the article published and before the readers.

For each story, one should have a specific purpose, a specific public and a specific magazine. There should be a point to make or a certain story to tell to a particular auidence.

Subjects for magazine articles related to conservation or natural resource management are abundant. People like to read about natural resources. Topics can include observations, new ideas, research results, management methods, problems, controversies, jobs or the people involved in natural resource work (but the article must be well written and interesting).

It generally is best to write from an outline. The following six parts are suggested. First, the title or "head" is carefully planned. This, along with the first sentence or two, constitutes the "hooker" and must attract attention when the reader is scanning the magazine. Next, the subject is stated. This involves the introduction and the problems or situation involved. After that, the subject is defined. The main points are explained further. Contrary views can be stated. Fourth, the subject is discussed. This portion eventually will constitute the main body of the article. Examples, details, observations, and experiences are logically incorporated. The fifth part of the outline is to apply the subject. Results are given and comparisons made. The last part of the story is the summary. Important points are restated in a new and fresh way.

John Gartner, in a paper presented at the 1961 annual convention of The Outdoor Writer's Association, named six different types of writing. The *Narration* is telling the story in a chronological sequence. The "Me and Pete" story often is all narrative. This approach may be dangerous if used in excess, although it does make a story move.

Dialogue must be natural and suit the character speaking. It must do one or more of three things: characterize the speaker, advance the story, and inform the reader about something he should know.

Exposition means to explain something in terms of reason as opposed to *Description* which explains in terms of the senses. All forward movement ceases when using exposition, so it can be dangerous. Exposition often can be combined with other types. Description is close to exposition and should be used in the same ways.

Introspection delves into the mind of the main character. The reader and the author think with him. This technique is excellent for a change of pace and is used much by the fiction writer.

Dramatic Action is produced with a combination of techniques to create a scene which adds to the story. This also is a good way to start an article. The reader is shown what is happening; he is not just told about it.

The mixture of the six techniques can be compared with a steak dinner. All meat, all potatoes and gravy, all salad, all vegetables or all dessert are not nearly as tasty as a proper mixture of them all. So it is with writing for entertainment (and education on the side). All parts or techniques must be combined in correct proportions for the best results.

As stated before, titles are important in popular writing. They should be short, usually of 10 words or less, and must attract attention and create interest. It is noted that titles of popular articles often have main words starting with the same letter of the alphabet. "How *Bad* is *Bruin*" is the title of an article about bear predation. "*Bucks* and *Bows*," a take-off on a once popular song, is an article about archery hunting for deer. "*Backroads* for *Buckskin*" is about access roads into back country for deer hunting purposes. The alliteration gives the title a pleasing, catchy effect. Some shocking words also can be incorporated as eyecatchers to motivate and command the interest of the average person. "The *Rape* of Our *Rivers*," a possible title concerning misuse and pollution of rivers, "*Babes* are *Starving*" about winter loss of deer), or "*Murder* of *Mother*" (about hunting females) might be examples. Charles Hjelte (1959), Chief of Publications for the Colorado Game, Fish, and Parks Division, gave several possible types of titles for outdoor stories (Appendix I).

Titles of scientific articles in technical journals should tell as briefly as possible exactly what the article is about. The reading audience, for the most part, will be those interested in the content for professional reasons. Therefore, a catchy title is not necessary or desired for a technical publication. Many guideline publications on "How to Write Technical Articles" are available. Two of the most popular are the *Style Manual for Biological Journals* published by the American Institute of Biological Science (1972) and W. O. Nagle's (1960) publication, *Making Your Technical Writing Useful.*

The first sentence in the first paragraph of a popular story is equally as important as the title in gathering attention. Hjelte (1959) listed several types of starting sentences used in leads for natural resource management stories for outdoor magazines (Appendix J). Combinations and variations are possible.

The first few paragraphs comprise the "lead." They seem to be most difficult to write. These also are some of the most important words of the article. They must attract and hold the interest and curiosity of the reader and, therefore, must not be too long. They, too, are the attention grabbers, the interest formers and the "want to read what follows" creators.

PESTICIDE PRIMER

PESTICIDE : A CHEMICAL USED TO CONTROL OR DESTROY UNWANTED PLANTS OR ANIMALS.

SHORT-LIFE PESTICIDES : THOSE WHICH BREAK DOWN RAPIDLY.

> EX: MALATHION IN DAYS.
> METHOXYCHLOR IN MONTHS.

"HARD" PESTICIDES : THOSE WHICH REMAIN UNCHANGED FOR LONG PERIODS OF TIME IN THE ENVIRONMENT. (YEARS FOR DDT)

OTHER EXAMPLES : ALDRIN, DIELDRIN, ENDRIN, CHLORDANE, LINDANE, AND HEPTACHLOR.

MOVEMENT OF PESTICIDES : WATER, WIND, DUST, AND ANIMALS HAVE MOVED HARD PESTICIDES TO ALL TYPES OF ENVIRONMENTS IN ALL PARTS OF THE WORLD TO AREAS WHERE THEY HAVE NEVER BEEN USED.

> EX. ANTARCTIC

SELECTIVE PESTICIDES : CHEMICALS THAT AFFECT TARGET SPECIES ONLY.

> EX.- LAMPRICIDE - KILLS ONLY LAMPREY LARVAE.
> PYRETHRUM - KILLS INSECTS, BUT NOT BIRDS.

BROAD-SPECTRUM PESTICIDES: CHEMICALS THAT AFFECT MANY SPECIES:

> EX: DDT, MALATHION

DIRECT KILL : SOME PESTICIDES ARE TOXIC ENOUGH TO KILL SOON AFTER TREATMENT.

Reproduced from Michigan Conservation magazine.
Story by Ozz Warbach.

Figure 73. Cartoons and caricatures can attract interest and increase understanding.

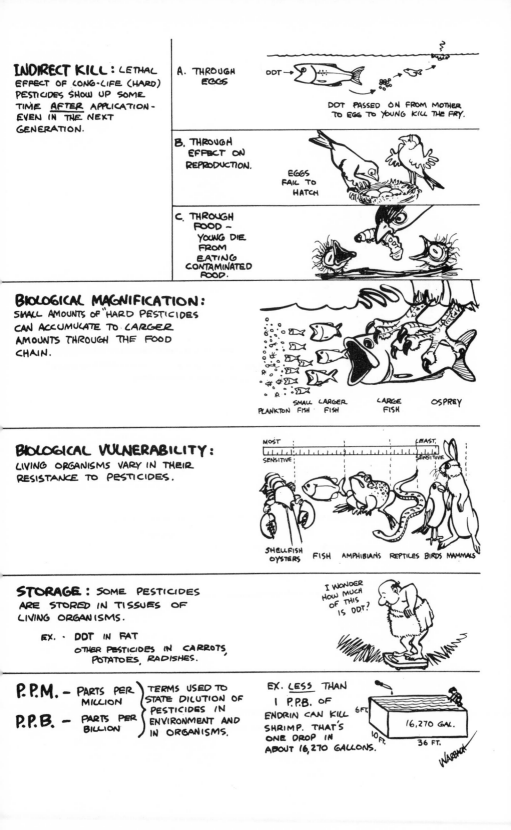

INDIRECT KILL: LETHAL EFFECT OF LONG-LIFE (HARD) PESTICIDES SHOW UP SOME TIME _AFTER_ APPLICATION — EVEN IN THE NEXT GENERATION.

A. THROUGH EGGS

DDT →

DDT PASSED ON FROM MOTHER TO EGG TO YOUNG KILL THE FRY.

B. THROUGH EFFECT ON REPRODUCTION.

EGGS FAIL TO HATCH

C. THROUGH FOOD — YOUNG DIE FROM EATING CONTAMINATED FOOD.

BIOLOGICAL MAGNIFICATION: SMALL AMOUNTS OF "HARD" PESTICIDES CAN ACCUMULATE TO LARGER AMOUNTS THROUGH THE FOOD CHAIN.

PLANKTON SMALL FISH LARGER FISH LARGE FISH OSPREY

BIOLOGICAL VULNERABILITY: LIVING ORGANISMS VARY IN THEIR RESISTANCE TO PESTICIDES.

MOST SENSITIVE   LEAST SENSITIVE

SHELLFISH OYSTERS FISH AMPHIBIANS REPTILES BIRDS MAMMALS

STORAGE: SOME PESTICIDES ARE STORED IN TISSUES OF LIVING ORGANISMS.

EX. · DDT IN FAT
OTHER PESTICIDES IN CARROTS, POTATOES, RADISHES.

I WONDER HOW MUCH OF THIS IS DDT?

P.P.M. — PARTS PER MILLION

P.P.B. — PARTS PER BILLION

TERMS USED TO STATE DILUTION OF PESTICIDES IN ENVIRONMENT AND IN ORGANISMS.

EX. _LESS_ THAN 1 P.P.B. OF ENDRIN CAN KILL SHRIMP. THAT'S ONE DROP IN ABOUT 16,270 GALLONS.

16,270 GAL.
6 FT
10 FT.
36 FT.

WARECKA

People work in different ways. Some write fast, others slowly. Some rewrite only once, others have to write a story many times. An effective approach for some is to write the first few paragraphs slowly and carefully, then to write the rest of the article as rapidly as possible. The author doesn't worry about minor points of grammar or punctuation. These can be corrected in later editing. The important thing is sequence and to get all of the facts down in a logical order. Then the manuscript is put away to "cool off." After several days or weeks, the final editing and polishing can get the material ready for publication.

It is difficult to give an average length, since the length should be fitted to the magazine and the subject. Conservation magazine stories generally average from 1,000 to 2,000 words. This is from four to eight double-spaced pages. First efforts usually end up too long rather than too short. Too many authors try to touch on several topics with one effort. It is far better to deal with one subject fully than to partly uncover several.

Pointed incidents and examples result in specificity. Anecdotes can be used for humor plus entertainment and to increase clarity and understanding. Action, adventure and controversy also create interest. Vocabulary should be in keeping with the intelligence level of the audience. For example, technical jargon does not belong in a sportsman's magazine. There is no point in the author trying to show how smart he is. The writer must remember that the important thing is to put the message across to the reader. Most authorities agree an educational level for the 8th or 9th grade is about right for the average magazine story. This is easily checked by having a high school freshman read the story and see if he understands.

The article should be written so it can be scanned. This can be done with the help of certain tools, such as headings and sub-headings, boldface type, underlining and italics. The use of colors and illustrative materials, such as tables, charts, photographs, cartoons and caricatures or drawings, is helpful (Figure 73). But, an illustration should be used only if it will attract interest, increase clarity or add to content. A picture of an apple may add little to a story about orchard damage by rabbits.

Photo-stories also are popular in outdoor writing. These usually consist of from 6 to 12, 8 x 10 inch, glossy photos that, along with the captions, tell the complete story. Normally less than one page of manuscript will accompany a photo-story. Quality again is the key to success.

Data and statistics may be necessary in a technical manuscript, but they should be omitted from a popular or semi-popular story unless absolutely necessary to prove a point. People do not like to mull over a mass of figures when reading for pleasure. They simply will not read the story.

Most magazine articles do not require documentation with references. Credit must be given where necessary, but references should be kept to a minimum. Ideas incorporated usually are not new or original. Footnotes are not used, nor is a bibliography necessary.

A popular article should be as personal as possible. People like to identify themselves with the tale and have their questions answered. Names, places and conversation help. The author must invite reader participation.

The writer should never forget that he is trying to influence people's thinking and to change public opinion. The ultimate goal is motivation and action of a specific public. Therefore, key points should be repeated and included in a different way in the summary. This can be done in a closing paragraph or sentence in order to leave the reader with the desired thought in mind.

Conservation writers who have aspirations to publish should try for the unusual slant or aspect or try to fit an immediate market need, such as a current controversy, a crusade or a revolutionary research interest, such as saving a near extinct species or development of a new census method. These approaches greatly increase the chances of having an article accepted for publication.

Once the process is complete, the question and problem are to get the article published. A query is sent to the editor of the publication for which the article was designed. This may be done before the story is completely written. This query is in the nature of a letter which gives the idea, length, a summary and other characteristics of the story, such as number of pictures, special angles and illustrations. Often an outline also is sent. Naturally, the query must be the best effort possible because the article will be accepted or rejected on this basis.

The editor will give a positive or a negative reply. With a positive reply, the procedure is under way. It is not unethical to query more than one editor, but after an acceptance has been given, the article has been promised to a certain publication and that is where it should go.

Most magazine editors like to have articles well in advance of the desired publishing date. A minimum of two months is suggested and six months is better. To illustrate, if an article is written about hunting deer during a November season, it should be in the publisher's hands by early summer. The phrases "June in January" and "Christmas in July" are appropriate. A department calendar of coming seasons and events helps to coordinate timing (Appendix A).

If the article is rejected the first time, it can be submitted elsewhere. Or, the approach can be changed, corrections made as per editorial comments, and it can be sent again to the same editor.

Some natural resource management administrators and outdoor writers make a strong case for using freelance writers to get the story told. Arguments are that the freelance writer has more ability, and this ability is realized by the editors of magazines. Thus, a direct route is through the freelance writer to the editor. Many professional freelance writers will even query editors regarding possible interest and acceptance. Dangers are possible distortion of the facts and a lack of credit for the natural resource manager with the original idea. A freelance writer with ability, however, can be the easiest route to publication.

Most natural resource management publications, such as state conservation magazines, do not pay for articles. Many of their inclusions are written by professionals of the parent organization or a similar agency. But, money should not be, and generally is not, the driving force for the natural resource manager to write for popular consumption. Altruism in the true sense, the betterment of the profession and the world, behooves all who have the ability and something worth writing about to publish it for people to read.

Pamphlets and Brochures

Too many natural resource agencies tend to measure communications by the number of pamphlets, bulletins or booklets distributed to their many publics. These have a place in the dissemination of information for educational purposes or for announcing a coming event, but are too slow for most public relations work. However, use of pamphlets and similar publications can be an excellent method for making a public aware that a situation exists.

Pamphlets also are used as an informational medium for routine news where immediate action is not necessary. Often they are sent on request after being advertised in some other way. They are used to explain involved operations or to interpret nature to those that will take the time to read them. A pamphlet mailed to all employees may assure the agency of complete coverage within a limited time. In this instance, a pamphlet is faster than a regularly scheduled house organ and has the advantage of informal intimacy with insured accuracy.

Bulletins and pamphlets are used to appeal for a cause, such as desired legislation, a clean-up campaign, a landowner-sportsman cooperative organization or to sell or explain a method of management or a coming short course (Figure 74). Some petroleum companies have issued excellent pamphlet publications relative to range and soil management. The west coast tree farms use bulletins to advertise their operations. Hunting maps and regulations are pamphlets that are issued by most states. These pamphlets convey methodology and instructions to hunters. Again, simplicity and ease of understanding are paramount.

Figure 74. Pamphlets are an excellent method to disperse information or to advertise an event.

Attractiveness cannot be overstressed (Figure 74). Regardless of the intended purpose, pamphlets and bulletins should be well written, interesting and understandable. If directions are important, a map should be included. Pamphlets should be constructed to carry a certain message to a certain audience. Clarity and simplicity are the keys to understanding.

The main point is that conservation messages must be put in front of the publics in such a way that they will be read and understood. How about in comic books instead of the gore, sex and crime stories? The Canadian Wildlife Service has done this (Figure 75). People, especially youth, read these publications. Why not on milk cartons or breakfast cereal boxes? With a little persuasion, public service companies or other businessness will incude brochure inserts in monthly messages or bill statements.

Annual Reports

Too many agencies consider the annual report to be a necessary evil instead of an important source of information. It usually ends up as dry as the desert, but shouldn't. People expect data and statistics in an annual report; therefore, such a publication offers an opportunity to make such matters known and available. Items such

Figure 75. Few conservation messages are published in comic book form.

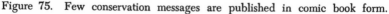

as the financial situation of the agency, problems, personnel changes, summaries of jobs, inventories and predictions can be included. But, it all should be written in an interesting and attractive way. The annual report offers the organization a chance to advertise its expertise, and it should be utilized to the fullest.

Each annual report should have a keynote issue or theme. This is changed from year to year. Natural resource management agency examples might include an accelerated research program, a particular phase of management, history of the organization, the increasing number of users or access problems (Figure 76).

Simplicity and accuracy, plus attractiveness, again are key prerequisites for an annual report (Figure 77). Rosenthal (1967) stressed that style and uniqueness also are important. The technical level should be that of the average newspaper reader, or about that of a freshman in high school. The publication must not be too long; 30 pages, printed on both sides, generally are enough. One-half, 15 pages, can be devoted to the theme, and the other 15 pages to the state of the organization, including accomplishments, desires and budgets.

A LOOK BACK

A 65-Year History of the
Colorado Game and Fish Department

1961 ANNUAL REPORT OF THE COLORADO GAME AND FISH DEPARTMENT

Figure 76.   Annual reports should include a central theme and statistical data
about the organization.

Rosenthal (1967) suggested a page size of 8½ by 11 inches. He also advocated liberal illustrations, with one page of illustrations, including pictures, figures and graphs, for each page of type with much white space and adequate margins. Statistics should be presented in graphic form as much as possible. The graphs and charts should be in color and must be kept simple. Captions and subheadings in the annual report increase understanding and ease in reading.

The rating chart for conservation magazines also is applicable to annual reports. This is presented in Appendix H. A checklist such as this offers an opportunity to evaluate and compare publications.

Figure 77. An annual report should be simple, attractive and accurate. Color and design are especially important.

Policy Manuals

Policies should be put in writing. The accepted way is to publish and make available a collection of all policies in a manual. Thus, the rules and regulations of the organization are available for all employees to read and to follow. This manual should be considered the "Bible" of the organization. It must be kept up-to-date and pertinent since its purpose is to provide the employee with a guide to conduct in all matters.

The policy manual should be simple in organization and must not confuse the employee or create "red tape" in an operation or duty. A table of contents is necessary with subjects grouped into definite categories. This publication is another vehicle to welcome a new employee to the agency with a letter from the supervisor or director. The organization structure and history can be given on the first one or two pages. Suggested inclusions, besides definite policies on specific issues, are employee benefits, working conditions and employee responsibilities. A loose leaf manual offers the opportunity to keep the publication current by adding or subtracting pages as policies change or new ones are added.

All characteristics of good writing are as important here as elsewhere. The written material should be short and to the point. Symbols and other illustrations break up the monotony. Art, headings and subheadings aid in rapidly scanning a section or locating a part. The material must be readable and understandable or the whole reason for a policy manual is lost.

Letters

Letters, although mass produced, can have the connotation of a personal, sincere, individual message if signed individually. The impact can be great. This approach often is used by an administrator to inform employees of some critical happening. The message is direct and to the point. The speed of this type of communication can be very rapid.

One difficulty with letters, as with any written communication, is readability. The key again is for the message to be simple, clear, straightforward, accurate and concise. This approach to communications also can be very expensive but generally is very timely. It should be used within an organization only when the seriousness or importance of the message warrants the approach.

So called "trash mail" and "sucker lists" have detracted from letters as a method of selling an idea or informing a public. If the letter is not outstanding and does not have the personal touch which gives it importance, it will probably end up in the wastebasket, unread.

Other drawbacks to letters are that there is no face-to-face contact and no questions can be asked and answered immediately. Such is the situation with the written method of communications and other mass media. Usually no illustrations, color or caricatures are included in letters, so their attractiveness depends completely upon neatness, briefness and arrangement.

Many letters are branded "propaganda" and discarded as such. Every effort to stress the personal nature, the truth and the importance of a letter should be put into practice. If the letter is not read it all has gone for naught.

Bulletin Boards

Bulletin boards are an excellent place to post current laws and decisions for internal public consumption. They should be kept current and interesting and considered as a location for news bulletins. Bulletin boards, if used correctly, are one of the most effective methods that can be used in stopping rumors within the organization. They are industry's most used approach for bringing printed comunications to the attention of employees.

Someone in the organization should have responsibility for the bulletin boards. They do not take care of themselves. This individual should be guided by a definite set of regulations related to posting procedures, approval of items, preparation, duplication and actual posting of notices. All copy should be screened before it is posted.

Figure 78. Bulletin boards should be kept neat and up to date. Most are not.

Color, art work and neatness help to build employee readership. Material must be current and important. A cartoon in *Stars and Stripes*, a service newspaper in World War II, depicted this. Sad Sack, the cartoon character and also a soldier, was looking at the bulletin board. In the corner under sheaves and sheaves of paper was a notice that read, "All men will fall out at 1400 hours and proceed to cross the Delaware," signed, G. Washington. Bulletin boards characteristically are allowed to become cluttered and to gather out-of-date information. This must not be permitted (Figure 78).

Information Racks

Information racks are used to make magazines, reprints, newspapers, pamphlets and bulletins available for people to read during leisure or waiting hours. The material is free and is distributed in this manner to those who want it. It is not known just how important these reading racks are, but they can contribute to information dissemination, good morale, health, safety, mental and spiritual nourishment and education.

Reading racks should be organized for the specific public, whether that public is made up of employees of the organization or external visitors. Location of the offerings can regulate the audience. If material is for internal consumption, it can be placed in the cafeteria or lounge. If for an external public, the information rack can be placed in the outer office or foyer near the front door.

Someone should be responsible for organization and maintenance of reading racks just as for bulletin boards. This individual should keep a record of the number of publications put in and taken out. It is imperative that materials be available for the people to see, take and read.

Information racks are widely used by large businesses. There is no obligation for the employee or visitor to pick up the materials. This in itself has certain appeal because the acquisition of information is strictly voluntary. An opportunity simply is made available for the individual to avail himself of materials. These can be read during coffee breaks, at lunch hour or at home.

Some materials included on information racks can be about the business and its accomplishments or problems. Other information may concern such topics as buying a house, how to obtain scholarships, education opportunities or any other subject for the good of the cause, the agency and the person reading the material. The reading rack allows the organization to communicate on subjects that are difficult to discuss or that otherwise may not be mentioned.

Television

There are approximately 800 commercial television stations operating in the United States. An additional 500 non-commercial or educational television stations also are on the air. Other commercial and educational stations are being planned. Closed circuit TV is widely used in teaching. Over 90 per cent of American homes have television sets (Anonymous, 1968). These sets operate an average of fr⌐m five to six hours per day (Bluem, Cox, and McPhereson, 1961). Theoretically it is possible to reach nearly 50 million people with one program transmitted in the vicinity of the nation's five largest cities and a nationwide telecast can contact over 100 million people. Satellite television relay stations make worldwide telecasts possible.

Money spent on television advertising ranks second only to newspaper advertising (Anonymous, 1960). These statistics indicate tremendous audiences and interest. It is well to remember, however, that contact is not communications, and any television program can be turned off with a flip of a switch.

If a cost-per-individual contacted were computed, the figure for television would be low. Other advantages of using television in public relations and information and education work are: people in all classes can be reached, including both city and rural; the medium holds interest and creates understanding, because programs can be seen as well as heard; and timeliness in relation to current happenings can be easily controlled.

Problems in Use of Television

One of the main problems encountered in using television in natural resource information work on commercial stations is that of scheduling. Many shows first go on the air as unsponsored public service programs at a certain, agreed upon time. This time may be sold to make room for another show; a sponsored one that pays the station for time used. The natural resource program then is given a less desirable time, and that again is sold. The length of the program may be cut several times to make room for paid commercials. These events are understandable, because a commercial station is a business and must make money to stay in operation.

The solution seems obvious. The natural resource agency can buy time or else obtain a sponsor. The first possibility usually is prohibited by cost and policies of a public service organization. The only alternative is to interest a sponsor.

The next question to be answered is, "What sort of sponsor?" A sporting goods store may be interested. Many outdoor programs are sponsored by breweries. Both of these possibilities usually are turned down by state or federal agencies. The sporting goods store is rejected because the natural resource management agency, a public service organization, cannot sanction one store and its products over competing sporting goods stores. The brewery offer is not accepted because, realistically, some people would be prejudiced by the product. The ultimate sponsor should be a business in no way connected with a product that might offend, such as alcohol, tobacco or with natural resource management. The first, regular television program of the Colorado Game and Fish Department was sponsored by the largest plumbing, heating and sheet metal business in the city. They were the sponsor for five years, and then the sponsorship changed to a major petroleum company. Seemingly, better station cooperation also was obtained with sponsorship.

Another closely allied problem is, "Who will do the commercials?" A member of the sponsoring company or the station should do the selling. If a conservation agency official does the commercials, the person presenting them must be out of uniform.

Complete agreement on length of commercials is needed. With a 15-minute program, the sponsor should receive no more than three minutes for advertising purposes. This usually is presented in two, one and one-half minute segments as they best fit the rest of the show. A sponsored, 30-minute program should include no more than five minutes of commercials.

There are no commercial or advertising problems if the program is presented on an education channel. These stations are endowed and depend strictly upon gifts or grants for operating funds. If an educational channel is used, the viewing audience will be much smaller. The education "stigma" appears to keep many people from watching programs on an educational channel. Most watch TV to be entertained not educated. Natural resource management programs can compete on the commercial channels. This is attested to by the many "Outdoors" and "Outdoorsmen" type programs on national telecasts today.

A situation may arise in which another medium, such as a newspaper, may claim that the natural resource agency is favoring television over the newspaper medium. This problem requires delicate handling and an explanation that no preference is intended. This can become a real problem and usually never works in reverse. Television or radio station personnel do not seem to care how much material is written for newspapers or magazines.

Difficulty in studio arrangement and timing may be encountered with a live program. For example, there may be three minutes or less to move equipment and "props" (ranging from aquaria filled with water to live mountain lions) into the studio and to get them arranged. There also is the problem of straightening up before the next show can go on. These obstacles can be overcome with adequate manpower and studio space. Stations with two studios or one very large studio, would not present this problem for live shows. Kinescopes and video tapes are other solutions, as they allow the earlier filming of a show for later release.

With each new show it becomes increasingly difficult to present outstanding subsequent programs. Repetition in any series of television shows is best avoided if possible. After a few years, many of the better program ideas have been used once, twice or even three times. This problem may be solved by dividing the responsibility for programs between two or three people. It seems to be effective in offering a variety of program ideas. Gilbert (1956, 1960) gave lists of wildlife management programs for television and radio that have been well received.

Another solution to the above problem is to operate with a series of programs rather than a continuous weekly report. The usual group of shows sold to a sponsor is for 13 weeks. This allows a break and a chance to evolve new program ideas between the end of one series and the beginning of the next.

The time required to prepare and present a good television program can be overwhelming. As an individual gains television experience, however, he becomes increasingly confident and needs less preparation. The average time at the start will be about eight hours of preparation for a 15-minute program. This figure includes everything from the hours of worrying and trying to get ideas for the next show to leg work in assembling props.

Not everyone can do, or wants to do, television work. It takes a certain kind of personality to succeed. In some, this personality can be cultivated. In others, it is never present; and in others, the personality is present but the desire or will is lacking. A natural resource management employee capable of doing good television work is even more rare than one that can speak well over the radio or write well.

Suggested Techniques

Logical steps in presenting a television program are given by many authors (Tonkin and Skelsey, 1953; Levenson and Stasheff, 1954; Chester and Garrison, 1956; Hubbell, 1959; Thomas, 1960; and Bluem, Cox, and McPhereson, 1961). These are supplemented by personal findings learned through experience with several television series.

After clearing with supervisors, one needs to make initial contact with the television station. This must be done in person, and the individual should have several of his best program ideas available in written, outline form.

The public interest approach regarding natural resources should be stressed with the television station. It can be pointed out that a television program on natural resource management will be a valuable and timely public service in that it will answer many questions of the audience. Also, the program will have an excellent viewing public from the standpoint of audience size.

The length of the programs and the scheduling time should be decided as early as possible. One must realize that it may be necessary to start with a less desirable time and work toward a better time. If a good show is produced, the station usually will arrange a good time. The first Colorado Game and Fish Department program settled in a 6:45 to 7:00 p.m. slot on Tuesdays. It followed regular sports and preceded the news. This was ideal time. After trying several 30-minute shows, it was decided that for one person doing a continuous sequence, the 15-minute long programs were better. For single shows, or for programs in a short sequence, a half-hour effort has the advantage of longer contact time.

Spot announcements are frequently sent to TV stations for them to use on public service donated time at their discretion. These vary from 10 seconds (10-25 words) to 60 seconds (120-150 words) in length. One or two slides or short film clips often are used in conjunction. A short, terse, vivid spot announcement that attracts attention, tells the viewer something and tells him to do something can be very effective (Appendix K).

One should solve all problems of a sponsor and commercials as soon as possible. All persons concerned will feel better when the show has a definite air time and running period. For a particularly important issue, it may be a good idea to buy prime time.

In developing an idea for a program it is best to work from an organizational calendar (Appendix A). It is possible to have interesting presentations and at the same time to promote the natural resource agency and its efforts. For example, one or two programs on bighorn sheep can be scheduled a week or two before the bighorn season. Programs can be arranged to explain new laws or regulations to the public. To further illustrate, new tagging regulations can be discussed before the big game season. Television programs can be an important asset to any natural resource management agency in disseminating publicity, information and instructions.

A person doing television work must keep in constant touch with his superiors. They may want to start the publicity programs for a certain problem or proposal long before that particular situation is known to the public. For example, if the organization wants a certain piece of legislation passed in the winter, publicity and the selling program may commence the previous spring or summer. Also, all programs that touch on policies of the conservation agency must be cleared before presentation.

It is a good idea to decide what is to be accomplished with a given program. The show should be mentally pictured. One should visualize what he is going to show and say, then it should be written down. The accepted way is to draw a line down a sheet of paper one-third of the width in from the left margin. The left one-third of the sheet is used for the video notes things to be shown). The right two-thirds can then be used for the audio portion (that to be said). The format, or blueprint, for a television program on hunting with a bow is shown in Appendix L.

The program should usually be discussed with the station director before showtime. This means it is necessary to arrive at least one-half hour early. The director knows studio limitations and can advise regarding physical limitations. After experience is obtained, this process may be necessary only for unusual programs.

After it is determined that the show has potential, materials and data must be collected. One must not overlook personnel. It is well to check and double check who and what is needed. People must agree to appear when wanted. Visual aids and props should be chosen carefully. They can make or break the entire program. Too many visuals or props may succeed only in cluttering the set. As a rule of thumb, one visual aid other than slides or films, is about right for three minutes of viewing.

Motion pictures, as well as kinescopes (a 16mm motion picture of a TV show) and the more popular video tapes now used for instant replays of sports events make possible repeated showings. Film also facilitates the viewing of creatures and scenes that cannot be shown "live" on television due to time, size or distance. Films decrease costs, but they do not have the effectiveness of a live program. Motion pictures should be used on television only when the subject is impossible or impractical to portray in any other way. Too many television programs of natural resource management are simply an often used and much seen motion picture.

Film clips, short motion picture sequences that are narrated in the studio, seem to be particularly effective in natural resource work. Other films, especially made for television, should be from 12 to 14 minutes or 27 to 29 minutes long. This allows time for commercials or spot announcements. Most studios prefer 16 millimeter film taken at 24 frames per second, which is sound speed.

Several large corporations produce outdoor motion pictures which are available and can be used on television. However, some of these are cluttered so badly with the corporation's product that they are not suited for use because of impromptu commercials. All commercial films should be previewed to see if they contain too much advertising or any advertising which may be objectionable. For example, a film showing one make of truck performing difficult feats in a hunting camp might be objectionable to another automobile company, especially if the second company is sponsoring the program!

All motion pictures should be checked before use on television. Those found to be badly scratched or having torn or badly worn sprocket holes should be rejected.

If slides are to be used, one should check the types of slide mounts the station equipment will accept. Slides can be mounted in glass for protection from fingerprints, dirt and scratches. Slides a little on the light or "thin" side are better as television seems to darken the effect. These are overexposed rather than underexposed. The slide sequence should be kept moving rapidly. About four to six slides per minute seem about right. Slides especially are good to illustrate spot announcements. All slides should be thoroughly previewed before showing. Carelessness is the only explanation for the wrong picture or an inverted image. This may be the responsibility of the station's engineering personnel, but the natural resource manager is the one who is blamed and looks foolish.

A size ratio of three units high to four units wide is suggested for posters, flip cards or black and white photographs. Vertical slides should not be used. These proportions are pleasing to the eye and are comparable to dimensions of most television screens. About ten per cent of a chart or picture is lost around the edges when photographed with a television camera. Therefore, essential information and points of interest must be concentrated toward the center.

Pictures and charts need to be large enough to maintain detail when reproduced on television. It is best not to use any smaller than 8 by 10 inches, although 5 by 7 inch photographs can be used if necessary. Low contrast charts, black on grey or white on grey, show up better than those with high contrast. Matte finish photographs will not reflect light and cause glare as will glossy prints. A good practice to use with all pictures and charts is to tilt the top of the picture or poster slightly outward. This will point any light glare downward and not into the camera. A dulling spray also can be applied to the print or poster as a last minute precaution. The actual object, if it can be used on television, generally is the best visual aid available.

Two rehearsals before the actual presentation are ideal. A walk-through or "dry-run" rehearsal need not be in the studio. It is wise, however, to hang up a tin lid or paper to represent the TV camera. Guests then can become accustomed to talking to this "camera" when not talking to another person. This preliminary rehearsal affords a chance to check the pace, take a rough timing and most important of all, it gives guests a chance to become familiar with procedures, including cues and talking to the single "eye" of a camera. As a result, everyone will be more relaxed during the aired program.

A dress rehearsal incorporates the use of all equipment and individuals exactly as it will be on the air. This rehearsal is used for accurate timing, tailoring, adding and subtracting. This is the time to detect and correct all errors. For example, the door on a deer trap may stick. It is far better to have this happen during a rehearsal than on the air. The dress rehearsal should not be concluded until everything is exactly right.

Many large television shows have a camera rehearsal in addition to the two already mentioned. This usually is not possible for natural resource programs due to individual time as well as station time. Actually, most natural resource shows go on the air without any rehearsals at all.

A copy of the final program outline should be reviewed with the program director before air time. He is the boss of all station activities relative to the program. Proposed movements should be indicated as nearly as they can be predicted. Time needed for each segment can be decided. Very few shows go exactly as planned. Better shows often are those where the unexpected does happen. Regardless of how calm a person thinks he is, if animals are used, they still can sense nervousness and anxiety. Tame animals often revert to their true, wild nature. In one instance the topic involved skunks and their place in nature. A docile, descented pet was used. This pet bit the handler's finger to the bone. He pried the skunk's mouth open with his other hand, and the skunk bit another finger to the bone! Blood was gushing, but the audience thought the show was excellent. They remembered what was said because the show was alive! Actually, there are three kinds of natural resource management television programs: the kind that is planned, the kind that is done, and the kind one wishes had been done after the program is televised.

To maintain good relations with station personnel, the studio should be cleaned up immediately after the program. This may involve only simple straightening and moving out, or it may involve mopping the floor or some other operation that takes more time. The cleanup *must not* be left for the floor manager, the camera man and personnel of the next program.

Any television show involves one more step, the "follow-up." A critique of the program should be held. Did the program accomplish the objectives? Did it incite questions and discussion? What were the strong and weak points? Complete notes will help avoid repetition, will aid in case a repeat of the program is wanted at a later date, and will provide a permanent record that can be used time after time.

There are many additional suggestions which have not been presented. These are listed.

1. The program should be publicized as much as possible. It is only good business to have as large a viewing audience as can be arranged.
2. Natural resource agency employees must make friends of the television station personnel. Absolute cooperation is necessary. A program can be helped or greatly hurt by the cameramen.
3. Television station staff should be allowed to take their normal responsibilities. An outsider must not attempt to tell them how to do their jobs.
4. A specific subject is better than a general subject. It is best to develop one idea or topic well rather than to skim over a broad subject or to touch lightly on several topics.
5. Clearances and copyrights for all materials used must be checked. This includes photographs, films, maps and music. Some educational films, in addition to requiring special clearance, may not be used on shows which are preceded or followed by other programs on which alcoholic beverages or tobacco are advertised. It is impossible to be too careful in checking and avoiding any legal implications.
6. It is wise to dress appropriately for the occasion. For example, if showing how to skin a deer, a person should not wear a suit and tie. A soft, checkered, flannel shirt, open at the collar, goes very well with a program on natural resource management. Jewelry can reflect lights and should be used with care.
7. Large areas of black and white clothing should be avoided. This creates a "halo" around the area. Pastel colors such as blues, greens and yellows are better television colors than blacks and

whites. Pinks or corals look like flesh on color TV and can embarrass. Buttons should be buttoned and zippers zipped. Vertical lines give an illusion of slimness, horizontal lines make the person look broader. Spots and contrast also broaden.

8. The camera shows the real person. It doesn't lie. All precautions should be watched and care taken to enhance the appearance. Bad points, such as lack of a shave and rumpled clothing seem to be accentuated. Make-up is used with color TV and covers up some blemishes. Bald spots can be dusted with powder to stop the shine. A new hair cut should be avoided as the performer looks scalped. Hands and nails must be clean.

9. The backdrop or background is important. A scene which suggests the out-of-doors, such as a fireplace with guns hanging over the mantel, is good. The working table can be rustic, such as the type that ordinarily is found in a hunting cabin or camp.

10. Introduction and announcements should be as brief as possible.

11. Every program needs an "attention getter" at the start. This may be a shot of a live animal, some other unusual visual, or a very intriguing question. The purpose is to attract the audience. The next job is to retain their attention.

12. Much "show how" and little "tell how" should be used on television. The best type of show is the demonstration where something was shown and explained. Viewer involvement is the key to success. An amateur lecturer is deadly to any television program. Interviews have an advantage of taking less preparation because an expert is helping. There also is a change in voices and faces for the audience to hear and see, therefore the interview is much better than a straight lecture. An occasional round table or controversial discussion offers variety. Spot announcements can be made especially applicable and timely to promote special programs, such as hunter safety during hunting season.

13. The correct attitude is important. A person should be interesting, cheerful, personable, sincere, alert, friendly, informal and always himself.

14. A performer should not slump or appear unnatural. One should sit on the edge of the chair. A good way to relax is to yawn just before the "you're on" cue.

15. A person must talk slowly, even more so than on radio. Conversation should be simple, frank and convincing. There is no need to project. Terms too technical for the viewing public should not be used. This especially is important at the start of a program when trying to capture an audience.

16. One should never read a script on a natural resource management television program. It is all right to use an outline or cue sheets, referred to as "idiot sheets" by the professionals, but there is no excuse for obvious reading.

17. A performer should talk as if to one person.

18. The speaker should look either at the camera or another individual to whom he is talking on the program. The "live" camera, the one sending the picture out over the air, always will be indicated by a red light being on near the lens. Cue signals by the floor manager also will help the talent to look at the correct camera. Talent should not look at a monitor set in the studio when they are on camera.

19. There should be no reference to last week's program. Not all of the current audience may have seen it. Nor should the audience be labeled by a certain classification, such as "you fishermen," or "you ranchers." Some viewers are not fishermen or ranchers.

20. All movements must be slow so the camera can follow. The camera can be thought of as a person watching.

21. An object must be shown for at least 30 seconds. The viewing public requires that long to be fully aware of the item.

22. Objects that are being shown should not be obscured by the hands or body.

23. The number of people in an average scene should be limited to two or three. More than this gives an impression of disorder and diverts attention.

24. Gestures should not be overused. It is not necessary to wave the hands to illustrate every point.

25. Obvious accidents should not be ignored. They may liven up the program and will create informality.

26. The time must be watched closely. One should know exactly how long the closing remarks will take. In this way it is possible to end right on time. Time cues will be given by the floor manager. These should be understood before the program.

27. It is a good idea to have some "cushion material." This can be included or left out, depending on how the time is going. Routine news releases are excellent for this purpose.

28. It is wise to keep one spare, complete program in readiness at all times in case key personnel do not show up or collapse from fright. It is best not to assume a thing. Motion pictures can be used for substitutes if necessary.

29. Television results are hard to measure. Telephone calls and letters give only a rough index of the viewing audience size. A method often used to measure the size of a viewing audience is to offer a free piece of literature to all that write in. One host for an outdoor program in New York asked that Conservation Clubs in the state send in their patches or emblems. These were used on the set and also indicated the magnitude of the viewing audience (Figure 79). Various indices, such as the Nielsen Index and the Crossley Reports, are calculated for larger programs.

Figure 79. Popularity of television programs can be indicated by having the viewing audience ask for, or send in, certain materials, such as conservation club emblems.

Television will be used more and more by natural resource agencies to further necessary objectives of management and to promote good public relations. The medium comparatively is new and there is certain amount of fear related to its usage. Very few state or federal agencies have made the most of TV. Those agencies that have used television in information and education work are most laudatory. Others consider it as being too expensive, time-consuming and difficult. A bad television show is really bad, but most turn out on the positive side.

Television is still not the complete answer for all public relations and education work. Competition from commercial programs with rich sponsors and professional talent is great. Senses of sound and sight are combined with movement, music and color, but the audience cannot ask questions directly. There is no personal contact. These factors are extremely vital if some issue has arisen where personal presentation and group discussion is the best solution.

Radio

Radio became an important mass medium in the early 1920's. The peak of popularity was reached in the late 1930's and early 1940's. Since that time, and with the advent of television, the growth of radio has continued, but at a much slower rate.

In 1964 there were approximately 3,900 AM and 1,100 FM radio stations in operation in the United States. These numbers have increased each year. Ninety-seven per cent of all homes have radios for a total of over 60 million homes with more than 200 million radios in use. Some homes have three or more radios per family. Eighty-five per cent of the automobiles in the United States have radios in them. Over 20 million radios were sold in 1967. This compares with 10 million television sets sold during the same period. Radios are turned on for an average of three hours per set per day. Although money spent for radio advertising ranks behind that spent for advertising in newspapers, magazines and on television, it still totals nearly 650 million dollars (Anonymous, 1968). These statistics certainly attest to the importance of radio as a contact method.

When one considers the changes in radio since World War II, it is apparent that radio may have been influenced by television but has adjusted accordingly. This adjustment includes transistor radios which have made listening possible anywhere and everywhere (Figure 80). The quality of radio reception also has been improved.

Radio programming has changed in recent years. The public service approach has replaced the entertainment connotation in radio broadcasting. The long, dramatic program previously common on radio before the advent of television is no longer popular. Network domination appears to be decreasing. Radio programs are mainly of local interest with much news and music. Programs move fast and hit hard. Spot announcements are frequent, and most programs are either 5 or 15 minutes long.

The advantages of radio contact in communications are many. The magnitude of the audience reached by radio is great and the amount of effort expended per person contacted is small when compared with other mass media. Timeliness is easily controlled, space and time are conquered rapidly, intimacy is present as the person is met in his chosen surroundings and the cost per person contacted is extremely low.

Radio has the advantage of being personal and available. It is in the hunting camp, in the automobile or is present while the listener is resting with eyes closed. The lady of the house can be ironing or doing some task where visual concentration is needed and still be listening to the radio. Farmers have radios in their barns or with them in the fields. Cowboys and landowners can put a radio, no larger than a package of cigarettes, in their shirt pockets while riding or plowing in their fields. Many rural areas, especially in the

Figure 80. Recent developments have made it possible to listen to radio almost any time or place.

western part of the United States, still do not have quality television reception and have very tardy mail deliveries. These rural people constitute one of the most important publics in natural resource work. Radio is a good means of contacting them.

In recent years the Colorado Wildlife Division, in cooperation with the Colorado State Highway Patrol, has organized the "Buckskin Network" to get emergency messages to the big game hunters in the field. Most of the citizen band radio clubs also help with the operation. Commercial stations in the vicinity of the hunting area broadcast messages at certain times. Hunters are told of these broadcast times and frequencies when they enter the hunting area.

Ease of transporting, using and quality of portable recorders make radio especially adaptable for natural resource field work or on-the-spot recordings. I have made tape recordings with excellent results while listening to sage grouse on their booming grounds, while in an airplane counting elk, while at game check stations and while in duck hunters' blinds. Vividness and reality are easily obtained in this way.

Less preparation is needed for a radio program than for a television show or to write an article. No props are needed. Instead of visuals, music and various sound effects help establish the desired mental image. However, it is still necessary to entertain the audience, to relax and inform them, as well as to educate them. Therefore, one always should strive for the utlimate in quality. The audience must be interested in the program or it will be turned off.

Problems in Use of Radio

In addition to comparable television problems and disadvantages of scheduling, sanctioning, lack of personal contact and a lack of talent and training in natural resource organization personnel, we must add a great problem of passive listening to the problems connected with using radio as a communications method. This problem is foremost in that many people listen to their radios without knowing what they are hearing.

Radio is one-dimensional because only the sense of sound is used. The image created must be in the listener's mind. There is no picture on paper or on a screen. This "theatre of the mind" must be so vividly portrayed that the audience not only listens but also associates itself with the idea or proposal being broadcast. Talent and the utilization of many techniques and facilities are necessary to interest, motivate and stimulate a public to action when contacted by radio.

As with television, a radio message can't be folded up and put aside for later digestion. Radio is an immediate medium and the message effectiveness generally depends upon a "one shot" effort at contact and understanding. A program once missed is usually gone forever.

The problems of sponsorship and scheduling for a natural resource radio program are acute. The scheduling of many conservation programs is changed repeatedly and many programs may not be broadcast at all. This problem occurs because most natural resource management programs are broadcast on public service time. Perhaps more effort should be made to pay for the time used or to find a sponsor to pay for it. Or, an agreement should be made with the station to schedule the program permanently in one time spot, whether sustaining or not, so a regular listening audience can be established.

Concentration on radio talent and efforts seemingly has decreased. Radio now appears to be sort of a stepchild to television. In many natural resource departments radio receives the time and talent that remain after the demands of television, newspapers and magazines are satisfied. It should not be this way. Radio is not a panacea for all communications problems but it is a very important means of communicating with many people. Considerable effort should be expended to insure a high quality production.

Suggested Techniques

Many of the hints given for a good television production are equally effective in developing a good radio program. These include program publicity, contacting station personnel well in advance of the first program, making an effort to attain and maintain friendly terms with station personnel, being on time and staying within time, pointing a program toward a specific public, developing programs after doing opinion research, striving for local interest, working from an organization calendar or schedule, using an "attention getting" introduction, covering one topic well rather than covering several halfway and keeping a log of completed programs. Many suggestions for good radio program production are listed in Levenson and Stasheff (1954) and Chester and Garrison (1956). There are additional techniques or suggestions that might be helpful, especially for conservation agency personnel.

Most radio programs done by natural resource management personnel are prerecorded for later use. A good tape recorder with a high quality microphone will help achieve a good program. Commercial stations use single track tapes (recorded across the entire width) at a speed of 7½ inches per second. Slower speeds (3¾ or 1⅞ IPS) can be "dubbed" to other tapes at the standard 7½ IPS speed in the studio, but fidelity is not as good at slower speeds. Many, excellent portable tape recorders are now available at reasonable prices.

Prerecording on tape allows easy program editing. It also is possible to tape a program for simultaneous use by several radio stations. The *Colorado Wildlife* radio program is taped each week by personnel of the College of Forestry and Natural Resources at Colorado State University in cooperation with the University Audio-Visual Service. These tapes are reproduced, and copies are sent to approximately 20 stations located throughout the state of Colorado. This program is 15 minutes long and has been broadcast each week for over ten years.

A person always should be on the alert for good program ideas. When an idea occurs, it should be written down. One should keep a file of good program ideas to draw upon.

It is best not to read a script on a radio program unless absolutely necessary. An air of informality derived from conversation lends intimacy that does not come from reading. Few people have the ability to read so it cannot be detected as such. A few errors even add to the desired "air of informality." However, it is always a good idea to have an outline script or format to follow (Appendix M).

The outline script includes a carefully timed, written, introduction and closing. This allows for necessary stretching or shortening in the middle of the program so that it always ends on time. The script should consist of no more than one, double-spaced sheet for a 15-minute program. Certain words can be underlined for emphasis. Pauses for effect also can be marked on the script. A rehearsal, or at least a review, of the outline before broadcast time with all participants increases confidence and is a good precaution against triteness and redundancy.

The introduction of the script and the broadcast should tell who, what, when, where, why and how. Also a hint should be given of what is to follow. The introduction should take no more than 30 seconds to one minute, and is used as the "hooker." Sound effects help.

Commercials or public service announcements are best included at natural breaks in the program or at the end. The closing summarizes in a sentence cr two the information that has been given plus inviting the audience to listen the next time.

If the radio performer has the right attitude toward the job, a big step toward a successful program has been taken. The idea for the show should be thought through completely and visualized in the mind of the talent. Enthusiasm and desire are prime requisites for success and will make errors and lack of ability and experience less noticeable.

A person using radio should enunciate distinctly, avoid sibilants and speak slowly. Words such as get, just, probably, and February should be pronounced the way they are spelled, not "git," "jist," "probly," and "Febuary." An average of 25 to 30 words per 15 seconds, with no more than 140 words spoken per minute, is suggested for the average broadcast. News can move faster (approximately 180 words per minute), because there is no attempt being made towards a conversational tone.

So called "picture phrases" where something is vividly portrayed in words set the "theatre of the mind." "The magnificent bull moose gradually rose out of the mists of the shallow lake as our canoe glided silently forward." This sentence is an example of a picture phrase.

Dialogue should be simple and non-technical. The use of gestures and facial expressions will cause body movement to incite naturalness in the voice. For example, one can count the fingers while counting on the air. Actually counting something usually makes it sound better. Contractions are a natural way of speaking and help a radio message sound natural. The goal is to be informal, informative, enthusiastic, at ease and yourself. To communicate, the message must mean the same thing to the recipient as to the sender; therefore, all meanings must be absolutely clear.

Music and sound effects are not used enough on natural resource management programs. They can set the stage for any radio production. Here is a place for the imaginative person to excel. The sound of a duck quacking, an elk bugling; the sounds heard from a herd of cows, a tree being cut or a running brook can attract attention and act as a prelude to the message that will follow. The same sounds and music can be used as a cushion at the end of the program to fill the extra 30 seconds when the talent runs out of something to say.

Conversation and remarks should be controlled as if talking to only one person. This creates desired intimacy. If a mistake is made in grammar or pronunciation, it is suggested to continue and not attempt to correct the error. To err is human, and humanization is desirable. Of course, one should be as accurate as possible and should avoid "uhs" or other speech errors.

A tap on the table sounds like a cannon shot over the air. Rustling of papers sounds like rain or hail on a tin roof. Many of these extraneous noises are the result of nervousness and must be carefully avoided. It is absolutely necessary to be sure that the microphone is turned off before remarks are made that are not pertinent to the broadcast. Books have been written about such remarks and careers have been ruined because of them.

The selection of program types should be based upon the abilities of available personnel and the peculiarities of the situation or topic being discussed. With the *straight talk* or *feature* type radio program, one person attempts to explain or relate something to a listening public. The effectiveness of this program type depends upon the individual's ability. The listener must be met on familiar ground and held with human interest so he will continue to listen.

News programs attempt to inform the public of current happenings. News should be immediate and different. Radio and television have taken over the "extra" edition of the newspapers. "When you hear it, it is news. When you read it, it's history," according to radio personnel.

The *interview* program uses one or two guests. One person acts as moderator and knows, or pretends to know, little about the subject. A good interview depends upon a good interviewer. He should ask the questions. To avoid embarrassment, questions should be written out and reviewed with the guests (the authorities or experts) before the program. Questions should be such that the answer will be in the form of a narrative or comment; not yes, no, or a number (Appendix N).

The guests will do a better job if they are made at ease early in the operation. Questions can be reviewed in a warm-up just before air time. Unnecessary comments by the host, such as "I see" and "uh-huh," as well as trite phrases, "would you mind tellings us," and "our time is about gone," do not help a program.

A *debate* or *round table discussion* can be used advantageously in natural resource management radio work when some important community issue is involved. The length of the program dictates the number of people that can be involved. These programs should be at least one-half hour long to be effective. The moderator must keep the discussion under control at all times so no one is left cut and to control especially argumentative individuals. As an example of a natural resource management debate or discussion program the question was discussed whether or not a large water impoundment near the community should be constructed. The advantages and disadvantages of the impoundment were made known to the public by the discussion.

On the spot or *remote* broadcasts especially are good for natural resource management programs. Currently available tape recorders are small, low priced and some are powered by transistors and batteries. They can be taken anywhere the natural resource manager works and they can be used with the assurance cf quality reproduction. A tape recorded at 7½ inches per second, 1200 feet long, will play for 30 minutes. This allows ample time for most field efforts or interviews. Tapes can be edited, erased or added to in the studio. Associated, natural background noise will increase authenticity.

Terse, repeated, vivid *spot announcements* can be of great help in promoting a natural resource management venture. These generally are read by station personnel and should be from 10 seconds (about 20 or 30 words) to one minute long (150 to 200 words). Spot announcements should be clever, catchy, forceful and sharp. A suggested form for a spot announcement is included in Appendix O. Each announcement should be on a separate sheet.

An example of a spot announcement that was successful in putting a message across to a hunting public consisted of a shot, a scream and a voice saying, "Don't take sound shots. See your target before you shoot." This took 15 seconds. The hunters remembered the message. Their attention was obtained, they were told something, and they were told to do something.

Another example of an effective spot announcement consisted of the sound of fire burning and the announcement that "The forests are as dry as popcorn. Be careful with your smokes and fires." The U. S. Fish and Wildlife Service used spot announcements in recent years when canvasback and redhead ducks were protected (Appendix P). These spot announcements were made to encourage purchase of duck stamps and were sent to radio stations all over the nation.

Radio is here, there and everywhere. It is an inherent part of our daily lives. It is intimate and flexible. It is depended upon and taken for granted. Again, it is not the sole answer, but it is an extremely important mass medium that should be used "in addition to," not "instead of." As with other mass media, radio is most effectively used at the interest and awareness stages of adoption. It can be used as a reminder in the later stages.

MISCELLANEOUS COMMUNICATIONS METHODS AND AIDS

In addition to previously discussed personal appearance programs and mass media methods of communications, there are other ways to contact and influence people that really do not fit either of the two categories. Some may look on these as only techniques of contact. Other people and organizations put great faith in these approaches as methods of influence.

Displays and Exhibits

The value of displays and exhibits often is questioned by personnel of many natural resource management agencies. Are the results worth the time, money and effort needed to put up a grass or tree display at the state fair, to maintain a glass fish truck for parades (Figure 81) or to keep a conservation exhibit van moving about the

Figure 81. The Colorado Game, Fish and Parks Division maintained a glass tank fish truck for many years that was used in many parades.

state? These questions have not been answered. It can be said, however, that displays and exhibits do interest people. Therefore, contact is made. The quality, the impact and the message of these efforts must rest with each individual display or exhibit and organization (Figure 82).

Figure 82. Displays and exhibits are used widely by natural resource management agencies. Their effectiveness in communications depends upon quality of
the exhibit.

As with other methods of contact or communication, it is wise
to aim a specific message at a specific audience. Factors to consider
include age, education, occupation, background, interest, and
whether urban or rural.

To be successful, the display or exhibit must be more than an
oddity. There should be a story or lesson present in addition to attracting attention and entertaining the viewers. One of the best
exhibits relating to natural resource management that I have ever
seen told a vivid story while making a comparison between a clean,
well-kept campground and a rundown, littered area. The display
was attractively organized with model installations. It was very interesting, and the message was present.

Displays and exhibits have habit value. People are used to seeing interesting things in a certain window or showcase. They will
go out of their way to see what is next, if the exposition continues
to maintain quality. The exhibit should be changed regularly and
often, yet it should remain long enough for all interested to see.

A display or exhibit should focus attention on a given point away
from the exact center of the area but at eye level. The theme should
be one that can be grasped at a glance. This requires simplicity in all
detail. One theme, well worked out, is better than several treated
in part.

Four major points are the maximum for a single theme. These
closely related points should be grouped under a single, attractive

title. An arrangement of the major points from left to right is natural since this is the direction of reading in our culture. One major point, the first, should lead to another, the second, and so on. Informality and attractiveness are increased if the main or starting point is not in the exact center of the display.

It is better to have a positive theme than a negative one. Generally, it is not productive to lament what has not been done or has been lost, except to aid in concentrating attention upon what can be done, what should be done or what has been saved.

Colors and lights, when used effectively, can be a great attractant to an audience. Color combinations and adequate lighting add or subtract from the overall quality and impact. Pastels are suggested with certain colors more appropriate for certain things. For example, blue is a cold color and can be used for effect to depict water and ice. Red and orange are warm colors and often are used for fire and heat. The actual color of the object should be used where possible (green-vegetation, brown-soil, etc.).

It is easy to coordinate displays with an organization and its activities. They offer a chance to familiarize people with mottos, badges, emblems and signs. During the hunting or fishing season the display can illustrate species or techniques of harvest or management. Equipment or tackle can be used and models or mounts draw attention. Cartoons or humor command interest and hold attention. Slides on a mechanical changer offer variety. Live animals attract viewers, but great care must be taken that animals used in displays are neither mistreated in any way nor give the appearance of being mistreated. There should be a message of conservation, sportsmanship or good natural resources management in each display or exhibit.

The display or exhibit first should be outlined and constructed to scale on paper. This makes mental visualization much easier as well as allowing a specific check on materials needed, on measurements and on sizes. Size is relative and all items should correspond. Objects must be large enough to be seen easily and all must be labeled. The labels should be large and clear. If items are donated, appropriate credit must be given.

Supplemental literature often is made available at a display to furnish information and to answer questions. Another approach is to have viewers indicate interest by signing a pad. Supplemental materials then are sent to them.

If a person mans the exhibit, he or she, too, is on display. The prime requisites are that he take the initiative in friendly conversation with the viewers, be interested in answering questions and that he be able to answer them. A uniform and badge will identify the person as belonging to the organization. He should be available and on his feet, not in the corner hidden by a newspaper. If the booth is to be attended, it should be attended at all times it is open. The area around the display also reflects the organization and should be kept neat and orderly at all times.

A display should be designed to attract the viewer so he will stop and look. This process takes less than a minute. If the opportunity is missed in that time, the viewer is gone. If the attention of the person is gained, he wants a closer look. He becomes interested in the display or exhibit. If he remains long enough to study it, an attitude toward the message or idea is developed. The end product, as it is with other communications methods, is to have the viewer or recipient become motivated enough by the display that he will form an opinion and then a belief. He will act on the belief as circumstances permit. The ultimate goal is to have the viewer motivated so he will exert his influence toward changing attitudes, opinions and beliefs of others.

Displays and exhibits are widely used by state and federal natural resource management agencies. In 1968, 49 of 50 state conservation departments used them to some extent (Wildlife Management Institute, 1968). Their cost is relatively low especially after the first effort since many materials can be used more than once. Their popularity indicates value, or they would not be used so widely. Suggestions for a display and a rating sheet are presented in Appendix Q.

Staged Events and Open Houses

A staged event is a promotional venture used to increase publicity of an idea or effort. It is a dramatization of a news event whereby an occasion is made more vivid. The public often attends to witness the event rather than the main activity. To illustrate, the director of the conservation agency, the supervisor of the national forest or the governor of the state may cut a ribbon to open a certain widely publicized, badly needed, access road. A parade might be used to herald the start of fire prevention week or anti-litter week. The so common "queen" contests which choose a pretty girl to represent and promote the original idea or venture are all staged events.

Another example, construction of a new lake for fishing might soon be completed. This lake cost the conservation department thousands of dollars to build. The department plans events to attract an audience and to get deserved publicity for its efforts. There might be, among other things, fly casting contests, free coffee and doughnuts and prizes for certain tagged fish that are caught. While people are being attracted by the events, contests or free material, they can be confronted with the good work that the organization has done in making this lake available to the public. All of this can put deposits in the "Bank of Good Will."

If a staged event is planned to herald an accomplishment, it must go smoothly. Much advanced planning is necessary. It must be done well or it should not be done at all, because negative results are possible. Little things are important, such as availability of adequate parking space, toilets and an adequate supply of refreshments. People do not like to wait or be left out. Events must click like clockwork. A photographer should be present to take motion pictures and still pictures for later newspaper, magazine and television publicity. Every advantage to the organization should be obtained from the accomplishment and the staged events.

Publicity is necessary before and after the event takes place. All media should be used to attract attention to the coming occurrence. After the happenings, follow-up pictures and stories will aid in obtaining the greatest value from the occasion.

An open house is a staged event of sorts, yet it is different in that the publicity usually is not pointed toward some certain item or deed of the organization but toward the entire effort. An open house can take place any time, at any natural resource agency facility and simply gives the public a chance to see the internal operation of some phase of the organization's activities. An open house often is used to "show off" a new facility (Figure 83). It also affords

Figure 83. An "Open House" where the Colorado Wildlife Division showed the facilities of a new fish hatchery to the public.

families of employees an excellent chance to see where the breadwinner works and to meet the boss.

This technique is especially useful to impress groups, such as legislators; or the governing board, including the Wildlife Commission or the State Board of Agriculture, with the facilities available and the work being done. The Colorado Wildlife Division has used the open house technique to show people their Little Hills Big Game Research Station and the work carried on there. The technique has been used by Colorado State University at its summer campus. The U. S. Forest and Range Experiment Station in Fort Collins, Colorado, had an open house to herald the opening of its new building. The advantage of personal contact is present. It is possible to show how things are done, why they are done, what is done with money that is available or why more funds are needed.

An open house should be well planned with all arrangements made in advance so that visitors can see and learn as much as possible in the time available. A definite itinerary should be developed and each person on the tour should have a written copy of the itinerary to aid in explanations. An interested and capable guide must be present to explain things and answer questions. Tours need be of the proper length—neither too long nor too short. Explanations must be simple and interesting. Groups should not be too large for all persons to see and hear well. It is a good idea to give some small souvenir and refreshments generally are appreciated by everyone.

Scott (1960) suggested seven committees with specific duties to plan a successful open house. The *steering committee* is responsible for the overall decisions. Its responsibility also includes close correlation of times and schedules. The *promotion committee* handles all publicity and announcements, within the organization and with external publics, before and after the actual happening. The *preparation committe* is responsible for facility readiness, safety and space coordination. Exhibits, displays, demonstrations, features, decorations and speeches are planned by the *special events committee.* The *tour and guide committee* coordinates the flow of traffic and assignment of guide duties. Refreshments, first aid, playground supervision and greetings are handled by the *reception and hospitality committee.* The last committee, *traffic,* is charged with parking problems, ingress and egress of automobiles and control of other modes of transportation.

Scott (1960) also stated that adequate planning for an open house should start at least two months ahead of the date. Announcements and advance publicity are suggested at from six to seven weeks. Brochures and itineraries must be made ready one month before the happening. Letters of invitation are sent to especially important people, including employees, press, radio and television stations at D-day minus three weeks. Hard sell publicity, such as posters, picture stories, spot announcements and repeated newscasts should start from one to two weeks before the open house. On the spot publicity of the open house and follow-up stories should be included in the planning and should take place during and after the event.

An open house, if correctly conducted, will prove to the community that the organization is a good component and a good citizen. Other businesses will find a good neighbor and an ally. Good working conditions and happy employees reflect benefits and safety. Economics can be interpreted and misconceptions corrected. This is a chance to develop employee and community pride.

Some large organizations or facilities have a continuous open house rather than making an event out of it for a short time. An example is the Patuxent Wildlife Research Center of the U. S. Fish and Wildlife Service. However, visitor numbers can get out of hand to the point where workers are constantly bothered, or staffing for tours and explanations is impossible. At Patuxent, Maryland, the Fish and Wildlife Service has installed five-minute recordings that are started by pushing a button. The U. S. National Park Service uses this approach at many of their museums and visitor centers. The recordings explain the facilities and work to the visitor, but direct contact and spontaneity with questions and answers are lost.

It also is possible to have self-conducted tours where visitors are given or sold a program or rented a pair of earphones. Each numbered stop in the program corresponds to a certain station on the tour and written or taped messages explain that situation.

The open house is another method of achieving deserved publicity for a job well done or an accomplishment successfully completed. Credit should be earned. It simply is good business.

Telephone Habits

This area of contact is set aside as a special unit because it is so important and yet is so frequently overlooked. As the basic field man is "Mr. Organization" to those with whom he comes in contact, the person answering the telephone represents the organization.

I recall one instance where a 10:00 a.m. call to a local natural resource agency office and an inquiry for Mr. "John Doe" received the reply, "He ain't showed yet." The stenographer should not tell the world that Mr. Doe was late to work! Her grammar was atrocious and a nasal twang didn't add much to the conversation. Needless to say, impressions of the organization, Mr. Doe, and the stenographer all dropped considerably.

But perhaps this was not the fault of the stenographer. Why not have a secretarial applicant talk over the telephone before hiring her? A pleasant voice can set the stage for an enjoyable and beneficial conversation. The administrator was lax in that he apparently had not instructed the secretary in how the telephone should be answered.

The person making the call should be told the name of the organization or the department, immediately. If the person answering the telephone has certain rank or status, he (or she) should give his (or her) name. Otherwise, the secretary can say "Mr. Doe's Office." Under no condition should the secretary give her name in the original greeting. A "May I help you" can complete the original greeting. Grunts, snorts, and wheezes can be very distracting. "Uh-huh's" and "I see's" are unnecessary.

Figure 84. Photographs can show "before and after" changes. Note upright, dead tree in upper, left corner of both pictures.

Figure 85. Photographs are used in census, sex determination and age determination of wildlife.

If an individual is out of the office, the secretary can use tact by simply saying he is not available. She also can offer to take a message or to have him return the call.

Telephones should be manned at all times during the working hours and should be answered before the second ring. After the conversation, it is wise to let the caller hang up first. It is not polite to give the impression that you are hanging up on someone.

Telephone protocol should be established for the benefit of all concerned. Once decided upon, it should be followed. The main two points, however, are to be courteous and helpful.

Photography

Photography is a very popular hobby. It also can be an exacting art. As an artist creates with his paint and brush, the photographer creates with camera and film. Color, contrast and composure are all important components of each artist's product. Some even consider it more exacting and more difficult to arrive at a high quality production with camera than with palette and paint. This is because the entire picture is produced as a unit, all at once, and cannot be conceived in parts or at different settings. Once a shot is missed, the expression gone, the animal moved, or the lighting changed, the identical picture probably never will be available again.

Photography has many uses in the natural resource professions. Timber cruises and range surveys are done with aerial photos. They can show before and after changes (Figure 84). They are used in census efforts of wildlife (Figure 85). New heat sensitive films make possible aerial photographs that indicate the presence of any "hot body" on the ground. Infrared films are used to determine species components of forests. They also are effective in showing changes or degrees in the state of health of an orchard or a field of grain or other crop. Who is to say what increased uses modern science will find for the photographer and photographs? The natural resource manager must use this tool and use it wisely.

The adage "One picture is worth a thousand words" has merit. Photographs are used, and should be used more, to illustrate technical reports, popular articles and newspaper stories. A picture of an event increases interest and authenticity, both so important in writing or speaking concerning natural resource happenings.

Cameras and Exposure

An expensive camera with high quality shutter and lenses does not necessarily produce a good picture. On the other hand, a good picture can not be taken with an inferior camera and materials. One other element, a careful, knowledgeable, capable person or persons must be present to compose the picture and produce the desired result.

A camera consists of a light-tight box with a lens, a shutter and a view finder. A picture actually can be taken with a light-tight box with a tiny pinhole poked in one end and a piece of unexposed film placed at the end of the box opposite the hole. The hole acts as the lens. A finger or flap over the hole acts as the shutter.

The lens usually is the most expensive part of a camera. It refracts or bends the light. It also can magnify or reduce image size and increase or decrease the "field of view" or the area of space in the picture.

Generally speaking, the more elements in a lens, the better its quality. A meniscus lens has a single element. A doublet lens has two elements and an anastigmatic lens has more than two elements. Meniscus and doublet lenses are found in cheaper cameras with fixed focusing (about 10 to 15 feet) and let in fixed amounts of light.

The focal length of a lens governs the image size and is the distance from the lens to the film when the camera is set at infinity. This also is very close to the distance across the negative at the diagonal. A camera with a 50 mm. lens, which is about average for most miniature or "slide" cameras, theoretically will produce an image size nearly equal to the way it appears to the human eye. A 135 mm. lens on the same camera will produce an image size approximately 2.6 times larger (135 ÷ 50). A 300 mm. lens will magnify six times; a 400 mm. lens will magnify the image size eight times. Each time the specific image size is magnified, the field of view or the area covered by the picture, will become increasingly smaller.

A wide angle lens decreases the image size and increases the field of view. It is especially useful in photographing large expanses of territory or large groups. The image size with a 35 mm. lens will be approximately 3/5 the size if the photo were taken with a 50 mm. lens.

The quality of a lens is best indicated by the f/stop. This refers to the size of the lens opening. This is one of the two settings necessary to regulate exposure of the film. To get the f/value of a lens, the focal length is divided by the diameter of the largest lens opening available. For example, if a lens with a focal length of four inches has a diameter of the largest lens opening available of one inch, the f/value of that lens would be f/4 (4 ÷ 1). The lens with the largest opening (smallest f/number) generally is of the best quality.

Going up or down the sequence of f/numbers changes the amount of light allowed to enter the camera. Each larger number on a camera decreases the f/stop and the amount of light by approximately one-half. For example, an f/16 setting will allow about one-half the amount of light to enter as will an f/11 setting. By the same token, an f/8 setting will allow twice the amount of light to enter as a setting of f/11 will. Again, f/stop controls the size of the opening, or by analogy, the size of the window.

The f/stop also controls the "depth of field," a term used to describe the range of distances in which included objects will be in sharp focus. With a large opening and small f/number (f/2.8, f/3.5, f/4, etc.) the depth of field is much shorter or smaller than with the larger f/numbers or smaller openings, such as f/8, f/11, f/16, etc.

The second setting necessary to regulate exposure is the shutter speed. This can be likened to the shade of a window and how fast it is drawn or how long the curtain is left open. The more expensive cameras have a wide range, including both faster and slower shutter speeds. No camera should ever be hand-held at a shutter speed slower than 1/25 of a second. Camera movement causing a blurred picture is one error than can never be corrected in the darkroom.

Shutters are generally of three types based upon location in the camera. The "before the lens" shutter is found on less expensive cameras. The spring mechanism is similar to a safety pin and it is very undependable. A "between the lens" shutter usually is composed of meshing leaf blades. It is very dependable and is found on some cameras of high quality. One big disadvantage is encountered in changing lenses. When a lens is changed, the shutter also must be changed. Also, when the lens is removed, film in the camera is automatically exposed because the shutter is removed or the shade taken from the window.

A "focal plane" or "behind the lens" shutter can be likened to a curtain located behind the lens and in front of the film. This allows the lens to be removed without exposing the film and facilitates free and easy interchange of lenses. A focal plane shutter is found on reflex cameras where the picture usually is composed on ground glass as the photographer looks through the lens. Focal plane shutters are prone to wear out, leak light and may malfunction upon occasion in very cold weather.

Shutter speed is calibrated in seconds or fractions of seconds. A shutter speed of 1/25 second is half as fast as 1/50 second, therefore will let in twice as much light. T and B settings are for time exposures. T stands for "Time;" when the shutter is tripped, it will stay open until tripped a second time. B stands for "Bulb," and when the shutter is tripped, the release must be held down for the aperture to stay open.

Putting the f/stop and shutter speed together can be a problem. The window size (f/stop) and the time the shade is up or the speed with which it is drawn (shutter speed) control the amount of light allowed to enter. The following settings let in approximately the same amount of light, and exposure is nearly identical. Numbers in parenthesis are for a camera with different calibrations. Depth of field increases from f/2.8 to f/16.

f/stop	Shutter speed (fractions of a second)
2.8	1/800 (1/1000)
3.5	1/400 (1/500)
4	1/200 (1/250)
5.6	1/100 (1/125)
8	1/50 (1/60)
11	1/25 (1/30)
16	1/10 (1/15)

A blurred picture also can occur if the shutter speed is set too slow. Animal movement, such as a bird flying, requires a fast shutter speed to stop movement (1/500-1/1000 second) and a comparable, small f/number (large opening) to regulate the exposure. This leeway, available with most good cameras, is necessary for natural resource management photography.

Another part of the camera is the view finder. An "optical," or "second lens," view finder consists of a separate window. The picture is composed through one window and taken through another. This can cause some problems of parallax, especially in closeup work, where the view composed through the view finder is not exactly the same as that taken by the lens.

Parallax problems are nonexistent with single lens reflex cameras They allow the photographer to look through the lens with which he will take the picture. This is done with a mirror inside the camera set at a 45° angle. The mirror reflects the image onto ground glass. When the image is sharp, the picture is in focus. When the shutter is tripped, the mirror flips out of the way and the film is exposed.

Many cameras, both with optical and ground glass view finders, have split-image focusing. This is an easy to use aid in accurate setting of distances. For example, in photographing a tree, if the picture is not in focus, the top of the tree will not be in line with the bottom. When the adjustment is made and the top is in line with the bottom, the picture is in focus.

What camera is best? It's difficult to say. Individual people have different preferences. Generally, the 35 mm. cameras are best for slides and only slides. Some people will disagree, but for black and white work where a large print is needed, the cameras using larger film are suggested. Finiteness decreases and fuzziness increases with enlargement of a small negative. Any error, scratch or dirt on a 35 mm. negative will be enlarged with the negative. Care can overcome this, but the average photographer will get better black and white prints from larger negatives.

The advantages of 35 mm. cameras are many. Their comparative small size makes them much easier to carry. Easily interchangeable lenses are available. The single, best camera for all jobs for the natural resource manager probably is the 35 millimeter camera.

Film

Light is reflected as radiant energy in varying amounts from objects. The light reflected from objects has different wave lengths, colors and intensities. This light is focused by the lens onto the film. The film is coated with various silver salts. With chemical processing, the silver salts are changed in proportion to the amount of light energy that struck them. Thus, an image is produced.

The *film speed* is the film's sensitivity to light. The higher the speed of the film, the less the exposure time needed. Some films are so fast that a fairly high quality, printable negative may result if the picture is taken by the light given off by one candle. The faster the film, however, the coarser the grain. A print made from coarse grain, fast films often will appear fuzzy or blurred. A fine grain film with slow speed usually is better to use if enlargements are needed, adequate light is available and the subject is relatively stationary.

The film manufacturer provides information with the film. This ASA (American Standards Association) rating of film speed can then be used in setting the light meter. A photographer should become familiar with one film and its capabilities because a light meter is not always available or time is not available to use it.

Color photography, in the popular sense, to produce 35 mm. slides is easier than black and white photography. The photographer exposes the film and then sends it in to be processed. Only a few, more serious, amateurs process color film. A quality black and white print will more frequently result if the photographer exposes, develops and prints his own pictures. Greater care usually is given to the operation than if it is done commercially.

A good picture can be ruined with poor developing, or it can be enhanced with good developing. Nor does a good negative necessarily mean a good print or enlargement, even though a good negative is requisite to a good print. It is impossible to get a good print from a poor negative, but some faults, such as composition, exposure and size can be minimized in the darkroom.

Color is a property of vision when the lens, whether in the eye or camera, responds in different ways to the stimulation of different wave lengths of light. If this stimulation received by the lens is not a fairly uniform distribution of many wave lengths, but rather is primarily one wave length (*monochromatic*), a color is picked up by the lens. As with black and white photography, the light is reflected to the lens by the objects around us. It is not necessary to reproduce a given radiation wave length, or mixture of wave lengths to simulate a given color, but it is necessary to produce an effect on the brain or film that will match that effect created by a certain set of wave lengths.

Most color films are coated with layers of emulsion. Each layer is sensitive to different colors; combinations of blue, yellow, green and red. Certain wave lengths of light pass through some of these layers to others of these color sensitive layers. Thus, a combination of colors is possible.

Composition

Regardless of how expensive the camera and how much knowledge one has of its mechanical operation and regardless of care in choosing and processing the film, the composition of the picture is an integral part of the result. True, if enough film is exposed, sooner or later a good picture may happen. The good photographer, however, creates, composes, uses light and shadows and produces good results much more frequently.

The first step in composition of a photograph is to have a definite purpose or objective in mind. Of course, some efforts are fortunate accidents. However, a picture is an aid to communications. It is a way to help tell a story or to make a message clearer and more meaningful. One cannot always wait for that lucky chance.

Figure 86. Perspective in a picture refers to depth or an illusion of distance. This can be attained by having objects in the foreground and background in focus.

Figure 87.   A background to establish or indicate size is especially important in closeup photography.

Backgrounds and foregrounds can add or detract much from a photograph. *Perspective* refers to depth, the three dimensional approach that often is wanted. For example, a close object in focus in the foreground may give perspective or depth to a mountain range or canyon also in focus in the far distance (Figure 86). Other times it may be advantageous to throw the background and foreground out of focus. This may be true if the object, such as a bird or mammal, will nearly fill the entire frame or if objects in the foreground and background are undesirable. Depth of field is primarily controlled by the f/stop.

What kind of background is best? The answer depends on many factors; the purpose, the object being photographed, colors, what is available and many other factors. For outdoor work, blue sky often makes a good background. Natural backgrounds lend authenticity. But, a background can be too beautiful and detract from the purpose of the photo. For example, an azure sky with fluffy clouds will detract from the picture of a forest and the desired feeling of a Ponderosa Pine environment. A piece of black cloth and a piece of white cloth in the camera bag can be a very handy background for closeups.

Composition also includes location of objects in the picture. The *rule of thirds* accepted by most photographers states that the main points in the photo should not be in the exact center but should be located off to the side. If the frame of the picture is trisected on two adjacent sides by evenly spaced lines, these lines will cross at four points. These points are where the main attractants in the photo should be located. It is best not to have the picture bisected by a horizontal or vertical line. The reason? Irregular or asymmetrical objects theoretically are more pleasing to the average person (Figure 88).

Proportion, too, is important. How big should an object in a picture be? A good rule of thumb with wildlife is to have the bird or mammal fill half the frame—if you primarily are interested in the animal. If environment occupied is the purpose, the animal should be much smaller so the habitat in the vicinity can show. It also is possible to get too close and end up with nothing but fur or feathers (Figure 89).

If possible, the subject should be in a graceful, natural position. If a man is involved, he should be dressed and posed in a natural way.

An animal in motion should be entering the frame, off center. Abnormal, unnatural photographs can detract from the main message and the purpose of the picture and actually may tell the wrong story. The viewer may concentrate on the awkward picture rather than upon the message that is being communicated.

Miscellaneous Comments and Equipment

A good light meter is indispensible to the beginning photographer while getting acquainted with the camera and film. After that it should be used only for the unusual shot where light problems are evident. Too many people use the light meter as a crutch and can't take a picture without one. In many natural resource management situations there simply is not time to use a meter, and the person who is completely dependent on one will not get the picture. Many modern, 35 mm. cameras have built-in light meters which measure the available light through the lens. For the most part, these are excellent and relatively foolproof, until the battery runs

Figure 88. The main point of interest in a photograph should not be in the exact center.

down. They also take time to operate, but will function regardless of the lens on the camera.

There are many kinds of filters. Some "filter out" certain colors of the spectrum and enhance others. Some filters are used to cut haze for distant shots. Other filters make the use of a restricted film possible in additional situations. Generally, filters are grouped into three categories. *Contrast* filters are shades of orange and red. They are used to make the sky appear darker, to make clouds appear lighter and fluffier, in other words to exaggerate the shadows, the light portions, and the dark portions of a picture. *Correction* filters are generally yellow or blue. They are used to decrease effects of haze and dust, to make objects in the distance clearer and also to make clouds stand out. A correction filter is used if indoor film is to be used outdoors. *Polaroid* filters reduce glare and reflection (Figure 90).

Figure 89.   A rule of thumb for proportion is to have the animal or object fill
one-half the frame.

When a filter is used, exposure must be corrected. If the stated
"filter factor" is 2, this means that the filter will cut the amount of
light by half and thus the exposure must be doubled, either in shutter speed or f/stop. The average photographer really has very little
use for filters. They should be left for the true professional where
ample time is available. One exception, a very pale haze filter can
be left on the lens at all times. It never harms because there is no
factor, and it will protect the camera lens.

Flash pictures most often are taken indoors. Flash can be used
to increase light, accentuate or decrease shadows and to develop
perspective or depth. Seldom is a flash picture needed outdoors,
unless in a dark forest, in a lair, to reduce shadows or for a closeup. However, much natural resource management work is done in
the laboratory, in holding pens or similar places where flash is
necessary to get the picture. A "guide number" is given when flash
bulbs are purchased. This number, plus the speed of the film and
the distance of the object, will give the f/stop (Guide No. ÷ Distance = f/stop). "Strobe" lights and other electronic flash units are
more expensive, but eliminate the need for bulbs.

Closeup photography can be handled in three ways. First a long
focal length (telephoto) lens can be used. Second, tubes or bellows
can be placed between the regular lens and the camera box. This
increases the focal length and results are similar to using a long
focal length lens. With both of these methods the depth of field is

greatly decreased and focusing must be exact. Available light also is often changed as the camera is placed closer to the object.

One or more closeup lenses also can be used for closeup work. These auxiliary lenses are put on the camera like filters and act as

Figure 90. Shadows can make a photograph distinctive and more appealing. Both pictures show browselines. Perhaps the stark reality without shadows is more forceful.

Figure 91.   Contrast is important in photography. These identical pictures show different degrees of contrast.

a magnifying glass. Closeup lenses are quicker and easier to use than the first two methods for closeup photography. Depth of field is equally exacting and requires careful consideration. When using a closeup lens the quality lens of the camera is covered with an inferior piece of glass. This reduces the quality of the camera lens to that of the glass. For exacting, detailed, precise work, the bellows and tubes or another lens on the camera are suggested. For average closeup work, say of flowers or flower parts, the closeup lens combination usually is adequate.

Many faults in black and white pictures can be corrected in part in the darkroom. Parts of the negative can be enlarged or cropped out. Segments can be darkened or made lighter by covering part of the paper under the enlarger. Underexposed negatives can be timed accordingly in printing or enlarging to give a usable picture. Contrast can be increased by using "hard," contrasty, white papers (F3 or F4—Figure 91). By the same token, contrast can be decreased by using a soft, off-white paper (F1 or F2). Glossy papers and pictures should be used for reproductive purposes. Matte, dull papers and pictures generally are best for framing and for television.

Like any other valuable equipment, expensive cameras should be insured. When a vehicle or home is broken into, cameras often are the first items taken. A good policy is to keep them in a rather obscure place or container. For example, one may carry cameras in the car in an empty, 50 caliber, machine gun, ammunition box available at most war surplus stores. This metal box is dust proof and light tight. In addition, it is waterproof and can be used as an extra seat. In case the car is burglarized, cameras and equipment worth many dollars usually will not be touched. The thief probably will think the box contains tools. If the camera equipment were in an expensive, leather case, it probably would be taken.

Cameras and equipment should be treated as the precision, expensive items they are. Lenses should be capped when not in use. Dust on the lens will show on the picture. Lenses can be cleaned with lens paper or a very soft camel's hair brush made for the job and available at most photography stores.

A filing system is suggested for negatives as well as for slides. The method of filing depends upon the individual, but negatives should be protected with cellophane envelopes. This facilitates viewing, as the envelopes can be seen through, as well as protecting the negatives from dirt and scratches.

EXTENSION SPECIALISTS

The Cooperative Extension Service came into being in 1914 with the passage of the Smith-Lever Act. This act provided federal funds to be allocated on a state matching basis to land grant institutions. The act was to be administered by the U. S. Department of Agriculture and stated that money was to be used to conduct research and to disseminate results and information.

Professions originally incorporated under the Smith-Lever Act were agriculture and home economic oriented. Results have been an important part in the success of modern agriculture. County agents and home demonstration agents are an accepted part of the average, rural community. Since its inception, the act has been broadened to include other professions, such as horticulture, agronomy and some areas in the broad field of conservation or natural resource management.

Extension specialists are common at the state levels in fields of forestry, outdoor recreation and in range management, especially in the western states. In 1967, all 50 states had one or more extension positions in outdoor recreation. Cornwell (1967) stated that 22 states had a wildlife extension specialist. Most of these have one man covering the state, several have two and a few states have three or more wildlife extension specialists. These men have nearly as many titles as there are individuals and the programs are extremely varied. States without extension specialists in the various conservation areas are constantly indicating a desire to have such positions and people.

Administrators of the Federal Extension Service agree that conservation has a place in extension work. The Soil and Water Conservation Specialist in the Federal Extension Service for many years also took care of the wildlife responsibility. A Wildlife Extension Specialist in the Federal Extension Service was authorized in 1968. In addition, the Federal Extension Service operates in many areas of forestry, outdoor recreation and other related programs.

The start of most natural resource management extension work is lost in obscurity. Bode (1937) gave Iowa and Texas credit for the first wildlife extension specialists in 1935. More recently, the U. S. Fish and Wildlife Service does approach extension work in some areas by teaching techniques of trapping and rodent and predator control to landowners. They also are responsible for pesticide surveillance.

Extension jobs are administered in many ways. Many are entirely funded from federal or state grants. In wildlife work, however, the individual usually is employed in a cooperative venture. Universities may furnish offices, administrative guidance, secretarial help, equipment and expenses. The conservation agency's share often is a grant of money, vehicles and equipment. Arrangements vary greatly with the state. Participation in the program by the state game and fish department appears desirable, however, as it does increase cooperation.

It is easy to see that the keyword to success in wildlife extension is cooperation. This can be fabricated by definite policies, goals and lines of authority and responsibility. Successful operation in some states is facilitated by an advisory board governing the individual's work. This board is often composed of representatives from the game and fish department, the department of natural resources in the university and the extension service of the school. In some instances, an individual is on the board to represent outside interests. Utah, for example, has one member from the Utah Wildlife Federation on their board (Crane, 1960).

The extensionist specialist can be thought of as a link in the communications process. He can be likened to a catalyst in a chemical reaction. The extension specialist is a connection between the outside publics and the conservation department or the natural resource profession. Since he is not a member of the conservation department, he can sell the department program and ideas without being accused of "blowing his own horn" or "feathering his own nest." He also is relatively free from political influences and internal pressures that may affect a conservation department employee. In addition, the extension agent often has prestige that is associated with anyone connected with a university. Some extension specialists have faculty titles. They usually work at state or regional levels and can influence many.

The extension specialist seems to be particularly effective in reaching the very important landowner public through the county agent. County agents have the confidence of the farmers and ranchers and are community leaders by job and ability. The extension agent can influence and motivate the county agent, who passes the message on to the landowner public. This chain of communications can be very effective in rural farm areas with problems of user access and harvester-landowner relations.

Facilities and equipment of both organizations, the natural resource management agency and the university, can be used by the agent. He also can call upon speakers from both agencies when special talent is needed. However, the natural resource extensionist has a job that often appears to fit into no agency. He is not a part of the conservation agency, and in some states he has not been accepted as part of the university extension service. Doubts and frustrations can result. Perhaps this is inherent in a new position and will change in time.

There may be some animosity on the part of information and education workers of the conservation department who feel their job, rights, and prerogatives are being infringed upon. There undoubtedly are plenty of problems to go around. Extension agents can attempt to influence an entirely different public than department officials or they can attack problems from another angle. The two categories of workers should cooperate and supplement, not duplicate, each other's work.

When there is a lack of coordination and cooperation between extensionists and conservation department employees, the natural resource extension agent soon develops a lack of interest. Results diminish as interest decreases. Many extension agents become frustrated because of a lack of guidance or help with some of their efforts. Some conservation departments appear to have only a passive interest in extension work and in other natural resource agencies the objectives of the extension position are not defined.

Some extension workers focus their attention on forums (Severy and Pengelly, 1956). Others write bulletins or concentrate on radio and television. Some extensionists work mostly with youth, while others work primarily with one or several adult groups. Still other extensionists act only as "trouble shooters" in that their efforts are pointed at problems as they arise.

One very effective method of extension education is the short course approach used widely and by many personnel of states. These concentrated, workshop type efforts often are pointed at teachers or county agents. Both are leaders, and in turn they will influence many.

Coordination between the natural resource management agency and individuals doing extension work is definitely needed so the experiences of one can benefit others. This coordination is being brought about to a limited degree for the wildlife profession by an annual, Wildlife Extension Specialist's meeting held in conjunction with the North American Wildlife and Natural Resources Conference. A good starting point for further coordination would be continuance of the wildlife extension position in the Federal Extension Service and the possibility of arriving at a common title for the state positions.

The extension specialist position should not be filled by a beginner in the natural resource management profession. The man must have technical training and experience in natural resource management, so he can write and speak with authority. He must have a demonstrated ability to contact people and to communicate with them. But, there must be more than ability. An interest and a desire to do a job beyond the normal requirement in the natural resource management professions also is needed.

Among educational efforts, cooperative extension remains the relatively "Unsung and Silent Service." The efforts of extension specialists in the natural resource professions in dealing with people are slowly being accepted in natural resource management as they have been accepted in the traditional agriculture complex.

THE PUBLIC RELATIONS PROCESS

Planning is the key to success in most endeavors, and the job of promoting good public relations is no exception. As the good researcher plans his project in light of specific objectives, the capable, efficient public relations practitioner also plans every effort.

Many public relations activities are the "fire-putting-out" type rather than the "fire prevention" kind. A well organized effort at good public relations, at selling an idea (fire prevention), makes combating poor public relations (fire-putting-out) unnecessary. It also is similar to a football game; a good offense is the best defense a team can have. If the team or organization is constantly on the offensive in creating a favorable image and in explaining operations, they will not have to be on the defense by erasing a poor image or making excuses for failures and poor public relations.

The steps in the organized public relations process, as given by Cutlip and Center (1964), are fact finding, planning, communications and evaluation. Wells (1966) refers to the SPACE approach, with each letter in the word "space" standing for a step in the operation (seek facts, planning, advising, communication and evaluation). I have added to these and separated several. The steps in the process then are: (1) define the problem or situation; (2) be sure the solution or decision is good for the people and the resource; (3) establish definite goals; (4) collect facts in relation to the situation and the specific publics involved; (5) develop a plan; (6) gather necessary items and materials; (7) indoctrinate and organize personnel; (8) communicate with the public(s); (9) conduct the operation; (10) constantly evaluate the entire process; (11) publicize the good job that was done; (12) organize and file materials and data for future reference.

The problem must be understood thoroughly and agreed upon by those who are responsible. It is necessary to have a clear picture of the goal to be reached. Is this the kind of venture that should be promoted? Is it definitely good for the people? Is it good for the resource? Are time elements such that a workable schedule can be arranged? Have we tried anything like this before? If so, what happened?

For example, let us postulate that we have too many bighorn sheep in an area. The range is overused and the herd may starve or succumb to disease unless surplus sheep are harvested. What are the objectives? Is a season the desired goal? If so, it should be established firmly that the amount and methods of harvest are in accord with good wildlife and range management. The specific details of the proposal should be clarified. How about long term goals or management methods in future years? Every possible contingency must be anticipated and messages made ready for the various publics, including the internal publics, because the organization *must be in accord* with the season.

Fact finding involves much research in relation to the specific publics concerned with the venture. Guesswork should be kept to a minimum. Are there any internal problems to be overcome? Who are the external publics involved? Have these groups been sorted out? Listening to individuals in these publics is one of the best techniques which can be used to determine attitudes, opinions and beliefs. Where does each public rest relative to the adoption or rejection sequence? Data concerning the people that compose the publics should be collected and kept in a handy file. What are the obstacles to be overcome? Are there adverse attitudes? What communications media are available? These communications "tools" should be correlated with objectives. Does the department have the confidence of the public? Is there organized opposition? Where should public relations efforts be concentrated? Who are the leaders for and against the season? What does the particular public know about bighorn sheep? Who owns the land involved? What do the landowners involved think about such a hunt? These and other questions need to be answered. The more facts, the less guesswork and the less formidable the opposition will be.

After all possible facts concerning the project and the important publics are gathered, screened and organized, it is time to develop a major campaign and alternate plans. The operation must stay within policy boundaries. Accurate timing and the communications methods to be used must be decided upon. Budgets must be worked out. Specific target publics must be selected for each phase of the operation. Planning and evaluation *must be continuous* throughout the project.

Personnel who are to be involved in the operation must be alerted and oriented to their responsibilities and schedules. Specific responsibilities for specific items facilitate completion and excellence. Complete indoctrination is necessary because these people will indoctrinate or try to influence others.

Props, pictures and other materials must be gathered together. A well planned operation can be a failure unless the needed visual aids and other items are available. A talk may fail unless certain illustrative material is used to increase clarity and achieve understanding.

After all steps in readiness are complete, the communications plan is set into motion. This seldom goes so smoothly that no changes are necessary. Thus, alternate decisions probably will have

Figure 92. Results of a successful operation should be publicized. This puts deposits in "The Bank Of Good Will."

to be made and other plans developed. These changes result from periodically sampling the public's opinion and from bi-directional communications. If a good job of communications is done, the people will understand and will be in agreement that a bighorn sheep season is necessary.

After the idea of a bighorn season has been accepted by the external publics, the dates for the harvest are set and the hunt takes place. The public relations men must keep their fingers on "the pulse" of the publics so that something does not go wrong at the last minute. Results are measured periodically and evaluation is a *constant* process. To illustrate, steps may have been taken for agency personnel to guide hunters into the back country where the largest herds occur. This modification of plans may have been the result when dissatisfaction was voiced by hunters after hunting success during the first first days of the season was lower than anticipated or desired.

When the season is over, the entire operation should be given a total, final evaluation. An effort to contact people involved (sheep hunters, landowners, agency personnel and others) very frequently is in order. If this is a small public, the contact can be done personally. With a large public, other contact methods, such as questionnaires, telephone polls and similar sampling methods may have to be used for the evaluation process.

THE PUBLIC RELATIONS APPROACH

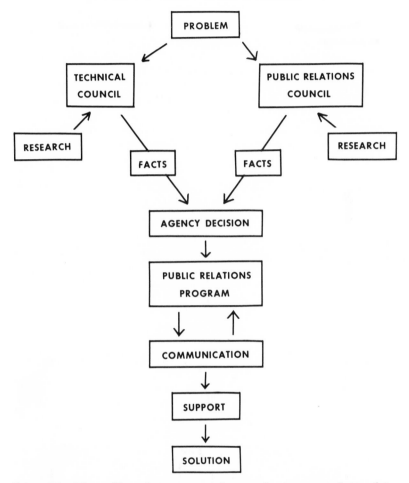

Figure 93. The public relations approach must be incorporated in solving biological problems and in having the results accepted.

Questions to be asked and answered in this final evaluation include the following: Were the goals achieved? Was the cost within reason for the results? How did the various publics react to the season? Was there opposition? If so, where did it originate and why? There are many other questions peculiar to each issue or operation.

Results (hopefully favorable to the organization and to the management method) are then publicized (Figure 92). This should be done as carefully and completely as possible. An attractive bulletin may be in order in addition to commonly used mass media methods of radio, television, magazines and newspapers. Assuming the results were mostly positive, some of the negative aspects should be disclosed. These bad points are least damaging if reviewed openly and not left to be uncovered by remaining opposition.

The final stage in the operation is the follow-up process. This is the "wrap-up" so that experiences, information and materials can be used in future work. The details, successes and failures should be recorded, organized and retained. A scrapbook or file of all news releases, radio and television program outlines, stories, notes, publications and reports on the effort will set the stage for similar efforts at a later date.

Public relations aspects should be incorporated with biological facts in solving a problem. Both are important (Figure 93).

TRAINING OF THE PUBLIC RELATIONS MAN IN NATURAL RESOURCES MANAGEMENT

The public relations man is both a specialist and a generalist. He must have knowledge of the profession that employs his services. In addition, he must have high qualities of character, curiosity, honesty, judgment, courage, thoroughness, tact, personality, humor, imagination and patience. He needs skills in communications, aptitude in expression and ability in administration. He must like to work with people and have a desire to understand people, their cultures, how they think and act and why they think and act the way they do. This man bridges the gap between the organization and its many publics. He interprets the agency to its many publics and the publics to the agency. He is tremendously important to the success or failure of an operation and of the entire organization. He must be an expert to do this job.

It appears that some people are born with greater qualities of personality and the ability to communicate. Some like to work with people more than others but most natural resource managers prefer to work with the resources; soil, water, plants and animals. Characteristics and abilities necessary in public relations can be developed to a certain extent in most people, some more than others, but desire is a major factor. Desire and the basic qualities must be there to work with.

Current efforts toward public relations by natural resource management agencies usually start, and stop, with an attempt to contact a public, often just any public, or to disseminate information. In 1950, Jack Culbreath wrote that "most organizations take a bright young fellow who can write or speak and put him in the front office with a title of public relations director or something similar. This man then writes, publishes and talks. He spends a lot of time giving speeches the boss doesn't want to give and writing stories and releases that the boss doesn't want to write." The situation hasn't changed much in the last 25 years. This is not public relations, because this is no more than contact or putting out information. This work often is done by someone in the organization who is not trained, is not particularly qualified or is not even interested in doing the job. Actually, the information and education man in some conservation organizations is the misfit, the fellow who couldn't pull his share in other jobs or who couldn't get along with fellow workers in those jobs. Such certainly should not be the case.

Abilities and characteristics of the individual are paramount, but generally the public relations man in natural resource management first should be a professional natural resource manager. Is it not far better to make a mistake in writing or speaking than to err in the

227

accuracy of basic information or principles being promoted? The trained natural resource manager is the least dangerous! Many people agree with this philosophy.

Others disagree to some extent with the above approach to the training required for a public relations man in the natural resource management professions. Some people believe that a person should be trained primarily in the arts of communications, journalism, the humanities and the principles of public relations; and secondarily trained in the natural resource management professions. Some believe that a public relations man can pick up the natural resource management knowledge needed while on the job.

Ideally, training should be acquired in journalism, public speaking, photography, the humanities and public relations. I believe this should be in addition to, and second to, a natural resource management background. Preferably, much training should be done in college and before the man is on the job.

Hiebert (1965) stated that at least 280 institutions of higher learning were offering courses in public relations. Five of these schools offered Master's degrees specifically in public relations. The Ph.D. degree was only obtainable in public relations through another field of interest, such as education, journalism or sociology.

At the present time nearly one-half of the people working in natural resource management information and education positions have a degree in some phase of natural resource management. Three out of four gained their media and communications knowledge through experience. Most administrators agree that the most desirable, new employee hired to work in public relations is one who has majored in the natural resource management area with added training in humanities and the communications arts. Therefore, it seems that the ideal public relations worker in natural resource management is adept in both public relations and natural resource management.

Such a man is rare, but with an awareness of need, some will be trained. In 1959, Colorado State University offered the first public relations course designed for the natural resource manager. Since its inception as a problem course offered to students on a volunteer basis, it has developed into a required offering in the wildlife biology curricula and a desired elective for other majors. A similar course was started in 1960 at the New York State University School of Forestry. The course, *Interpreting Forestry to the Public,* is designed to train the forester to present his specialized subject so that it is of interest to the outside publics. The University of Wisconsin developed a curriculum in conservation communications in 1968. Cornell offered a short course in Public Relations for Natural Resource Managers in 1970. Some phase of public relations in natural resource management is now being taught in at least six other major universities.

A graduate program in public relations in the natural resource management professions virtually is unknown but has many possibilities. Research would be in the fields of humanities and often is not accepted by the biologically oriented professions. Perhaps this also will change with time.

It seems logical that universities make provisions for undergraduate work in natural resource management to be supplemented by graduate work in the public relations areas. This would require flexibility in the undergraduate program to allow advanced, technical courses in natural resource management, normally required for graduation, to be postponed until graduate work. Thus, more basic courses in humanities, communications and related public relations arts could be taken during the undergraduate period when credit can be obtained for them.

A college degree plus experience is suggested for the individual doing information and education (public relations) work in natural resource management. A Master's degree is desirable for this position. With the advanced degree, many additional courses can be taken. The Doctorate degree is now mandatory for most extension positions at the state level. Field experience in natural resource management should be a prime requisite for an information and education man in the profession.

Recent trends indicate that agencies are beginning to realize the importance of training competent individuals for public relations work in natural resource management. Some organizations, such as The National Wildlife Federation and Resources for the Future, have established fellowships and grants for graduate work in the fields of public relations in natural resource management. The Outdoor Writers Association of America offers a fellowship in outdoor journalism. National resource management agencies are commencing to hire men multi-trained in natural resource management and public relations for vacant or newly created positions in information and education work. Universities are starting to provide the training needed to prepare students of natural resource management who also are interested in public relations work.

There is a difference between public relations and information and education work. The public relations man attempts to mold public opinion through knowledge of culture and predetermined opinions of the publics. He is an important part of the organization at the policy making level. He is counselled by management and in turn counsels them. By contrast, the information and education employee's main job is to supply information to the publics. He may try to educate but usually is not concerned with predispositions or culture. The rank of the information and education employee in the organization usually is below that of management. Virtually all conservation agency "public relations departments" rightfully should be called information and education departments.

CASE STUDIES

The case study approach to analysis and learning is widely acclaimed by educators. Reading about an actual event and the chronological happenings that took place gives the student of public relations an insight into the planning, or lack of it, and the results that followed. It is hoped that these selected case histories of actual happenings will set the stage for better planned and executed attempts at public relations efforts in the natural resource management professions.

A suggested outline for case study in public relations work is included as Appendix R. It should be pointed out that each case is different and all are not suited to the same approach and outline.

The cases presented are the results of student efforts in advanced classes at Colorado State University. In each case, credit is given to the student that originally compiled the information. Some editing and further analysis were done. I wish to thank the students and the organizations involved in the case studies.

One factor stands out in most natural resource management efforts at public relations. The side, and there are sides, *that is on the defensive*, either by force or choice, *usually loses* the battle or issue. It appears that the best idea is to *keep on the offensive* by explaining the happenings and by educating the publics interested in the natural resource management operations.

CASE 1

The Yellowstone Elk Controversy

(Alan Woolf, 1967)

Objectives

This case study will include the history of the Yellowstone elk controversy, and an attempt will be made to focus attention on the events and opinions leading to the decision by the National Park Service to terminate the direct-reduction program during the winter of 1967.

Case Situation

Policies

The policies involved will be presented in two parts: first, the policies of the National Park Service; and second, the policies of the other natural resource agencies involved in the management of the Northern Yellowstone elk herd. The policies adopted by the

230

Park Service are the heart of the controversy. These policies have not been fully presented and explained to the many publics that are involved and concerned with the management practices of the Park Service. Following are some of the more important aspects of National Park Service policy pertinent to the Yellowstone elk controversy, and the sources of these policies:

$\left(\text{Act of August 25, 1916 establishing the Park Service:}\right)$

"The service thus established shall promote and regulate the use of the Federal areas . . . . by such means and measures as conform to the fundamental purpose of the said parks, ..., which purpose is to conserve the scenery and the natural and historic objects and the wild life therein and to provide for the enjoyment of the same in such manner and by such means as will leave them unimpaired for the enjoyment of future generations."

"That the Secretary of the Interior . . . . may also, upon terms and conditions to be fixed by him, sell or dispose of timber in those cases where in his judgement the cutting of such timber is required in order to control the attacks of insects or diseases or otherwise conserve the scenery or the natural or historic objects in any such party, monument, or reservation. He may also provide in his discretion for the destruction of such animals and of such plant life as may be detrimental to the use of any of said parks, monuments, or reservations."

$\left(\begin{array}{l}\text{Advisory Board on Wildlife Management appointed by Secretary of the Interior Udall (The Leopold Report) March 4, 1963:}\end{array}\right)$

"In recent years the National Park Service has broadened its concept of wildlife conservation to provide for purposeful management of plant and animal communities as an essential step in preserving wildlife resources . . . . unimpaired for the enjoyment of future generations."

"As a primary goal, we would recommend that the biotic associations within each park be maintained, or where necessary recreated, as nearly as possible in the condition that prevailed when the area was first visited by the white man, a National Park should represent a vignette of primitive America."

". . . . observable artificiality in any form must be minimized and obscured in every way possible . . . . In the same category is artificial feeding of wildlife . . . . Fed elk deplete natural ranges. Forage relationships in wild animals should be natural."

". . . . every phase of management itself be under the full jurisdiction of biologically trained personnel of the Park Service . . . . Reducing the numbers of elk in Yellowstone . . . . is part of an overall scheme to preserve or restore a natural biotic scene. The purpose is single-minded. We cannot endorse the view that responsibility for removing excess game animals be shared with state fish and game departments whose primary interest would be to capitalize on the recreational value of the public hunting that thus could be supplied. Such a proposal imputes a multiple use concept of park management which was never intended, which is not legally permitted, nor for which can we find any impelling justification today."

"Direct removal by killing is the most economical and effective way of regulating ungulates within a park. Game removal by shooting should be conducted under the complete jurisdiction of qualified park personnel and solely for the purpose of reducing animals to preserve park values. Recreational hunting is an inappropriate and non-conforming use of the national parks and monuments."

The contents of the Leopold Report are extremely important because it has been accepted by the Park Service as a guideline for park policies and objectives.

(A Cooperative Management Plan for the Northern Yellowstone Elk Herd and its Habitat—December 1963:)

"The animals indigenous to the parks shall be protected, restored, if practicable and their welfare in a natural wild state perpetuated. Their management shall consist only of measures conforming with the basic laws and which are essential to the maintenance of populations and their natural environments in a healthy condition."

This cooperative management plan is signed by the National Park Service, Montana Fish and Game Commission, Wyoming Game and Fish Commission, and the U. S. Forest Service.

(Long-Range Wildlife and Habitat Management Plan for Yellowstone National Park—September 1964:)

"Objective: To attain a balanced relationship between plants and animals and between different species of animals, thus providing an optimum opportunity for the park visitor to observe and enjoy wildlife and plant resources of Yellowstone National Park under conditions which will reflect healthy animals in an appealing, natural environment."

The specific programs for the Northern Yellowstone elk herd can also be considered Park Service policy. The policies of the other natural resource agencies concerned with the management of the Northern Yellowstone elk herd are stated in the cooperative management plan that was formulated and signed in 1963. The policy statements of the agencies co-signing with the Park Service are:

Montana Fish and Game Commission: "To produce and maintain a maximum breeding stock of big game on all suitable lands of Montana, public and private, in harmony with all other uses of such lands, and consistent with the available forage supply, and to utilize, through public hunting, the available crop of big game produced annually by this breeding stock."

Wyoming Game and Fish Commission: Their policy statement conforms closely with the statement of the Montana Fish and Game Commission.

U. S. Forest Service: "The Forest Service recognizes that responsibility for elk stocking rests with the states. In order to insure coordination of uses, the Forest Service will determine the appropriateness of individual projects . . . ."

"Breeding stock now exists on most National Forest areas where elk production and management is desirable. It rarely will be necessary to build up additional supplies of elk by artificially stocking. Of more importance is the determination and correction of envionmental or other factors that limit the natural increase . . . . The agreement will also provide for herd controls to keep populations in balance with the habitat."

"This policy does not provide for widespread stocking without individual study agreements. Future stockings will depend on individual study findings."

The important statements regarding this controversy are contained in several documents, none of which have beeen given a great deal of publicity. They are the "Leopold Report," a cooperative management plan for the Northern Yellowstone elk herd (Leopold, 1963), and the long-range wildlife and habitat management plan for Yellowstone National Park. Another important document containing figures on the current elk status and the reasons behind the reduction program is the 1966-67 wildlife management plan for Yellowstone National Park.

Budgets

Until 1964, no specific provision was included in the Park Service budget for wildlife management, and all expenses for management came from contingency funds within individual parks. Wildlife management measures received money from the Park Service budget only if they were related to other park activities.

The costs of live-trapping elk are shared by the Park Service and the agencies receiving the elk. The receiving agencies pay helicopter and shipping costs, with no charge being made for the animals. Helicopter charges have varied from two to ten dollars per animal trapped. The Park Service pays all other costs related to the elk reduction program. This includes salaries, trap construction (estimates for new traps, specifically designed for trapping elk with helicopters, are approximately $15,000 each) and related expenses. Additionally, approximately $100 per hour rental for helicopters used for driving elk to hunters beyond the park boundary and elk censuses are paid for by the Park Service.

Leopold (1963), in the advisory board report to the Secretary of the Interior said that trapping and handling of a big game animal usually costs from $50 to $150 and in some cases, much more. Even with receiving agencies paying a small portion of the cost, this amounts to a large sum of money spent by the Park Service to trap elk. In addition to the financial burden on the Park Service, Jack Richard, author of an article in the February 21, 1965 Sunday Empire, the magazine of the Denver Post, also pointed out the economic problems of Montana and Wyoming. Richard wondered how long these two states could afford to accept live-trapped elk costing from $12 to $20 per head and still charge their resident hunters $5 for a license. Of course every elk hunter is not successful. Much additional money is spent by hunters for food, lodging and other items.

Basis for Opposing Arguments

The arguments revolve around several basic problems and approaches to these problems. One view is that elk reductions in the park are not necessary. One aspect of this view is that there may be an over-population, but since it is a National Park, the herd should be left alone for nature to take its course.

The Park Service in turn can point to research, including range exclosures, that indicates the harmful effects the elk herd has had on Northern Yellowstone winter ranges Very little controversy exists over whether or not a reduction is necessary. As for letting nature take its course, it has been pointed out by the Leopold Report that management is necessary in National Parks if park objectives are to be met; namely, to preserve the flora, fauna and scenic features of the area.

Another argument against letting the animals starve was well put by Pengelly (1963). He pointed out the inevitable cycle of overpopulation, overgrazing, moisture retention, soil deterioration and the replacement of desirable plant species by less nutritional species. This cycle would further damage the range and reduce the carrying capacity for all ungulate species. While elk normally can reproduce their number in five years, it takes up to 50 years or more for vegetation to re-establish itself, and from 100 to 500 or more years for soil building and replenishment on eroded ranges.

Most arguments revolve around how the reduction should be carried out by the Park Service. Basically, there are five possible methods of herd reduction: 1. public hunting north of the park boundary; 2. live-trapping and transplanting; 3. "direct-reduction" by park personnel; 4. public hunting in the park which is not within the existing legal framework; and 5. introduction of large predators.

The first method of control, public hunting outside the park presently is used and has been for many years. However, it is not an effective control measure because the success of the hunt depends on weather, date of the hunt and the extent of elk movements. The widely varying kills shown in Table 9 indicate the lack of dependable herd reduction by this method. However, this method may be preferred by the Park Service as a method of herd control. The hunt is important to the economy of Gardiner, Montana, a small town just north of Yellowstone Park headquarters at Mammoth. The Park Service and the Montana Fish and Game Commission have cooperated for many years to achieve a maximum harvest from this hunt consistent with weather conditions and the live-trapping program in the park. The Gardiner-Jardine "Firing Line" has achieved nationwide fame and is talked about nearly as much as the direct-reduction in the park itself.

The local residents of Gardiner have mixed feelings about the elk situation in the park and the "Firing Line." Most residents recognize that the overpopulation exists but question if large reductions in the park are necessary. They would prefer to have the elk driven out for hunters. Although they do not think much of the "hunt" and the "sportsmen" involved, the Gardiner residents can not afford to have the hunt ignored as the main reduction method. Christopherson, writing for the Saturday Evening Post, (1952) gave a description of the Gardiner-Jardine Firing Line. He called it "one of the sorriest spectacles known to hunting."

Live-trapping and transplanting is the method of reduction strongly advocated by state conservation agency personnel of Montana and Wyoming. Again, the Park Service prefers this method to direct-reduction, but the success is limited by weather conditions. Beginning in 1963, helicopters were used to herd the elk into traps. This technique has greatly improved the success of live-trapping (Table 9). However, live-trapping and transplanting of surplus elk, in number large enough to have a great deal of effect is, at the present time—with present methods, impractical and uneconomical. Most of the nation's tenable elk range is already occupied and has all the elk it needs and can support (Madson, 1966).

The Leopold Report also considered the solution of live-trapping. The report stated: ". . . . Trapping and transplanting has not proved to be a practical method of control, though it is an appropriate source of breeding stock as needed elsewhere." The discussion of budgets, earlier in this case study, pointed out some of the costs and the live-trapping operation, both to the Park Service and the agencies receiving elk.

Table 9. National Park Service Elk Reductions, Northern Yellowstone Elk Herd, Yellowstone National Park.

Period	Hunter kill	Direct Field Reduction	Live trapping	Winter kill	TOTAL REDUCTION	Actual spring count
1934-35	2,598	223	444		3,265	10,647
1935-36	2,287	6*	551	89	2,933	10,112
1936-37	257	394	180	15	846	10,281
1937-38	3,587	11*	225	89	3,912	8,794
1938-39	2,971	—	307	533	3,811	10,976
1939-40	122	—	16	68	206	
1940-41	275	—	12	10	297	
1941-42	2,071	—	145	108	2,324	
1942-43	6,539	691	—	872	8,102	
1943-44	125	—	10	100	235	8,235
1944-45	403	—	—	300	703	
1945-46	2,094	—	73	250	2,417	
1946-47	3,069	—	76	475	3,620	8,513
1947-48	970	—	39	375	1,384	
1948-49	2,837	—	49	300	3,186	7,815
1949-50	40	518	316	184	1,058	
1950-51	1,265	500	312	217	2,294	
1951-52	3,198	52*	563	500	4,313	
1952-53	110	7*	165	50	332	
1953-54	422	171	216	241	1,050	
1954-55	763	13*	593	289	1,658	
1955-56	3,900	1,974	645	—	6,519	6,963 (helicopter)
1956-57	345	717	227	—	1,289	
1957-58	50	536	—	—	586	
1958-59	372	1,051	319	—	1,742	4,848 (fixed-wing)
1959-60	50	674	135	—	859	
1960-61	25	1,287	147	—	1,459	8,150 (helicopter)
1961-62	125	4,309	301[1]	476	5,220	5,725 (helicopter)
1962-63	530	619[2]	671	negligible	1,820	
1963-64	30	215[5]	906[3]	11	1,151	
1964-65	1,012	205[5]	687[4]	11	1,904	4,865 (helicopter)
1965-66	30	181[5]	1,059[6]	11	1,270	
TOTALS	42,472	14,354	9,398	5,541	71,765	

* Taken for museum specimens or biological studies.
[1] Includes 13 trap loss.
[2] Includes 215 for biological studies.
[3] Includes trap loss of 40.
[4] Includes trap loss of 22.
[5] Biological studies only.
[6] Includes trap loss of 35.

Direct-reduction by Park Personnel is the center of the Yellowstone elk controversy. This method was first used by the Park Service in 1934. Direct-reduction is used only when hunter harvest outside the park and live-trapping fail to reduce the herd to the desired level. Most of the opposition to direct-reduction comes from those who believe that live-trapping can accomplish the necessary reduction without resorting to direct-reduction and those who believe that the Park Service is usurping a recreational resource that should belong to sportsmen.

Public hunting in the park is not permitted under existing laws. Most Park Service personnel generally believe that the law should not be changed to permit hunting because it would endanger other park values. The Park Service policy follows the policy statement in the Leopold Report: ". . . . Such a proposal imputes a multiple use concept of park management which was never intended, which is not legally permitted, nor for which can we find any impelling justification today."

Sportsmen argue that the precedent for public hunting in National Parks has already been set in Grand Teton Park. However, the Park Service also points out that public hunting would not accomplish the necessary reduction. In addition, other parks values are endangered. During the 1961 Teton hunt, 23 illegally killed elk, 11 moose, 2 bears, and several coyotes were found by park rangers. As for hunting success, only half of the permits authorized from 1951 to 1962 ever were used with a hunter's success of 27 per cent (Trueblood, 1963). To accomplish the 5,000 herd reduction of 1962, nearly 20,000 hunters would have been needed. This figure only is a rough estimate because the Grand Teton winter range is much smaller and more accessible than the Northern Yellowstone winter range.

Artificial feeding has been suggested as an emergency measure, but this would be in complete opposition to Park Service objectives. The artificiality and additional problems in range management it would cause make this alternative undesirable.

Introduction of large predators, wolves and cougars, has been advocated by some. This method appears to have several serious drawbacks. Predators would be hard to obtain in the numbers necessary. They probably would kill other animals in addition to, and perhaps instead of, the elk. There is no reason why they should stay within the Park confines. Stockmen in the vicinity probably would lose animals and the National Park Service would have additional problems.

Present Park Service policy is to carry out the necessary herd control using public hunting outside of the park as the primary method. This is supplemented by live-trapping. Direct-reduction by rangers is used only when the other two methods fail to achieve the desired and needed reduction. This is the same policy first estab-

lished and used in 1934. Listed in Table 9 are the official Yellowstone Park elk reduction figures from all herd control methods from
1934 to 1966.

Politics

Politics enter the Yellowstone elk controversy from two aspects.
As with all public agencies, the National Park Service is responsible
to the people. This responsibility is manifested in the form of Federal legislators who exert financial control over the Park Service operations and political pressure at the higher administrative levels.
Legislators are an important internal public of the Park Service.
They can do much to help management practices or bring them to
a quick halt. The influence of Senator McGee (D-Wyo.) in the 1967
controversy is an example of how a Senator can influence park management policies.

Another effect of politicians came from the elected officials of
Montana and Wyoming. The Governors of these states were leading
the opposition to the direct-reduction program. The Governor of
Wyoming made the first public out-cry against the policy and his
condemnation of the Park Service quickly gathered support for his
contentions and charges.

History

Background

The Northern Yellowstone winter range that supports the controversial elk herd includes a maximum area of nearly 120,000 acres
in the northern half of Yellowstone National Park east of the Gallatin Mountain range. This area is reduced to less than 90,000 acres
of winter range during severe winters (U. S. National Park Service,
1964). The Northern Yellowstone elk herd shares this limited winter
range with mule deer, bighorn sheep, antelope, bison and moose.
White-tailed deer also were once present on this range and their
extinction is blamed on competition with elk.

The present winter ranges of elk in the Lamar and upper Yellowstone River drainages were not traditional wintering grounds in
1872 when Yellowstone National Park was created (Pengelly, 1963).
By 1881, park records show that 400 elk wintered in the Lamar
Valley. The winter herd increased rapidly and by 1892, the elk herd
on the northern winter range was estimated to number 25,000.
Heavy winter losses of approximately 5,000 elk were reported in
1892 and 1899, but the herd quickly recovered (Pengelly, 1963).
The herd reached its peak in 1914, numbering an estimated 35,200
head. During the severe winter of 1919-20, two thirds of the elk
herd died. Since then, the herd size has fluctuated between approximately 15,000 and 6,000 animals (Table 10).

The following estimates of the number of elk in the Northern Yellowstone elk herd for the years shown are the most accurate available. It must be understood that these are estimates, and that over such a long period, correspondence, news releases, etc., may have included figures that are somewhat varied.

Table 10. National Park Service Estimates of the Size of the Northern Yellowstone Elk Herd, 1892-1965.

Year	Estimated number	Year	Estimated number	
1892	25,000	1940	12,000	
1893	25,000	1941	12,500	
1897	15,000	1942	11,700	
1907	25,000	1943*	9,100	
1908	25,000	1944	10,500	
1909	30,000	1945	11,500	
1910	30,000	1946*	10,700	
1912	30,100	1947	9,600	
1913	32,200	1948	12,400	
1914	35,300	1949	11,000	
1916*	29,500	1950	12,000	
1923*	14,500	1951	12,000	
1926	14,000	1952	9,200	
1927*	13,000	1953	10,600	
1928*	14,200	1954	11,500	
1929	13,300	1955	11,800	
1930	10,600	1956*	8,300	
1931	10,600	1957	8,200	
1932	10,600	1958	9,000	
1933	12,500	1959*	7,200	
1934*	13,000	1960	7,600	
1935*	11,000	1961*	10,000	(helicopter)
1936*	11,000	1962*	6,800	(helicopter)
1937*	9,700	1963	6,100	
1938*	11,000	1964	6,700	
1939	10,800	1965*	6,900	(helicopter)
		1966	7,000	
		1967	7,200	

* Years in which actual count was made; figure printed is estimate based on count.

Park Service officials recorded their first observations of range damage due to elk abundance in 1911 (Pengelly, 1963). Important range investigations first were carried out in 1917 (Graves and Nelson, 1919), and again in 1930 (Rush, 1932). Although the problem was recognized, little was done to improve the situation. Authorization for the removal of elk by killing first was received in 1934 and 223 elk were removed by direct-reduction. Since that time, direct-reduction has been used as needed to reduce the herd when other methods have not produced the necessary success. However, it was not until 1949 that the first soundly thought out management program for the Northern Yellowstone elk herd was approved (Yellowstone National Park, 1964). The goal of this plan was to reduce the herd to 5,000 elk and maintain it at that level. Relatively large direct-reduction programs were undertaken in 1955-56 (1,974 elk); 1958-59 (1,051 elk); and 1960-61 (1,287 elk). These programs were met with some adverse reaction by some publics, but generally the press emphasized the Park Service's views and assessments of the situation and little opposition came to the surface. Most of the opposition came from sportsmen's groups who desired public hunting in the park.

The approximate goal of 5,000 elk on the northern winter range was not reached until the winter of 1961-62, when a total reduction of 5,220 was attained with 4,309 taken by direct-reduction. This reduction was much publicized and touched off an emotional explosion. The opposition consisted of two groups. They either had vested interests in the Yellowstone elk, or they were well meaning but poorly informed. Trueblood (1963) stated that "public understanding of the need of management is the most difficult problem of all. A vast number of people still grow misty-eyed because of the Bambi myth." Protests were made against the extermination of the elk. "Organizations were formed, and one of them—the Gallatin Elk Protective Association—sent out a bulletin: 'Dear Sportsman: Hang up your rifle forever . . . Even as you read this letter the most magnificent of American big-game animals, the elk, is rapidly on its way toward complete extinction" (Trueblood, 1963). This reaction was typical of the emotions generated by the 1961-62 reduction.

The Montana Fish and Game Department fearing adverse publicity, refused to cooperate with an extended season for hunters outside the park and the rangers carried out the reduction themselves. The opposition to the reduction relied primarily on emotions to halt the Park Service, but even legal action was attempted. An injunction to halt and prohibit further shooting was brought against Yellowstone National Park Superintendent L. A. Garrison by three Cody, Wyoming guides and outfitters represented by former Wyoming Governor, Milward Simpson. The injunction was dismissed in court, but U. S. Congressional pressure was threatened by Senator Joe Hickey (D-Wyo.) when the court action failed. This Congressional pressure also failed to stop the direct-reduction.

Although the controversy and its resulting publicity subsided, the situation was not resolved. The reduction ended for the year, but the elk problem remained. However, some efforts were made to solve the problem. An advisory board (Stanley A. Cain; Clarence M. Cottam; Ira N. Gabrielson; Thomas L. Kimball; and Chairman, A. Starker Leopold) was appointed to study the problem of wildlife management in National Parks. This board made its report (Leopold Report) to the Secretary of the Interior on March 4, 1963. The findings of the board formed the basis of present Park Service policy regarding wildlife management and park objectives and values.

To solve the elk problem further, a cooperative management plan for the Northern Yellowstone elk herd and its habitat was initiated. This cooperative plan was endorsed and signed by personnel of the U. S. National Park Service, Montana Fish and Game Commission, Wyoming Game and Fish Commission, and the U. S. Forest Service. In 1964, two additional steps were taken by the Park Service to improve the situation. First, money was allocated for wildlife management for the first time in the Park Service budget. With funds now included in the budget, Yellowstone Park initiated a long-range wildlife and habitat management plan. This plan set goals and removed management from a year to year basis.

The last direct-reduction until 1967 was carried out in 1962-63. Only one year after the major controversy, little opposition was voiced, and 619 elk were shot by park rangers.

Reasons for the 1967 Controversy
___

The 1967 controversy was merely a continuation of the attitudes, opinions, and beliefs that remained unchanged since the beginning of the Yellowstone Park direct-reduction program. The controversy reached its peak during the 1961-62 reduction, and emotions completely dominated any attempts to rationally evaluate the possible alternatives. The elk problem remained but the issues were permitted to become dormant. When the 1967 reduction was announced, political leaders in Wyoming and Montana (particularly Wyoming) claimed a lack of communication and cooperation on the part of the Park Service and quickly rallied support to halt the 1967 direct-reduction program short of its goals.

Publics Involved and their Tendencies

Proponents
___

Internal publics: National Park Service (includes numerous sub-publics such as administrators, rangers and naturalists, office staff, maintenance personnel, etc.). With the exception of one important internal public that will be discussed under opponents, the Park Service is united behind the concept of direct-reduction as a management tool. Most personnel do not like the job and regret the need to do it, however, they recognize the necessity.

External publics: Professional managers (this public also includes many sub-publics, some of which are opponents of the direct-reduction program). For the most part, professionally trained wildlife investigators recognize the practicality and economic advantages of the program and support the Park Service management plan for elk.

Park and Recreation "Conservation" groups: Although numerous and having diverse interests, most of these groups support the Park Service policy. They are strongly against public hunting in the park. However, many would favor live-trapping to reduce the herd.

Opponents

Internal publics: Some federal legislators are included because they approve budgets and policies. This important internal public of the Park Service generally is strongly against the direct-reduction program in Yellowstone. Almost all the pressure is from the legislators from the surrounding states of Montana and Wyoming, especially Wyoming. The legislators have advocated the live-trapping program and have not been trying to gain public hunting privileges in Yellowstone.

External publics:

State of Montana—Elected Officials
             —Fish and Game Department
                  —Commission
                  —Administrators
                  —Biologists, wardens, and others
State of Wyoming—Elected Officials
             —Game and Fish Department
                  —Commission
                  —Administrators
                  —Biologists, wardens, and others

Both of these states went on record as being opposed to the direct-reduction program. They prefer a live-trapping and transplanting program to control the herd. Wyoming even suggested artificial feeding as an emergency measure rather than direct-reduction.

Rocky Mountain States Game and Fish Departments: The personnel of these departments favor trapping and transplanting. Many administrators also advocate more state control of game management in National Parks. Some employees do recognize the need for direct-reduction and support the Park Service as individuals.

Local residents of Gardiner, Montana: This public includes many sub-publics such as guides, businessmen, motel operators and others. For economic reasons, they want the Park Service to devise means to provide more hunting opportunity, either outside the park, or inside the park. Most of these people do recognize the need to control the northern elk herd, either by hunting or other means if needed.

Montana and Wyoming guides, outfitters and other businessmen: These sub-publics favor public hunting in the park for economic reasons. Some will support live-trapping but most are strongly opposed to direct-reduction.

Sportsmen's groups (Montana, Wyoming, and other groups throughout the country): These groups for the most part, advocate public hunting in the park.

Media personnel: They recognize the need for some type of herd control but generally favor live-trapping or public hunting. A few persons completely support the present program, and some oppose any sort of reduction.

"The Great American Public:" This ill-defined and ambiguous public, consisting of numerous and unidentifiable sub-publics is against direct-reduction with only a few exceptions. The reasons are mostly emotional and because of publicity put out by opponents of direct-reduction. However, their support could be won by a well-planned public relations effort to foster a greater understanding of the reasons, issues and alternatives.

Campaigns and Communications

Media Used

Newspapers were the major medium used by both the National Park Service and the various opponents to the 1967 direct-reduction program. The Park Service relied heavily on news releases, while the opponents used statements and interviews very effectively. Because of nationwide interest in Yellowstone National Park, the issue was given extensive coverage from coast-to-coast. News media personnel also were quick to editorialize the issue since it generated much interest and was very controversial. Television also was used to disseminate information about the issue. However, the coverage given on TV was not sought by either side, information merely was used because of public interest.

The elk controversy has been given coverage in national magazines, Sunday supplements to newspapers and semi-technical publications for many years. Most of the reports stressed the need for reduction, but few gave support to the program of direct-reduction. Many technical publications and papers have been written about the issue stressing the various aspects of the controversy. They are perhaps the most objective reports, however, they have a limited readership.

Other Techniques

Personal contact, meetings, field-trips and other methods to explain their problem on a face-to-face basis have been used by the Park Service. Tours or interviews also were used. In most of the cases that were investigated, the media personnel frequently requested the interview or tour.

The only regularly scheduled meetings concerning the northern elk herd are those scheduled each Spring under the terms of the 1963 cooperative management plan. According to a Park Service press release dated December 6, 1966, consultations were made with cosigners of the agreement before firming up management plans for the Northern Yellowstone elk herd.

A public meeting on the controversy was held in Casper, Wyoming on March 11, 1967. This was a hearing requested by Senator McGee (D-Wyo.), a member of the Senate appropriations subcommitee. When this hearing opened, Senator McGee announced the end of the direct-reduction program for 1967.

Propaganda was used very effectively by those opposed to the direct-reduction program. In all of the newspaper articles that were reviewed, the only statements that could be considered propaganda by the Park Service were two that mentioned "saving the herd," and it "is the humane thing to do." Both of these statements may have been attempts to arouse the sympathy of the public. One other propaganda attempt by the Park Service was to use the testimonial technique. The original date to begin reduction was delayed so the Park Service advisory board (the Leopold Board) could investigate and report on the situation. This effort completely backfired when the press reported that the members of the board never even entered the park. This discredited the report of the board that endorsed a continuation of direct-reduction.

The opposition used a well-planned propaganda effort to halt the direct-reduction. They used "name-calling" effectively to appeal to the "common man" and termed the board an "aesthetic, intellectual group." They made many efforts to discredit the Park Service. Repetition was used often, and charges of "lack of cooperation with state officials;" "laxity in the trapping program;" and "lack of an adequate, responsible, and effective management technique" were leveled against the Park Service. Particular emphasis was placed on the "admitted goof" by the Park Service Director when he failed to pursue the live-trapping program further before initiating direct-reduction. Also, Wyoming Biologists were pictured as "experts" in the field of elk management, and inferences were made that they could have solved the problem had the Park Service sought advice.

The "testimonial" and "band-wagon" techniques were both used with effectiveness. Constant references were made to the "public" and the "people of Wyoming" by well-known state and federal officials of Wyoming. According to these officials, everyone but the Park Service was opposed to the direct-reduction. Loaded words were also used by the opposition, and the media personnel writing articles. Terms such as "butcher," "slaughter" and "wanton killing" were used in nearly every statement and printed article. Appeals to public emotions were also made by describing "frightened animals being herded and shot" from helicopters and snowmobiles. Verbal appeals to the public's emotions were supplemented by well-chosen pictures.

Economics or the "money angle" also were brought into the battle. Many references were made to the economic advantages public hunting possessed in contrast to the "costs" of direct-reduction.

"Card stacking" and the "red-herring" technique were used in statements by the opposition. Only part of the story was told and the complexities and consequences of the various alternatives never were mentioned.

The issue is complex and not all newspaper articles opposed the direct-reduction. Some articles recognized the complex problems involved and tried to give the public some knowledge of the situation. Generally, however, the press reported the Park Service management program in a negative light. Although recognizing the need to reduce the herd, either public hunting or increased live-trapping was preferred. Since the opposition made a determined effort to be heard, they monopolized the news reports and the Park Service was usually presented as; "but the Park Service said . . . ." Some articles that were opposed to the direct-reduction were either written by well-meaning, but ill-informed people or by those capitalizing on the sensationalism of the issue.

Results

Analysis of Techniques and Their Effectiveness

The opposition forced a halt to the 1967 direct-reduction program with an effective public relations effort that employed propaganda to make strong emotional appeals to the public. The Park Service was portrayed as "having an autocratic and untenable attitude" in carrying out the slaughter program in spite of overwhelming public protests.

The Park Service did not make a sufficiently planned and organized attempt to sell their elk management program to the publics involved. Their efforts mainly were to answer charges made by the opposition. The defensive posture taken by the Park Service did little to win public support. The opposition won by capitalizing on the lack of public knowledge and understanding, and was able to present their views in a favorable light.

Sequence of Events

December 6, 1966—Press release by the National Park Service announcing 1966-67 elk management plans.

February 13, 1967—The original announced date to begin the direct-reduction program. This date was postponed on February 11, 1967 so the advisory board could investigate the situation and report to the Secretary of the Interior.

February 27, 1967—Second date scheduled to begin direct-reduction. Reduction started.

March 11, 1967 —Public hearing in Casper, Wyoming. Senator Gale McGee (D-Wyo.), a member of the Senate appropriations sub-committee, acted as chairman. The halt of the 1967 direct-reduction program was announced at this hearing.

Basis for Success or Failure

Under the heading, Analysis of Techniques and Their Effectiveness, reasons were given for the failure of the direct-reduction program. However, the failure also was caused by other reasons. One major problem seemed to be a lack of successful communications with the state agencies concerned with the issue. The either real, or apparent indignation displayed by the state officials of Wyoming suggests that additional conferences and coordination with these officials could do much to reduce active opposition. Although a cooperative management plan has been in existence since 1963, either the provisions for cooperation are not being followed, or the Park Service is failing to publicize meetings and management decisions.

Perhaps the best reason for the failure was well stated by Trueblood (1963). "Probably nowhere in all the fields of human activity does the shadow of the past lie more heavily upon the present than in game management. Tradition's chilling taboos force administrators to do short-sighted things, blind the public to the true status of our game populations, and furnish politicians with emotion-charged issues."

Summary, Alternate Solutions and Future Possibilities

The basis for arguments, both pro and con were discussed early in this case study. The possibilities open to the Park Service basically constitute the same program that has been used since 1934. The need for direct-reduction remains dependent on the success of hunting outside the park and the live-trapping program in the park. Continued pressure undoubtedly will be put on the Park Service to permit public hunting in Yellowstone Park. This will not solve the elk program, and it may endanger park values and goals if permitted. The economic disadvantages of large scale live-trapping, as well as the inherent short-comings of the technique, may limit this method as an effective herd control measure.

The only solution to the problem is a dedicated effort to inform the public of the complexities of the situation and win their support to develop and carry out an effective herd control program on the Northern Yellowstone winter range. This program should be co-ordinated and in cooperation with the states of Montana and Wyoming. However, the Park Service should bear the responsibility for the program and should direct it. Above all, the management program, changes and the status of the elk herd should be well publicized.

Two quotes from Pengelly (1963) are the best summary of the situation, and hope for the future:

"Whether the agencies involved and the general public understand the biological, social, and legal aspects of this special case will largely determine its future handling. Public reaction will depend in part on the efforts of responsible and courageous conservationists who must conduct more basic research and explain the entire history and course of events—choices, costs, and consequences—in such a way that the public (hunters and nonhunters) will want to support proper management. There are some issues that cannot be resolved by popular vote, and this appears to be one of them."

"Management can only proceed as fast, and as far as the public will support it, and with complex issues such as these it will take time, skill, and courage to achieve such support. The initiative, however, rests with the agency entrusted with management responsibility."

Where do we go from here? The elk program has been around for a long time. Until public support is won, it will continue to be a problem plaguing the National Park Service and their attempts to manage the elk herd on the Northern Yellowstone winter range.

CASE 2

The Wyoming Fencing Controversy

(O. Burton Wastcoat, 1967)

Objectives

The objective in this case study is to evaluate the persuasive techniques, intentional or unintentional, utilized in the "Wyoming fencing controversy." No solution to the problem will be given, however a general trend has been noted. In this study objectivity will be one of the primary aims.

Case Situation

Shortly after the Civil War public lands in Wyoming were subjected to unregulated grazing. In 1934 the Taylor Grazing Act was passed by Congress and regulation to rectify earlier misuse began. It is accepted by factions in this controversy that it is virtually impossible to carry out conservation programs to minimize soil erosion, excessive run-off and deterioration of the plant cover if the numbers of livestock cannot be controlled. Concurrent with the efforts of the Bureau to adjust livestock numbers to the carrying capacity of the public rangelands, a means of defining allotments and limiting livestock use to the permitted numbers and areas of use is necessary. The construction of fences is thus an important and necessary facet of the range conservation and development program. Herding, as a means of control, is largely becoming uneconomical. The most practical means whereby sheep can be controlled as required, is by the use of woven wire fencing. (This statement does not give height specifications for fences, nor does it consider barbed wire fencing. Woven wire fencing is reported to be the most detrimental to antelope movement.)

"Grazing capacity of rangeland under woven wire fences can be improved. While this is almost certainly due, in part, to more intensive and better management, when sheep cease to be herded they are allowed to shift for themselves—finding their own bedgrounds and coming to water when they desire. They spread out and cover pastures more thoroughly, grazing places herded sheep never find. Grass breakage and trampling from having a band of sheep traveling over the range is almost eliminated. Dual use (sheep and wildlife), where both grass and browse are present, helps to maintain a desirable balance between these two types of forage. More economical use of the resource is thus assured. In sum, many serious abuses and misuses of the public rangeland can be eliminated through orderly woven wire fencing." This quotation is from the U. S. Bureau of Land Management Position Statement (1965). There appears to be some bias in favor of ranchers and the

Bureau's past policy. Serious abuse also may occur if the public is denied reasonable access if no gates are present or are great distance apart.

In 1950 the Bureau of Land Management and the U. S. Fish and Wildlife Service conducted a study on fence types. Their conclusions in this study provided the best information available at the time for development of suitable fencing on the public lands to meet the requirements of livestock interests, while at the same time protecting the public interest in the antelope and other wildlife resources (U. S. Bureau of Land Mgt., 1965). In the ten-year period after this study, 1,938 miles of fence were constructed on public land. Additional studies have been conducted but the results show that further informative studies must be made before definite recommendations can be made.

History

Since World War II, and more noticeably in the past few years, there has been increasing conflict between the users of public land in the Western United States. This case deals with the land of the Bureau of Land Management (hereafter referred to as the B.L.M.) in Wyoming. This controversy involves sheepmen, the B.L.M., and those specifically interested in conserving the pronghorn, also called antelope by most people. The current intense conflict began with the discovery, in early August, 1965, that a large ranch had constructed approximately 30 miles of sheep-tight fence on public domain and had the land posted against public hunting. This incident received state-wide newspaper coverage, both in print and photographs. Photographs showed no trespassing signs and deer and antelope lying dead by fence lines or hanging from them.

This utilization of emotion was the first attempt to attract the attention of the general public by those in opposition to the B.L.M.'s fencing policy.

Publics Involved

Bureau of Land Management

The B.L.M. is responsible for the management of the public lands concerned. In the past five years there has been a change of policy from "maximum benefit from the land at the present time for the adjudged most important user," to a policy of "the greatest good, for the greatest number, in the long run." The new policy involves consultation with all parties interested and a determination of the "greatest good."

Wyoming Game and Fish Department

This organization is charged with administering the wildlife resource, both on public and private land, for the perpetuation of species involved and for their harvest.

Wyoming Woolgrowers Association

Comprised of a great percentage of the sheep ranchers in Wyoming, this group is concerned primarily with their economic welfare. Policies that will maintain range land in a condition to provide feed for their sheep are their dominant interest. These policies may, or may not, be in keeping with B.L.M. policies.

Wyoming Wildlife Federation

A State Chapter of the National Wildlife Federation, this organization's stated objective is: "To create and encourage an awareness among the people of this nation of the need for wise use and proper management of those resources of the earth upon which the lives and welfare of men depend: the soil, the water, the forests, the minerals, the plant life, and the wildlife."

Wyoming Izaak Walton League

This organization is comprised of conservationists and sportsmen as is the Wildlife Federation. They are a Chapter of the National Izaak Walton League of America. One of their primary objectives is to preserve wildlife for future generations.

General Publics

These publics include unorganized sportsmen and conservationists, The Wyoming Cattlegrowers Association (involved because of possible future land use policies), Wyoming Chambers of Commerce in the areas involved, banks and other businessmen and interested segments of the general United States public.

In the definitions of the various publics there is apparent bias. This was not intended, but is merely a result of the stated objectives of the publics involved. It may be noted that no overt value judgment concerning economics or preservation of species has been made.

Communication Media and Techniques

Newspapers throughout Wyoming were the primary means of communication in this case. Extensive coverage was given, especially in areas where ranchers used B.L.M. lands as a supplement to their own land, and in areas where large hunter populations live.

Group contact was used in two cases. A forum was sponsored by the Game and Fish Department in Casper on October 9th. On this occasion any interested person was permitted to speak. On the 4th of November the Woolgrowers Association invited the B.L.M., the Game and Fish Department, and the two wildlife groups to their annual convention in Gillett, Wyoming. This meeting was also conducted as a forum.

Person-to-person communication was at a minimum, as was utilization of radio and television.

Emotion in reference to the "plight of the antelope" was stressed both in photographs and in writing. "The West, according to the popular ballad, is supposed to be the place where seldom is heard a discouraging word and the deer and the antelope play. Not any more! . . . the fate of the antelope . . . . The doom of the antelope may well be determined by the erection of fences . . ." (Johns, 1965). "The antelope will go the way of the buffalo. Antelope have never been faced with high barriers and they don't know how to cope with them" (Anonymous, 1965a).

Tom Bell (1965), President of the Wyoming Wildlife Federation, utilized the identification and nationalism technique of influence most effectively. He stated, "We want to let the public know the facts and make up their own minds. Sportsmen's rights are being jeopardized, and the out-of-state sportsmen's rights, when they enter a stockman's-dominated state are being jeopardized." Other statements also were effective. An example: "These lands don't belong to just the ranchers and hunters. They belong to everyone . . . . We need a lot more interest from the public. The Game and Fish Department and the outdoor groups can't do it all" (Anonymous, 1965a). Johns (1965) wrote that "we feel the wise use of these resources is important to the citizens of the State of Wyoming and that they shall be held in trust for the public-at-large in the United States."

Indignation was another technique used by Mr. Bell (1965) in his case against the ranch. "To add insult to injury, they posted No Trespassing signs on the fences on this public land." It comes as something of a shock to learn some ranchers are unethical and crude enough to claim large sections of public lands to which they have no more right than any other private citizen and then to ask the B.L.M. for a permit to make the fences legal.

Five of Starch's (1924) social drives were noted. A combination of "play-sport" and "pleasure" is possible due to their interrelation in this case. Fences were consistently blamed for the reduction of the antelope population in recent years. This reduction affects the leisure time of sportsmen, photographers and "nature lovers." "Economy" was used by all factions. Economy of natural resources and manpower have been noted. It should be pointed out that sheep are a stabilizing factor in the local as well as state economy, but it should also be pointed out that wildlife related recreation, including hunting, is Wyoming's third largest industry (after livestock and oil). "Efficiency" was used primarily by those in favor of fencing. It was stated that every major bank in Wyoming had been founded by sheepmen.

"Cooperation" in reaching an agreement or solution on the problem was stressed. Bell (1965) said, "We are fully aware that the great majority of ranchers are not only responsible and law-abiding citizens but are also the best friends and allies of our game animals." The president of the Wyoming Izaak Walton League, (Personal Interview) commented that "They (the B.L.M.) are pitting one side against another (stockmen against sportsmen) when they should be serving both." The president of the Wyoming Woolgrowers, agreed that "more cooperation and coordination in management practices was necessary" (Anonymous, 1965a).

The rancher attempted to use self justification and emotional tools in rebuttal to charges against him. He said that he could see nothing wrong with building fences if he thought they were needed, after he had stated that he was "the biggest landowner and sheep raiser in the State." He added that he didn't feel he had done anything that hadn't been done before (Anonymous, 1965a).

Sequence of Events

As previously noted, the current phase of the fencing controversy began in early August. The timing probably was unintentional and occurred only due to the discovery of the fence and signs. The timing, however, was the first major advantage for the wildlife groups since the antelope hunting season was near. Though not necessarily related, the Wyoming Game and Fish Department issued 10,000 fewer permits to hunt antelope in 1965 than in 1964, which represents a 25 per cent decrease. The first reaction of an individual would be to assume that fencing had caused a decrease in the antelope population, although the primary factors for the population decrease probably were the recent severe winters.

In the first week of September the Wyoming Wildlife Federation and the Wyoming Izaak Walton League had their attorney file affidavits stating that the rancher had constructed illegal fences which were a danger to wildlife and constituted the taking of public land for private use.

On September 30th Representative Henry S. Reuss (Democrat, Wisconsin) introduced a bill (H.R. 11359) in the 89th Congress. This bill was the result of a letter to him from members of the National Wildlife Federation. The bill called for the removal of any fence which impeded the movement of wildlife and also would make any further fencing illegal (Johns, 1965). This action probably had dual effects upon the general public. First, many recognized the possible severity of the problem from the wildlife economic standpoint. Secondly, many realized the detrimental economic significance such a bill could have upon Wyoming. Also, if all fences "impeding wildlife" were removed, land management could regress to the 1930's.

The Game and Fish meeting at Casper on October 9th was the final major event. At this meeting three groups (the Game and Fish Department, the B.L.M., and the combination of the Izaak Walton League and the Wyoming Wildlife Federation) issued policy statements with suggestions. Again wide publicity was gained for these three groups, as well as for the Woolgrowers.

In this controversy the sheepmen were on the defensive due to fencing by the rancher. Their basic issue was the economics of fencing in money saved, land improvement due to fencing and related wildlife habitat improvement due to formation of new water sources with increased fencing.

The wildlife groups stressed the detrimental effects of fencing upon antelope and the illegality of posting public property. They also stated they desired the "wise use of *our* natural resources."

The B.L.M., during much of the controversy, was being very discreet relative to past practices and enforcement of regulations.

Summary

The Wildlife Federation, the B.L.M., the Woolgrowers and the State Game and Fish Department all proposed compromises in this controversy. These proposals were prepared a way in so the opposition could gracefully change their opinions.

The B.L.M. director in Wyoming stated that fences on Federal land may have to be lowered and equipped with wildlife crossing devices and that more access points must be provided for recreationists. Also he added, public land use for livestock must be recognized and is necessary for maximum wildlife use.

Aside from proposed compromises, the only tangible result of this persuasive efforts is the opening of approximately 600,000 acres of private land for public hunting. If pressure is continued and public attention is "maintained," removal of much fencing and construction of access points could occur.

CASE 3

The Fate Of A Bill

(Louis E. Stephenson, 1966)

Objectives

The objective of this paper is to consider the persuasive elements that participated in the defeat of Amendment No. 3, The Right of Eminent Domain for the Colorado Game and Fish Department, freedom of game and fish funds from legislative control, and establishment of the Colorado Wildlife Management Commission.

The Bill

II. AMENDMENT NO. 3

Section 1.   The control, management, restoration, conservation and regulation of the bird, fish, game and wildlife resources of the state, including hatcheries, sanctuaries, refuges, reservations and all other property owned, acquired or used for such purposes and the acquisition, establishment and use thereof, and the administration of all laws pertaining thereto shall be vested in The Colorado Wildlife Management Commission of five (5) members which Commission is hereby created. One member, without voting power, shall be the Director of Natural Resources as created by law. The other members shall have knowledge of and have shown an active and constructive interest in wildlife conservation and management and shall be appointed by the Governor. At any time not more than two voting members of the commission shall be members of or represent the same political party. Not more than one voting member shall be a resident of the same Congressional District. Effective the first day of January, 1961 the Governor shall appoint one member for a term of two years, two members for terms of four years and one member for a term of six years and thereafter, as each term expires, the Governor shall appoint a member for a term of six years. The members of the Commission shall not be paid any salary, but shall be reimbursed for their actual and necessary expenses incurred in carrying out their official duties. If the Governor fails to fill a vacancy within thirty days, the remainder of the Commission shall fill such vacancy for the unexpired term. The Governor may remove a Commissioner for inefficiency, neglect of duty or misconduct in office, after first delivering to him a copy of the charges and affording him an opportunity of being heard upon not less than ten days' written notice. Any order of removal shall recite fully the charges made and the Governor's findings thereon and shall be filed with the Secretary of State.

Section 2.   The present Game and Fish Commission, as created by statute, is abolished effective January 1, 1961.

Section 3. The Commission may acquire by purchase or gift any property or interests in property necessary, useful or convenient for its purposes, and may exercise the right of eminent domain for the purpose of acquiring reasonable and necessary easements or rights of way for public access to and from public lands, in the manner provided by law for the State Highway Commission of Colorado.

Section 4. To execute the law and regulations pursuant to this Article there is hereby established a Director of Wildlife Conservation who shall employ and fix the duties and compensation of such officers and employees as he from time to time deems necessary, all subject to and in accordance with the Civil Service laws as provided by Article XII, Section 13 of this constitution, and said Executive Director and officers and employees shall be employed and hold office in accordance with said Article XII, Section 13. No member of the Commission shall be an appointee or employee of the Commission or Executive Director. The present Director of the Game and Fish Department, as heretofore established by law, shall be the first Executive Director of Wildlife Conservation, and all officers and employees of said Department shall continue as employees of said Executive Director under said Article XII, Section 13. In performing the duties herein specified, the powers and authority of the Commission and the power and authority of the Executive Director shall, to the extent practicable, be separate and apart from each other in that the Commission shall fix all policies and issue all regulations and the Executive Director shall administer and execute such policies and regulations.

Section 5. The license fees, moneys and funds arising from the operations and transactions of the Commission and from the application and administration of the laws and regulations pertaining to the bird, fish, game and wildlife resources of the state and from the sale of property used for said purposes, and all funds now in the Game and Fish Cash Fund shall be deposited with the State Treasurer into a Game and Fish Cash Fund and shall, with all interest thereon, be expended and used by the Commission for the control, management, restoration, conservation, and regulation of the bird, fish, game and wildlife resources of the state, including the purchase or other acquisition of property or interests in property for said purposes, and for the administration of the laws pertaining thereto, and for no other purpose; PROVIDED, HOWEVER, that the Commission shall allocate and transfer to the General Fund of this State each year such sums as the Commission shall determine reasonable and proper as compensation for general State services rendered to the Commission, but not to exceed two per cent (2%) of its gross revenues, exclusive of receipts from the United States Government. The Commission shall, on or before January 1, each year, prepare an annual budget of proposed expenditure for the following fiscal year, and submit copies thereof to the Governor and to the General Assembly, but such expenditures may be made by the Commission without appropriation by the General Assembly.

Section 6.   The Commission shall issue rules and regulations as may be necessary to issue licenses, to regulate bag limits, to fix seasons, to fix the means and manner of taking game, fish, and other wildlife, to establish refuges or sanctuaries and for internal management, and to accomplish all purposes incidental to or relating to the foregoing. Such rules and regulations not relating to the Commission organization and internal management, shall be filed with the Secretary of State and shall be effective not less than ten days after the completion of such publication as the Commission determines necessary to inform the public; PROVIDED, HOWEVER, that when the Commission determines that emergency conditions require the closing of any season in any area, it may do so on not less than 48 hours notice published in a manner determined by the Commission to give the public adequate notice. Such rules and regulations affecting private rights as are judicial or quasi-judicial in nature shall be subject to judicial review as provided by law for reviewing orders or rulings of administrative agencies and commissions. The Commission shall supply all persons on request printed copies of its rules and regulations not relating to organization or internal management, and the violation of any said rules and regulations of the Commission shall be a misdemeanor, punishable as provided by law.

Section 7.   This Article shall be self-enacting and self-enforcing, and all laws inconsistent with this Article or with regulations issued by the Commission hereunder shall no longer remain in force or effect. Laws not inconsistent herewith shall remain in effect or may be enacted in aid thereof.

The ballot title and submission clause to the proposed Initiative Amendment to the Constitution petitioned for herein as designated and affixed by the Secretary of State, Attorney General and Reporter of the Supreme Court is as follows, to-wit:

AN ACT TO ADD A NEW ARTICLE TO THE CONSTITUTION, CREATING A COLORADO WILDLIFE MANAGEMENT COMMISSION; AND A DEPART-   YES
MENT OF WILDLIFE CONSERVATION; AUTHORIZING THE ACQUISITION OF RIGHTS OF WAY FOR PUBLIC ACCESS TO PUBLIC LANDS; RESTRICTING THE USE OF REVENUES OF THE   NO
COMMISSION FOR GAME, FISH, AND WILDLIFE PURPOSES; PRESCRIBING THE POWERS AND DUTIES OF SUCH COMMISSION.

History

No piece of legislation just happens. There is a reason for each bill or constitutional amendment proposed; some fancied or real inequity or ill each new proposal would correct. Such was the case with Amendment No. 3, and before an analysis cf the persuasive factors that went into its defeat can be made, an effort must be made to review some of the factors leading to the proposal.

Part of the precipiting reasons for Amendment No. 3 can be traced to the geography of Colorado itself. Colorado, a state of 66.5 million acres of land has over 24 million acres of government owned land contributing to make Colorado one of the nation's greatest hunting and fishing states. This public land is for all intents and purposes surrounded by 39 million acres of privately owned ranch and farm land. These private lands in some cases block easy access to the public owned hunting and fishing areas and in many instances offered equal if not better hunting and fishing than the publicly owned lands.

During the years since the end of World War II the nation has turned from spectator sports to do-it-yourself recreation. Hunting and fishing have been one of the areas of greatest recreational interest. In addition to this increased interest in hunting and fishing, the population has changed from rural to urban. During the past 30 years the population has increased by more than 700,000 people. All of this growth took place in the urban areas. Non-farm population increased from 753,000 in 1930 to 1,600,000 in 1960; while during the same period farm population decreased by more than 50 per cent or from 283,000 in 1930 to 128,000 in 1960.

Most of Colorado's population live in a seven county area made up of Adams, Arapahoe, Boulder, Denver, El Paso, Jefferson and Pueblo Counties. This increased urban population coupled with the newly awakened interest in hunting and fishing brought the neophyte woodsman outdoors in ever increasing numbers. The hunting and fishing pressure on public lands and streams became more than the public lands could absorb and in many instances the private land owner made his land and streams accessible to these city dwellers turned hunter or fisherman. In other cases the sportsman found the private land posted, gates locked and in some instances even the easy access to public land blocked by the posted land of the ranches. What was the reason for these locked gates and posted lands?

One of the reasons for this, of course, was the fact that some of the land owners were using their land as private hunting and fishing preserves in order to have a source of additional income, but many of the lands that were posted were closed to hunting because of poor sportsmanship on the part of the hunters.

M. L. James and Son of Sedalia, Colorado, presented the ranchers' point of view in a letter to the Colorado Cattlemen's Association which was published in the March, 1956, issue of the *Cattle*

Guard. Mr. James gave a number of reasons for the ranchers' irritation.

First—Ten minutes in an alfalfa field will kill a cow. How would you like to have a fisherman or hunter leave a gate open between your alfalfa field and your pasture where more than a hundred head of cattle are grazing and that gate is two miles from your house? This has been done on our ranch.

Second—Our road up our creek is gumbo mud and we irrigate above it. Fishermen get stuck in the mud and think nothing of driving out in the alfalfa field, rolling down a ton of hay and cutting great ruts in the level field making it impossible to irrigate or run any haying equipment. It's also fun to drive through the field to some high hill to pick wild flowers, choke cherries or just for a view of the country.

Third—They must build a fire to make coffee—and have at different times set a pasture, field or old cattle shed on fire.

Fourth—They leave old lunch boxes, beer cans and old papers to blow—nothing frightens a saddle horse worse than an old box or paper.

Fifth—What is nastier than used kleenex or toilet paper? Would city people like it if we stopped behind one of their hedges to go to the toilet and left uncovered the toilet paper and what we left behind?

Such was the state of affairs in 1957 when the first serious effort was made to force the rancher to at least provide access to the public lands.

Case Situation

During the 1957 legislature a bill was introduced which would provide the Colorado Game and Fish Commission with the right of eminent domain. The ranchers recognized the seriousness of the proposed law and working through the Colorado Cattlemen's Association and through their executive secretary, they managed to defeat the measure. During the 1959 legislature essentially the same bill again was introduced and labeled H. B. 81. Once again the Colorado Cattlemen's Association (C. C. A.) was able to mobilize enough support on behalf of the ranchers to defeat the bill.

When it became apparent that it would be almost impossible to get the proposed legislation through the state senate and house, the proponents decided to present their case to the general public by way of an amendment to the state constitution. In order to do this, in October, 1959, the sportsmen organized the Conservation Council of Colorado, Inc.

By the first of January, 1960, it was common knowledge that the Conservation Council of Colorado, Inc., intended to sponsor some type of the constitutional amendment which would change the structure of the Colorado Fish and Game Department and at the same time give the Fish and Game Department the right of eminent domain. By April enough signatures were on the petition to have Amendment No. 3 added to the ballot to be voted upon by the citizens of Colorado in November.

The Cattlemen's Association had been closely watching the progress of the petition and were ready to undertake a strong campaign against the amendment. Using the *Cattle Guard*, the official publication of C. C. A., as his sounding board, David Rice (1959), the executive secretary, sounded the alarm in the April issue in his column, "As I see It." In his column Rice said:

"Petitions are now being circulated by an organization known as the Conservation Council of Colorado, Inc. It is reported that they have sufficient signatures to place this proposal on the ballot this fall. At first glance, it would seem that this proposal would only affect land owners adjacent to federal lands. Nothing could be further from the truth. As written, it directly affects every citizen of Colorado. In fact, it is an entirely new conception of state government.

In recent months we have seen many indications of the growing trend centralizing our state government with emphasis being placed on government by commissions and director of commissions. There are numerous commissions now carrying out duties prescribed to them by the Legislatures by law. Now comes this new threat to our democratic form of government—a proposal that would establish a commission as an independent body responsible to no one—the Governor, the Legislature, nor the people.

Do we want to embark on a policy in Colorado whereby we establish all of our commissions as independent bodies to spend our monies as they see fit—powers that should remain in the hands of our Legislators?

Our association has been very strongly opposed to any type of eminent domain rights for our Game and Fish Commission, but in this particular situation, it is my very firm opinion that the eminent domain is secondary and the threat to our democratic form of government is primary."

The first article against Amendment No. 3 presented the charges that were to be used over and over again against the proposed amendment. These four main arguments used against the proposed amendment were:

1. It would set up a state within a state by Constitution Amendment.
2. It gives the proposed Commission of five members complete control of a sizeable fund without any legislative check by the legislature and without any administrative check by the governor.
3. It is completely in opposition to the democratic form of gov-

ernment by establishing in the state constitution the power of this four-man commission to allocate and transfer to the General Fund of Colorado each year such sums as the commission shall determine reasonable and proper as compensation for general state services rendered to the commission, and goes further to limit this amount not to exceed 2 percent of its gross revenues. It appears that the philosophy behind this entire amendment is to gain all of the advantage of state law in requiring hunting and fishing licenses and the collection of fees thereon, but then to live apart from the state government and even pay the state government on the basis it bills itself for state government. The amendment thus sets up a little dictatorship instead of a democratic form of government to which most citizens are dedicated.

4. It provides a constitutional power of eminent domain for a use, that no matter how popular and worthwhile it may be, is secondary to such uses as the national security and welfare. We believe that provisions of this power for the purpose stated should not be a part of the State Constitution inasmuch as county commissioners and the State Highway Department now have this power for the purpose of road building. We do not believe it is good government for the Game and Fish Commission to be in the road selection business when it is constitutionally granted the right of eminent domain for public access to and from public lands.

Senator Fay DeBerard (1960) also spoke out against Amendment No. 3. Senator DeBerard, a Kremmling rancher, was serving his second term as senator from District 13, Rio Blanco, Moffat, Routt, Jackson, and Grand Counties. DeBerard was a highly regarded person. A graduate of Colorado State University in 1924, majoring in Animal Husbandry, he returned to Kremmling becoming a prominent rancher and citizen. A member of the Rotary and Elks Club, the Middle Park Hospital Board, Grand County Fair Board, Past President of Colorado Hereford Association and the National Cattlemen's Association, he was elected County Commissioner, serving seven years and served 20 years on the school board, 16 as president. In 1953 he was appointed to the senate and by 1960 had served nine years in the senate.

Speaking at the annual meeting of the Middle Park Stockgrowers Association, DeBerard (1960) is reported in the *Cattle Guard* as having said:

We're in trouble! I'm speaking of this eminent domain situation. Unless the stockmen really get out and work this fall—and I mean work—they'll be the victims of a program which has been pushed for seven solid years.

Right now different sportsmen's groups are engaged in securing signatures on a petition which would call for an amendment to be put on this fall's election ballot doing away with the present Colorado Game & Fish Commission.

In place of the present Commission, which for the past 18 months has been working very cooperatively with landowners working out mutual problems, a four-man ruling body would be formed.

I am not surprised by this current petition drive and I do not doubt but that enough signatures will be obtained to force a vote. That's why we must get out and properly inform the people what this is all about.

Seven years ago, when I first took my Senate seat, a sportsman's group approached me and said in point blank language that "some day we'll get the right of eminent domain to allow hunting and fishing on privately owned as well as public lands. It may take us 10 years, but we'll get the job done."

If this constitutional amendment changing the status of the Game and Fish Commission is put on the ballot, and okayed by Colorado's voters, it will give the new four-man body the right to condemn right-of-ways through any private land it wants. You can bet that such rights-of-way will utilize the roads which stockmen have built themselves, right through the barn yard in many cases. This proposed commission would not have to answer to anyone, not even the Colorado Legislature.

Organization, Campaigns and Techniques

From the very beginning of this campaign the antagonist managed to put the proponents of Amendment No. 3 on the defensive and during the entire campaign the supporters of the proposed amendment had to spend much of their energy denying charges rather than coming out in a strong stand for the amendment. Another technique was to use the members of the Conservation Council as scapegoats; picturing them as selfish, calculating men intent on destroying our democratic way of government.

By April sides were beginning to be formed and many of the major farm organization papers and periodicals joined the cattlemen in opposition to the proposed amendment. One such magazine that took a strong stand against Amendment No. 3 was *Western Farm Life*. Phil J. Patterson (1960) the managing editor and a "No-holds barred" editorialist, wrote in his April column *Ditch and Trail*:

Major farm organizations in Colorado, some of the state's legislative leaders and even sportsmen's organizations, have taken a stand against a proposed constitutional amendment in the state designed to create a new game and fish department outside all normal checks and controls.

The Conservation Council of Colorado set off the fireworks by terming the amendment an "access bill." For my two-bits worth these self-centered characters have a 'fanatical obsession' concerning the right of eminent domain and not only should rural groups be on guard against such rough-shod power-plays but so should urban dwellers. Sportsmen will have much more to lose if rural landowners' resentment is built up to a stage where all private streams and hunting acres now open are closed. Even the state's Game and Fish Commission rolled its eyeballs and dropped its fishing pole and creel over the land access coercion—the commission pointed out that the state and counties have the constitutional right of eminent domain in establishing roads for access in any area.

It will be something to watch in all western states as the push and lobbying for 'wilderness areas' and other disparities in land management are called for by the bird watchers. Research has proved time and again that 'managed resources' will produce more for all.

The central theme of dictorial control, poor government and the right of eminent domain already in the possession of the state and counties, appeared in this editorial as well as in almost all of the speeches, editorials and articles published against the amendment.

The opposition realized that even a 100% "No" vote by people in the rural areas without support of the urban population could not defeat the proposed amendment. It was also very apparent that in order to serve the support of the urban areas an effective organization had to be established. The solution to this particular problem was the formation of Coloradoans for Sound Government Incorporated (C. S. G.). Edwin C. Johnson, former U. S. Senator and Governor of Colorado, was made President of C. S. G.; David G. Rice, Jr., (Ex. Sec.—C. C. A.), Executive Vice-President; L. V. Toyne, Secretary of the Colorado State Association of Soil Conservation Districts, Secretary-Treasurer. The board of directors was composed of leading citizens from throughout the state.

The opposition was counting heavily on the prestige of such men as Ed Johnson to lend creditability to its statements. Senator Johnson was born in Kansas in 1881 and as a young man moved to Colorado just west of Craig, where he homesteaded. In 1922 he was elected to the house of the General Assembly where he served four times before being elected Governor in 1930. Two years later he was elected State Senator and was elected to succeed himself in 1942 and 1948. Senator Johnson was highly regarded in Colorado and so his name as president of the Coloradoans for Sound Government Committee immediately legitamized the organization. He was more than just a figurehead and his statements opposing Amendment No. 3 carried a tremendous amount of weight.

The person most responsible for the organization of C. S. G. and its success, if one person can be singled out, was David G. Rice, Jr. A native of Grand Junction, Colorado, he graduated from Colorado State University in Animal Husbandry in 1940 and served six years as a county agent in Elbert County and two years, from 1947 to 1949 as county agent in Delta County. Since that time he has been the Executive Secretary of the Colorado Cattlemen's Association. He is an exceptionally capable administrator, a highly competent organizer and promoter and probably one of the most successful lobbyists in the State Legislature.

The organizers of the Coloradoans for Sound Government made no secret of their objectives. The C. S. G. again stated the four main objectives to the proposed amendment and in addition used three sound psychological techniques, which were to be used continually throughout the campaign to develop a negative attitude toward the proposed amendment. The four objectives of C. S. G. and the incorporated psychological appeals were:

1. To defeat Amendment No. 3 which is the constitutional amendment prosoped to set up a new game and fish commission and abolish the present 8-man commission, placing a new 4-man commission in a "state within a state" outside of all legislative or executive control. (Fear technique. The implication that the amendment would destroy our democratic way of life.)

2. To acquaint the public with true aims and purposes of the small group attempting to place this serious affront to democracy into the Constitution of the State of Colorado. (An appeal to the loyalties, the norms and standards of the group, the Colorado citizens.)

3. To point out advancements already made in supplying adequate access to all public lands and plans of farm organizations and sportsmen's clubs to accelerate this movement now and in the future.

4. To point out what real, honest sportsmen could do to assist landowners who provide hunters and fishermen with the greater portion of their hunting and fishing. (An appeal directed to a person's pride and his identification with the group of honest sportsmen.)

The C. C. A. personnel realized that in order to be effective, the campaign would (1) have to be conducted at a grass roots level in order to persuade the rural voters and (2) if the urban population was to be persuaded an effective campaign would have to be conducted through television and newspaper, and that this would be costly. In order to achieve the first objective and at the same time raise funds for the second part of the campaign a number of local C. S. G. organizations in many instances built around the County Cattlemen's Associations were organized. Each local organization was given a quota to reach insofar as the fund drive was concerned. The $36,000 that was raised in this manner was used primarily on advertising.

The local units of Coloradoans for Sound Government were particularly successful because they utilized the two-way flow of communications extremely effectively. The local leaders were kept supplied with information regarding Amendment No. 3 including speeches, flyers, posters, bumper stickers and news releases. The local leaders in turn kept the entire community well posted on why Amendment No. 3 should be defeated.

Another technique used by the C. S. G. was group persuasion. Krech, Crutchfield and Ballachey (1962) stated, ". . . a situation in which a communication is addressed to a group largely composed of persons favorable to the communicator's position will greatly increase the effectiveness of his communication up the dissident minority." This technique of group persuasion was effectively used in both the rural and urban communities.

Throughout the entire campaign the *Cattle Guard*, circulation of nearly 5,000, was used to keep the ranchers interested in fighting Amendment No. 3. Many highly regarded cattlemen came out in strong opposition to the proposed amendment. The main points of a state within a state, complete control of the Game and Fish Department by a four-man board, a commission completely in opposition to the democratic form of government and uncontrolled power of eminent domain were restated in each speech, news release and printed article.

By September the drive to defeat the proposed amendment had been in progress at least six months and the executive committee of Coloradoans for Sound Government fearing that interest was on the wane sent to all the local units of the C. S. G. a letter including a reprint of a Denver Post poll that indicated that if the general election were held then, in September, 62% of the voters would vote for the amendment. The letter ended with this statement:

"You and your association must take the responsibility of seeing to it that your county committee is organized and functioning; meet the county quota; see that every voter in your county realizes that dictatorial power that will be given to four men if No. 3 passes."

In September the *Cattle Guard* also played on the fear that Amendment No. 3 had a very good possibility of passing. In an article entitled, "Rural Residents Need All Out Vote Drive," Tom J. Lawrie (1960), editor of the *Cattle Guard*, said:

"As hard as it is to believe Amendment No. 3 appears to have a good chance of passing . . ."

He went on to state why everyone should vote against No. 3 playing strongly on the fear tendency, by quoting from the proposed amendment the section which stated that the article shall be self-enacting and self-enforcing and all laws inconsistent with the article—shall no longer remain in force or effect, and then stating,

"This would mean water law changes if the board desired. For instance, if the water level in some reservoir dropped to a point the board felt was improper, it could rule no water should be released for irrigation purposes."

Lawrie ended his article by stating,

"This is absolutely the worst piece of legislation ever to come before the voters. From everyone's standpoint not just the ranchers and rural landowners."

In order to reach the urban voter a different tactic was used. Radio and television were employed as much as the budget would allow. Highly regarded urban organizations such as Colorado Young Democrats, Colorado League of Women Voters, Colorado State Chamber of Commerce, plus most newspapers and legislators were convinced that Amendment No. 3 was bad legislation and added their support to Coloradoans for Sound Government. Special speeches were prepared for spokesmen for these organizations to use in speaking before their groups. The speeches were loaded with references as to why this amendment was bad legislation. Such points as unregulated power, destruction of traditional checks and balances, destruction of the democratic processes of government and regulations of the four-man commissions taking precedence over the laws of the people's elected representative and governor were brought out in the speeches.

The speeches appealed to the identification of the sportsmen as honest sportsmen and their need to unite with the landowners to defeat this proposal. The sportsman was told that through cooperation they could have the best of recreational facilities in Colorado. Through use of the "blackjack" they could only bring back problems that had been slowly dissipated by means of democratic approaches. But most of all they must not accept deliberate destruction of democratic government. All speeches name-dropped. The names of person of recognized prestige opposed to Amendment No. 3 were liberally used throughout the speeches.

"Flyers" were distributed which told the voter why Amendment No. 3 was bad legislation, stressed the four main points against No. 3, and urged the voter to vote "No" on Amendment No. 3, the "Deliberate Destruction of Democratic Government." The leaflets included a list of leaders and organizations in opposition to No. 3 to lend credibility to the statements. Billboards were located strategically throughout the metropolitan area urging the voter to vote for democratic government by voting no on Amendment No. 3. Everywhere one drove or went he was likely to see either a billboard or a bumper sticker endlessly repeating the slogan, "Vote for Democratic Government. Vote no on Amendment No. 3."

Amendment No. 3 was news and consequently an almost uncountable number of inches of newspaper space was devoted to reporting the charges and countercharges being hurled back and forth between the principles or to reporting the many, many meetings held to either promote or defeat No. 3.

Fifty-seven major articles were printed regarding Amendment No. 3 in the Denver Post alone from the beginning of the campaign in January until the election in November. All of this served to keep the issues regarding Amendment No. 3 before the public eye. Perhaps more importantly many of the major publications took an editorial stand against the passage of this proposed amendment.

For example, in the October issue of the *Denver Post,* Roscoe Flemming (1960) devoted his column to Amendment No. 3. The column on this particular Saturday was entitled, "Amendment No. 3 Threatens Colorado With Absolute Czar." Fleming then went on to outline why Amendment No. 3 should be defeated. Fleming declared, "In fact, this body (Colorado Wildlife Management Commission) could discard all present law and make its own mandate; a combination of a true, non-elected legislature and a perpetual super-constitutional convention all in one; and all beyond reach of the people."

"There is no legal control, whatsoever over the commissioners, who are to be named for staggered six-year terms. The Governor names them but couldn't remove them save for cause so vague that any attempt at such removal would merely mean a long court fight."

"Every single law and regulation affecting Colorado Wildlife resources worked out painfully over many years woud be effectively subject to repeal January 1, 1961 and these non-elected men could rewrite the whole code at their absolute pleasure."

In this editorial, as in all other persuasive efforts against No. 3, the writers tried to convince their audience that this was dangerous legislation and appealed to them through the use of fear to vote against the proposed amendment.

Another technique that was used to persuade the urban sportsman to vote against the proposed amendment was the issuing of passes to the fishermen and hunters by the landowners that gave them permission to hunt or fish on their property and at the same time reminded them that their insured good fishing or hunting depended upon the defeat of Amendment No. 3.

Results and Summary

The sustained effort to persuade the voters to defeat Amendment No. 3 was successful, overwhelmingly so. The voters rejected the amendment by a vote of almost 3 to 1; 409,000 against to 185,000 for. The success of the campaign to defeat Amendment No. 3 probably was due to four causes:

1. The very nature of the bill itself. Although many people felt that all of the public lands should be readily accessible, many voters honestly feared giving the proposed Colorado Wildlife Management Commission the power to spend money without legislative approval or the power to repeal any law or regulation that the commission

considered inconsistent with the goals of the commission. Many people actually believed this amendment was bad government.

2. The campaign against the bill was very well organized and efficiently executed. By taking advantage of local leadership and actually utilizing the two-step flow of communication the effectiveness of the campaign was multiplied many times. The rural counties' local organizations were able to raise enough money to permit the Coloradoans for Sound Government to wage an effective campaign in the seven metropolitan counties that controlled the vote.

3. The persuasive techniques used were well planned and timed. The very fact that the campaign could enlist such personages as Senator Ed Johnson, Senator Fay DeBerard, Otto Maul, president of Colorado Cattlemen's Association and many others added creditability to the campaign. Repetition and restatement were used extensively to keep the issue in front of the public. Groups and group commitment were effectively used. The use of the fear technique plus the technique of discrediting the proponent of the amendment all helped in defeating the proposal.

4. Finally, the amendment was complex enough that despite the fact that a flood of advertising, news releases and public proclamations were made concerning the amendment, many people did not wholly understand it and so played safe by voting no.

Although the proposal was soundly defeated at the polls, it did bring to light both sides of the problems that had generated the amendment. Both sportsmen and landowners recognized the need of cooperation with each other and out of the reoriented viewpoint "Operation Respect" was formed. This program recognized the fact that there must be mutuality of respect between the landowner and the sportsman.

There are still unthinking sportsmen that throw beer cans in the hay meadows or shoot the prize Hereford, and there are still posted lands and locked gates, but the situation is improving.

APPENDICES

Appendix A

PUBLICITY CALENDAR (SIX MONTHS)
(Colorado Wildlife Division)

News Release—Distribution: Newspapers, Radio, TV, Other Agencies, Personnel, Legislators, Sportsmen's Clubs, Interested Individuals.

Month	Points to Stress
JULY	Fishing Report; Sportsmen of the Week; Magazine Promotion; Antelope and Bighorn Seasons (permits, etc.); Elk Permits; Conservation Courses (schools and colleges); Commission News; Grouse Season; Fur Regulations; Conventions and Personnel; Hunter Safety Report; Landowner-Fishermen Relations.
AUGUST	Fishing Report; Sportsmen of the Week; Dove Season; High Country Fishing; Hunter Safety Report; Bighorn, Antelope and Elk Drawings; Commission News; New Laws in Effect; Turkey Season.
SEPTEMBER	Fishing Report; Sportsmen of the Week; Commission News; Elk, Deer Season Preview; Migratory Bird (duck and geese) Populations; Antelope & Bighorn Resume; Rabbit Season; New Hunting Access Roads; Department Activities, etc.
OCTOBER	Fishing Report; Sportsmen of the Week; Commission News; Hunter Safety; Conservation Activities; Big Game Seasons; Pheasant Season; Turkey Season; Check Station Activities.
NOVEMBER	Sportsmen of the Week; Commission News; Migratory Bird Season; Winter Fishing; Hunter Safety; Conservation Activities.
DECEMBER	Sportsmen of the Week; Commission News; Licenses Sold; Hunter Safety; Research Activities.

Magazine—Distribution: Subscribers and Complimentary List.

ISSUE:	
JULY AUGUST	How and Where to Fish; Kokanee; Bear Season; Boating; Camping; Legislation; Warmwater Fishing Research; Trout Research; Department Activities; Big Game Review.
SEPTEMBER OCTOBER	Where and How to Hunt; Landowners-Sportsmen Relations; Big Game Research; Fur Regulations; Turkey Hunting.
NOVEMBER DECEMBER	Where and How to Hunt Ducks, Geese, Pheasants; Research and Management of Game Birds; Chukars; Landowner-Sportsmen; Winter Range; Index.

Personal Appearance Programs and Exhibits. Publics to Be Reached—Prime Movers—Ranchers, Farmers, Civic Groups, Schools, Youth Groups, Sportsmen, Legislators, and Teachers.

JULY	Hunter Safety; Nature Study, Conservation-Education (at camps); Planning Displays at State Fairs.
AUGUST	Hunter Safety; Nature Study; Conservation-Education (at camps); Display—Hunter Safety at State Fair.
SEPTEMBER	Big Game Seasons; Sheep Season; Hunter Safety; Dove Season.
OCTOBER	Big Game Seasons; Resume of Grouse Season; Hunter Safety.
NOVEMBER	Migratory Bird Seasons; Later Deer Seasons; Hunter Safety; Fall Game and Fish Activities; Winter Fishing; Pheasant Season; Conservation-Education.
DECEMBER	Winter Fishing; Late Deer Seasons; Department Activities; Federal Aid Projects; Legislative Needs.

T.V.—and—Radio Programs—Distribution: General Public.

JULY & AUGUST	Sportsmen of the Week; Magazine Sales; Brief Hunting Reminders-Big Game; Bighorn Sheep Information; Antelope Season; Elk Drawings; Commission Meetings; Fishing Report.
SEPTEMBER	Sportsmen of the Week; Hunter Safety Program; Antelope Season; Fall Camping; Turkey Season; Resume of Dove Season; Grouse Season; Konanee Fishing; Elk Drawing—reminder; Bighorn Sheep Season.
OCTOBER	Resume of Dove Season; Deer and Elk Season; Check Station Reports; Hunter Safety Instructions; Turkey Season Resume.
NOVEMBER	Big Game Season Progress and Resume; Pheasant Season; Hunter Safety; Migratory Bird Seasons; Conservation-Education.
DECEMBER	Pheasant Season Resume; Hunter Safety; Konanee Fishing; Department Activities.

Appendix B

SPORTSMAN OF THE WEEK
STATE OF COLORADO
DEPARTMENT OF GAME AND FISH

TO: All Field Personnel

FROM: Thomas L. Kimball, Director

We are continuing the "sportsman of the week" program in which the department's officers (WCOs, trappers, and wardens) will nominate a sportsman who has performed sportsman-like deeds or efforts directed toward bettering the sport of hunting and fishing.

Do not nominate those people who have merely been successful in getting a full bag or a magnificent trophy, but rather people who have done things such as saving lives, promoting good sportsman-landowner relationship, devoting their life to conservation, helping someone lost or in distress, and so forth.

From the nominees a sportsman of the week will be selected and will be given special honors on radio and through papers. We will award him a one year subscription to the department magazine "COLORADO OUTDOORS" and a special binder for the magazines.

Please choose your nominee with discretion. Send name of nominee and full details of his performance to the I & E division, attention, editorial section.

(Courtesy of Colorado Wildlife Division)

Sportsman of the Week—Application Form

Date _____

Name _____

Address _____

Telephone number (if possible) _____ _____

Special reason for nomination _____

_____

_____

_____

_____

_____

Nominated by: _____
          (Name and title of warden, trapper or W.C.O.)
          (Courtesy of Colorado Wildlife Division)

Appendix C

COMMUNICATIONS FLOW CHART

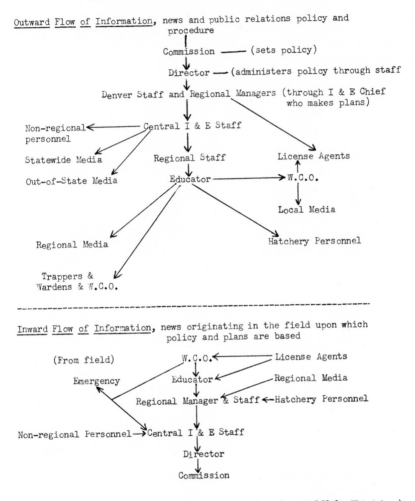

Outward <u>Flow</u> <u>of</u> <u>Information</u>, news and public relations policy and
procedure

Commission ——— (sets policy)

Director —— (administers policy through staff

Denver Staff and Regional Managers (through I & E Chief
who makes plans)

Non-regional ← Central I & E Staff
personnel

Statewide Media

Out-of-State Media

Regional Staff

Educator ————————→ W.C.O.

License Agents

Local Media

Regional Media

Hatchery Personnel

Trappers &
Wardens & W.C.O.

Inward <u>Flow</u> <u>of</u> <u>Information</u>, news originating in the field upon which
policy and plans are based

(From field)   W.C.O. ← ———— License Agents

Emergency   Educator ← ———— Regional Media

Regional Manager & Staff ← Hatchery Personnel

Non-regional Personnel → Central I & E Staff

Director

Commission

(Courtesy of Colorado Wildlife Division)

Appendix D

PLANNED MEETINGS SUCCEED (Anonymous, 1965)

As one sits through all-too-many meetings, conferences, and conventions, it soon becomes apparent that certain planning and operational procedures enter into the determination of a successful meeting. Therefore, a suggested checklist is here presented to aid planners in spornsoring a successful affair.

Before The Meeting

1. Firm up entire program well in advance.
2. Be certain speakers know their program time limits.
3. Outline program contents for publicity channels, including places and dates, as early as possible.
4. Complete planning for all physical facilities:
    a. Meeting and banquet rooms, including blackout needs.
    b. Hospitality and press rooms, and adequate exhibit space.
    c. Registration supplies, blackboards, audio-visual, and recording and public address systems, and qualified operators on hand.
    d. Signs and bulletin boards for guidance and directory purposes.
    e. Photographers and equipment.
5. Arrange for and invite displays and exhibits.
6. Provide for advance publicity (press, radio, TV), both in meeting area and far afield when applicable.
7. Line up local city support and participation—use your convention bureau and Chamber of Commerce.
8. Provide for Society dues collections and employment contact desk facilities in convention registration lobby or area.
9. Line up staff of hosts and hostesses, transportation facilities to and from stations and airports and local points of interest, and telephone service.
10. Printing of circulars, programs, tickets.
11. Facilities for handling money at registration and ticket sales periods.

During The Meeting

1. Start meetings promptly, using door prizes to assure prompt attendance.
2. Keep sessions and speakers on schedule (suggest use of belled timer).
3. Public address, recording, and audio-visual equipment:
    a. Have it ready and warmed up beforehand.
    b. Have qualified operators available.
    c. Assign blackout responsibilities.

4. Keep program on schedule.
5. Provide hallway display panel announcing current session inside meeting room.
6. Keep program on schedule (beginning to get the idea?).
7. Make a good photographic record of each feature of the program.
8. Keep the program on schedule (got it?)
9. Make adequate recording of important parts of program.
10. Staff hospitality and press rooms and transportation desk.
11. Arrange for press, radio, and TV coverage of meeting, interviews with outstanding personalities in attendance, and other excellent promotional advantages you have.
12. At least see that sponsoring officials are given due introduction and credit before the largest gathering (usually opening general session or the banquet) of the meeting.

After the Meeting

1. Express thanks in all necessary directions.
2. Use recorded materials to advantage in staff training and classroom teaching.
3. Use the transactions promptly, while they still have value.
4. Use publicity channels to:
   a. Circulate important actions where they'll do some good.
   b. Distribute usable well-labeled photos of meeting subjects to the person's local press area facilities (helps him, too!).
5. Announce date and place of next meeting.

Appendix E

SLIDE TALK EVALUATION

Name	Subject	
Item	Possible Points	Points This Presentation
Room set up	5	
Equipment quality (Projector, screen, pointer, change signal)	5	
Equipment operation	10	
Slide quality	10	
Slide arrangement	10	
Speech and pronunciation	10	
Commentary	10	
Speed	10	
Introduction	5	
Closing	5	
Knowledge of subject	10	
Miscellaneous	10	
Total points	100	

Comments

Appendix F

MOTION PICTURE PROJECTOR TROUBLE SHOOTING CHART

In case trouble is encountered in the operation of the projector, some suggestions are given for locating and correcting the trouble.

1. Projector won't run.

1. Check power supply, fuses in building, circuit and projector fuse.

2. Projection runs but bulb won't light.

2. Replace bulb.

3. Loud speaker hums but there is no sound.

3. Check if the exciter lamp is burning.

4. Exciter lamp burning, loud speaker humming but no sound.

4. Possibly photo-electric cell inoperative. In most instances turn over to repairman.

5. Picture flickering.

5. Re-thread, probably not engaging properly. Reform loops behind lens.

6. Sound garbled.

6. Film not tight around soundhead.

7. Lip movement and sound not synchronized.

7. Projector improperly threaded, too long or too short length of film between aperture and soundhead. Check size of lower loop.

8. If the film breaks.

8. Do not pin, tape or in any other way join the film together. Run off about two feet of the film and overlap the film on the take-up reel so that the friction between the two pieces of film will hold it together. Continue the show after this has been done. Indicate breakage when returning film.

Appendix G

MOTION PICTURE PROJECTION

When you show a motion picture without "incidents," without lost time or obvious fussing with the equipment, you gain the confidence of your audience. A poor show lowers your professional stature. You may not be a professional projectionist but you can offset that by careful attention to the following points:

BEFORE THE MEETING

1. Have necessary equipment including spare parts, bulbs, extra reels and extension cord.
2. Locate electric outlet. See that extension cord will reach.
3. Determine proper positioning of projector and screen.
4. Locate light switches. Decide who will handle lights.
5. For daytime meetings, be sure that the room can be darkened sufficiently.
6. Check type of current. This can be important in rural areas.
7. See that films have been rewound and are not broken.
8. Clean projector film gate and lenses.
9. Have film correctly threaded and focused, sound warmed up and ready to start.

DURING THE MEETING

1. Stay at the projector.
2. Do not project clear leader, leader numbers, etc. Cover lens with hand or leave light switch off until title starts.
3. Avoid sudden volume change. Start at "medium" and change slowly as needed.
4. If film breaks, unwind enough for 1½ laps around the take-up reel and rethread. Don't splice with scotch tape.
5. Switch off lamp (or cover lens) when "End" appears on screen.
6. Switch off amplifier when music stops.
7. Turn on house lights immediately.
8. Avoid rewinding during the meeting.

AFTER THE MEETING

1. Rewind films unless directed otherwise.
2. See that reels, title bands and mailing boxes are not switched.
3. Make out attendance record, if requested.
4. Return film promptly.

YOUR AUDIENCE MAY NOT SAY ANYTHING BUT THEY WILL NOTICE A GOOD OR BAD SHOW.

Appendix H

RATING SHEET FOR NATURAL RESOURCE MAGAZINES

ELEMENT	Guide	RATING				Guide
		Excellent	Adequate	Mediocre	Poor	
Cover	Pictorial Meaningful Provocative Color					Dull Black and White Too Garrulous Detracts
Design	Attractive Color					Cluttered Sprawling Black and White
Illustrations	Clear Comprehensive Meaningful Plentiful Revealing Comparative Color					Confusing Absent Sparse Too Profuse Blurred Black and White
Text	Comprehensive Interesting Well Written Well Organized Understandable					Poorly Written Poorly Organized Too Easy Too Hard
Printing	Crisp Vivid Sharp Good Layout Quality Paper					Sloppy Dull Poor Paper Blurred

Miscellaneous—add or subtract accordingly (Length, Timeliness, Size, etc.)

Excellent—20, Adequate—15, Mediocre—10, Poor—5, Lacking—0

Total possible points—100

Appendix I

TITLES FOR MAGAZINE ARTICLES

Following are examples of eight different types of heads or titles for stories. Give a headline some thought. The result should catch the reader's eye.

1. *Summary:*
   Maryland's Indians—Top Conservationists.

2. *Striking Statement:*
   The Riddle of the Quick-Frozen Mammoths.
   Predators Are Like People.

3. *Narrative:*
   The Town Turned Out For Archery.

4. *Descriptive:*
   Coyote Hunting in High Gear.
   Fishing For Prairie Dogs.
   Bumper Manna Supply for Wildlife.
   Cumberland Gap Historical Park New Tourist Attraction.

5. *Quotation:*
   A Lady by the Side of the Road.
   We'll Rough It!

6. *Question:*
   Why Protect Hawks?
   Does Your Shotgun Shoot Where It's Looking?
   What is Pellet Shock?

7. *Direct Address:*
   Mr. Sportsman, Meet The Land!

8. *Alliteration:*
   Purple Perch With Pink Polka Dots.
   Streamlining by the Streamside.

(Courtesy Charles Hjelte, Chief of Publications,
Colorado Wildlife Division)

Appendix J

LEADS FOR MAGAZINES ARTICLES

Following are examples of the seven basic leads for stories. The main thing to remember, though, is too keep the lead or introduction short.

1. *Summary:*
   From the beginning when Esau tasted his first venison, white man has always plundered, wasted and destroyed.

   A predator is any creature that has beaten you to another creature you wanted for yourself.

   The landed face of Iowa has seen many drastic changes since the advent of the first settlers.

   The life blood of the fisherman is expectancy.

2. *Striking Statement:*
   Nobody, as far as I have been able to ascertain, seriously wants to quick-freeze an elephant.

3. *Narrative:*
   Five men walked abreast along a power line right-of-way in Pennsylvania.

   When I reached southwest Colorado at the heights of the depression, the dust of the Texas plains was still in my nostrils and still stained my faded patched levis.

   It was a sparkling November day and my friend and I were hunting pheasants on a nearby farm.

4. *Descriptive:*
   Pampas grass is tall, sometimes growing over eight feet; it is brown-stemmed, looking almost like giant stands of wheat, and the head of this marsh grass is lacy and as soft as Italian velvet when the wind blows it against your face as you stand hidden in its growth.

5. *Quotation:*
   "Brown Gold." Thus did a successful marshland trapper describe that common but much sought-after furbearer—the muskrat.

   "We'll rough it! Yessir, we'll live right on the beach and battle the winds, sand and sun right on the tip of Cape Hatteras."

6. *Question:*
   Why are quail seasons in New Mexico held when they are?
   A Roman Catholic for President?

7. *Direct Address:*
   Girls, if you're worried about that double chin or "spare tire"— go fishing.

   So you got yourself an antelope license this fall?

   Do you dream of catching that "hanging on the wall type" trophy trout, but usually content yourself with the pan-sized variety?

   (Courtesy Charles Hjelte, Chief of Publications,
   Colorado Wildlife Division)

Appendix K

TELEVISION SPOT ANNOUNCEMENTS

Special Duck Stamp Sale Drive

(Only one photo of stamp and certificate and one address card enclosed.)

Announcement No. 1

VIDEO (Flip Card)	AUDIO
1. Cartoon No. 1 Homeless ducks.	The sale of duck stamps is off nearly 25 percent from a year ago. As a result, your Government's purchases of wetlands needed by waterfowl are being slowed down. To counter this trend, the U. S. Fish and Wildlife Service has launched a nationwide
2. Use pix of certificate and duck stamp (Zoom in on stamp)	after-season sale of these stamps. A certificate signed by the Secretary of the Interior is being given to each purchaser in recognition of this contribution to conservation. Send $3 to the Bureau of Sport Fisheries and Wildlife, Washington 25, D. C.,
3. Use address card	eries and Wildlife, Washington 25, D. C., and get your stamp and certificate.

Announcement No. 2

1. Cartoon No. 2 Flying ducks.	Ducks can't nest on the wing, but places where they can nest or rest are disappearing. Help save wetlands for waterfowl. Buy
2. Use pix of certificate and duck stamp	a $3 duck stamp and make a contribution to conservation. You'll also get a certificate signed by the Secretary of the Interior.
3. Use address card	Send your money to the Bureau of Sport Fisheries and Wildlife, Washington 25, D. C.

Announcement No. 3

VIDEO (Flip Card)	AUDIO
1. Cartoon No. 3 Duck on fence post.	You can't blame a duck for dreaming. Civilization is taking the duck marshes day by day. Conservationists are trying to save enough of them to assure generations of the future some of the opportunities we have to hunt, photograph, or just watch these

2. Use pix of certificate and duck stamp

3. Use address card

magnificent birds. Help them reach this goal. Buy a duck stamp, even after-season, buy a share in the future of America's waterfowl for $3, and get a certificate signed by the Secretary of the Interior in recognition of your contribution. Send your check or money order to the Bureau of Sport Fisheries and Wildlife, Washington 25, D. C.

Announcement No. 4

1. Cartoon No. 4
Thirsty duck.

2. Use pix of certificate and duck stamp

3. Use address card

The slogan of Wildlife Week for this year is to impress upon us that water is the key to our survival. Wildlife especially needs consideration in this respect, not only for itself but for the good that wildlife does mankind in general. A practical way to help wildlife is to buy a duck stamp in a special after-season sale now under way and add your money to that which is being used to buy wetlands for waterfowl. You will also receive a certificate signed by the Secretary of the Interior recognizing your contribution. Send your $3 to the Bureau of Sport Fisheries and Wildlife, Washington 25, D. C.

(Courtesy U. S. Fish and Wildlife Service)

Appendix L

TELEVISION PROGRAM FORMAT

CSU OUTDOORS
12:00 Noon, Saturday, September 3, 1964
To be taped 7:00 p.m. Thursday, September 1, 1964

VIDEO	AUDIO
Open on interesting visual to be used during program. (Arrow hitting target bullseye)	ET: UP MUSIC AND UNDER FOR:
	ANNOUNCER:
Super #1 (CSU Outdoors)	From KBTV, Channel 9, it's "CSU Outdoors" . . . A Program dedicated to you the people of Colorado who depend on our resources for enjoyment and livelihood. . . .
Super #2 (Colorado State University and KBTV)	Produced by Colorado State University, at Fort Collins, in cooperation with KBTV. Your host for today is Doug Gilbert, Professor of Wildlife Biology at CSU.
CU cf Gilbert	GILBERT:
	1. Introduce program
	2. Contest announcement
	3. Award prize and read letter
	4. . . . Back in one minute
Sound-On Film	ONE-MINUTE SPOT ANNOUNCEMENT
CU of Gilbert and Jones	GILBERT & JONES:
	1. Gilbert introduce Jones

CSU OUTDOORS   September 3, 1964

VIDEO	AUDIO
	2. Discussion— Why hunt with a bow?
CU of bows	3. Popularity of archery
CU of arrows	4. Bow types
CU of quiver, arm guard, shooting glove, etc.	5. Arrow types
	6. Other equipment
	7. Discuss current big game seasons, laws, dates, etc.

Slide (No. 1) of deer killed
with bow

Demonstration of "pull"

CU of Jones shooting

Sound-On Film

CU of Gilbert & Jones

Same shot used to open
program.

Super #1
(CSU Outdoors)

CSU OUTDOORS

VIDEO

Super #2
(KBTV and
Colorado State University)

8. Discuss past successes of Mr.
   Jones in hunting big game
   with a bow.
9. How does a bow kill?
10. Tips for archers
    a. Choosing equipment
    b. Hunting methods
    c. After the animal is hit
11. Demonstration of accuracy
12. . . . Back in a one minute
ONE-MINUTE SPOT
ANNOUNCEMENT
GILBERT:
1. Thank Jones
2. Remind of contest
3. End program
ANNOUNCER

That ends this week's "CSU
Outdoors," which featured your
host, Doug Gilbert of Colorado
State University.

September 3, 1964

AUDIO

Join us again next week for an-
other "CSU OUTDOORS." This
week's program, presented by
KBTV as a public service feature,
was produced by Colorado State
University at Fort Collins.
ET: UP MUSIC, HOLD AND
FADE TO REGULAR KBTV
FORMAT.

Appendix M

RADIO PROGRAM FORMAT

Colorado Game, Fish and Parks Division

Radio Script No. 45   For Use: November 1-8, 1968

Total Time—13½ minutes, with additional 1½ minutes for Commercial or PSA (Total 15 minutes)

Music: Up, hold, and fade to . . . .

Sound: Elk bugle (can be duck quacking, goose honking, or stream running)

Anncr: Hello everyone. This is *(Anncr's Name)*. Welcome to Colorado Wildlife! This show is dedicated to a better understanding of wildlife management and hunting and fishing problems in our great state. Here is our regular on the program, *(Official's Name)*, who is *(Title)*.

(First Name), what's our topic for today?

Topic—Big Game Seasons and Results

1. Deer Season

    A. Kill to date
    B. Reasons for such a heavy kill
    C. Best areas to hunt
    D. Special problems
    E. Miscellaneous suggestions

2. Elk Season
   (Same sub-topics as for deer season)

3. Coming dates and regulations of post seasons and special seasons

Anncr: Thanks *(First Name)*. That about wraps it up for today. We have talked about   *(General Summary)*
Be with us again next week at the same time when *(Title)* *(Name)* of the Colorado Game, Fish and Parks Division will be at mikeside with Colorado Wildlife. The Colorado Game, Fish, and Parks Division does not necessarily endorse the service or products advertised on this program. This is *(Anncr's Name)* reminding you that "A good sportsman takes only his share."

Music: Up, hold, and fade out . . . .

Appendix N

INTERVIEW TECHNIQUES FOR RADIO AND TELEVISION

1. Get all the background that you need on the guest and topic in advance of the interview.

2. Be at the studio to welcome guest well before air time. In TV ask if he has visuals; check and see that they are appropriate. Discuss visuals with director. When to show, how to be used, etc.

3. Get from guest the key points he wants brought out in the interview.

4. Brief guest as to the nature of the audience.

5. Arrange these key points in what seems the best possible order.

   For example:
   Q1: Brings out guest's position in his field; why he is visiting in this area; discovers for audience something about his personality; establishes him as a real living person, not just a representative of his organization.

   Q2: Something about his background, personal or professional.

   Q3: Leads into real topic: What are we going to talk about today? Why is this guest a good one to tell us about it?

   Q4, 5, 6: Developmental questions to bring out information or guest's point of view.

   Q7: Next to last, and most important question.

   Q: Last question, action desired and summary of interview; one or both.

6. Other patterns of arrangement.
   a. Chronological
   b. Geographical
   c. Divisions of audience; men, women, children.

7. General procedures:
   a. Plan area to be covered.
   b. Keep some interesting material for middle and end.
   c. Keep spotlight on person being interviewed.
   d. Make transitions from question to question, if at all possible. Use preceding answer as spring board into next question. At times you may have to clarify something said in an answer.
   e. Keep transitions short.
   f. Ask only one question at a time.
   g. Ask questions requiring comment and interpretation, or extending information. Avoid "yes or no" questions.

    h. Seize control of interview at end so you don't have to interrupt interviewee to end show.

8. DON'TS:
    a. "I see" "Uh-huh."
    b. Vocal pause: "er," "uh."
    c. Double barreled questions, or double questions.
    d. Restate interviewee's answers "in other words."
    e. Stalling; "Well, er, what I'd like to ask you is . . ."
    f. Asking potentially embarrassing questions, unless you have previously cleared them with the guest.
    g. Use obvious statements of greeting or force interviewee to reply when everyone knows you've met previously.

Appendix O

RADIO SPOT ANNOUNCEMENT FORMAT

Organization: *Colorado State Forest Service*

Length of Spot: *15 Seconds (25 words)*

Starting Date: *August 15, 1968*

Ending Date: *September 15, 1968*

Message: (Sound of forest fire, tape included) This is a bad month for forest fires. The woods are very dry and we need your help. Enjoy your forests, but *please* be careful. Thanks.

Appendix P

RADIO SPOT ANNOUNCEMENTS

The sale of duck stamps for the current year is down nearly 25 percent. Because these dollars are the only ones available for Federal purchases of wetlands for waterfowl, this important program faces a slowdown. In an effort to make up for some of the loss of revenue, the U. S. Fish and Wildlife Service has inaugurated a nationwide after-season drive to sell duck stamps to conservation-minded persons.

A certificate signed by the Secretary of the Interior, recognizing this contribution to conservation, is being given to each purchaser of a duck stamp during this campaign. To get a stamp and certificate, send $3 to the Bureau of Sport Fisheries and Wildlife, Washington 25, D. C.

❋ ❋ ❋ ❋ ❋ ❋ ❋ ❋

Keep 'em flyin' with your buyin' is a quick way of saying that the best way to assure waterfowl for future generations is to buy duck stamps today. All revenues from duck stamp sales go to the selection and purchase of wetlands for waterfowl. With the human population increasing, habitat ducks need is decreasing. We must preserve as much as we can but funds are needed. Send your check or money order for $3 to the Bureau of Sport Fisheries and Wildlife, Washington 25, D. C., for your stamp and conservationist certificate.

❋ ❋ ❋ ❋ ❋ ❋ ❋ ❋

Mr. and Mrs. America! Here is a message on conservation. Our wild waterfowl are in trouble. Drought has plagued them in their northern nesting grounds; man is encroaching upon their feeding and resting areas down the migration lanes.

This year, sales of duck stamps which finance Federal purchases of the wetlands the ducks and geese need are declining and the acquisition program is being hampered.

Help the waterfowl conservation program. Buy a $3 duck stamp in this after-season drive and receive a certificate signed by the Secretary of the Interior which notes your conservation effort. Send your check or money order to the Bureau of Sport Fisheries and Wildlife, Washington 25, D. C.

❋ ❋ ❋ ❋ ❋ ❋ ❋ ❋

Wildlife Week this year has the theme: *Water—Key to Your Survival.* Let's not forget our waterfowl. They, too, need water areas to survive.

Duck stamp sales, which finance Federal purchases of wetlands for waterfowl use, are off sharply this year. Wetland purchases will decline unless these revenues are increased. You can help. Buy a duck stamp now. You will get a certificate signed by the Secretary of the Interior showing you have made a special contribution to waterfowl conservation.

Send your check or money order for the purchase of the $3 duck stamp to the Bureau of Sport Fisheries and Wildlife, Washington 25, D. C.

(Courtesy U. S. Fish and Wildlife Service)

Appendix Q

DISPLAY SUGGESTIONS AND RATING SHEET

Displays are another method of "getting a message across," or communicating with, and influencing people.

I. Specific Values
    A. Habit value, similar to bulletin board.
    B. Easy to focus attention on a certain point.

II. Displays should have the following characteristics:
    A. Timely
    B. One subject only
    C. Simple
    D. Interesting (humor often adds this)
    E. Have eye appeal, including proportions and color harmony
    F. Have a positive theme
    G. Main point of interest should be near the center
    H. Be large enough (all writing should be of sufficient size to read without straining)
    I. Credit should be given to others providing help and materials
    J. Significant
    K. Will not offend people or groups
    L. Accurate
    M. No cruelty to animals

III. Steps in making a display
    A. Outline the idea, draw sketches
    B. Check on space, take measurements.
    C. Inventory—decide on materials
    D. Gather materials
    E. Install
    F. Check and maintain—at least once per day.

IV. Miscellaneous suggestions
    A. Do not include valuables. Cases have been broken into. If necessary, remove valuables at night.
    B. Do not use tacks on walls. Remove *all* tape at termination.
    C. Strive for a worthwhile, interesting idea. Displays can deal with any phase of Natural Resource Management.
        Examples:
        1. Recreation-Campground development, Anti-litter
        2. Forestry—Methods of harvest, Tree identification, Aging methods, Tools used.
        3. Range—Grass and shrub identification, Competition between animals.
        4. Wildlife—Identification, Aging methods, Safety during seasons, Record head measurement.

5. Miscellaneous—Archery, Mountain climbing, Fishery management, Watershed management.

DISPLAY RATING SHEET

Name(s) _____

Date _____ Subject _____

| | Points | | |
Item	Possible	Actual	Comments
Originality			
of idea	5		
of display technique	5		
Timeliness	10		
Color and lighting	10		
Neatness			
spacing and balance	5		
lettering	5		
materials	5		
Durability			
during the week	5		
at week's end	5		
Theme			
ease of understanding	10		
completeness	10		
simplicity	10		
unity	5		
initiates action	10		
Total	100		

Miscellaneous comments (add or subtract from final score accordingly) _____

_____

_____

Rated by _____

Appendix R

CASE STUDY APPROACH

I.   Objective(s)—(problem recognition)

II.   Case Situation—(problem definition)
    A. Policies
    B. Budgets
    C. Statements
    D. Surveys
    E. Basis for arguments (pro or con) relative to situation
    F. Politics

III.   History of Effort—(or lack of effort)
    A. Background information
    B. Reasons for present controversy or proposal

IV.   Publics Involved and Their Tendencies
    A. Proponents
        1. Internal publics—(and sub-publics)
        2. External publics—(and sub-publics)
    B. Opponents
        1. Internal publics—(and sub-publics)
        2. External publics—(and sub-publics)

V.   Campaigns and Communications
    A. Media used
    B. Other techniques
        1. Propaganda
        2. Samples and polls
        3. Personal contact
        4. Meetings

VI.   Results
    A. Analysis of techniques and their effectiveness
    B. Sequence of events
    C. Basis for success or failure

VII.   Alternate Solutions

VIII.   Summary and Evaluation

IX.   Future Possibilities

X.   Bibliography or Literature Cited

LITERATURE CITED

Albig, W. 1956. Modern public opinion. McGraw-Hill Co. New York, N. Y. 518 pp.

American Institute of Biological Sciences. 1972. Style manual for biology editors. 3rd Ed. Washington, D. C. 297 pp.

Anderson, M. A. 1957. The diffusion process. Spec. Rept. No. 18. Ag. Ext. Serv., Iowa State Coll., Ames, Iowa. 6 pp.

Anonymous. 1959. A national failure in conservation education. Conserv. News. 24(3): 5-7.

Anonymous, 1960. Television factbook. Television Digest. Triangle Publishers, Inc. Randor, Pa. 500 pp.

Anonymous. 1965. Planned meetings succeed. Wild. Soc. News. 101: 61.

Anonymous. 1965a. Wyoming State Journal. Lander, Wyo. Nos. 3, 17, 31.

Anonymous. 1968. Broadcasting yearbook. Broadcasting Publishers, Inc. Washington, D. C. 6 sec.

Badler, M. M. 1961. The audiovisual aid that will produce the best results. Pub. Rel. J. 17(11): 7-8.

Bell, T. 1965. Rocky Mountain News. Denver, Colo. Oct. 2, 7, 10.

Bernays, E. L. 1952. Public relations. Univ. of Okla. Press, Norman. 384 pp.

Bluem, A. W., J. F. Cox, and G. McPhereson. 1961. Television in the public interest. Hastings House Publishers, New York, N. Y. 192 pp.

Bode, I. T. 1937. Extension work in wildlife restoration. Trans. N. Am. Wildl. Conf. 2: 62-67.

Bohlen, J. M. and G. M. Beal. 1956. Instructor's guide-communications training program. Am. Assoc. Land Grant Colleges and Univ. Unit 1, Sec. 3. 6 seg.

Breth, H. 1948. Under the wildlife "blanket of ignorance." Trans. N. Am. Wildl. Conf. 13: 176-181.

Brion, J. P. 1967. How to build good will from a "hole in the ground." Pub. Rel. J. 23(3): 20-22.

Bromley, A. W. 1945. Evaluation of the New York state experimental cooperative landowner-sportsman controlled public hunting grounds program, 1939-1943. Trans. N. Am. Wildl. Conf. 10: 9-29.

Brown, E. K. 1959. Wanted—safe hunting. Proc. W. Assoc. State Game and Fish Comm. 39: 365-368.

————. No date. The Idaho conservation information forum. Unpub. Rept. 14 pp. (Mimeo).

Cain, S. A. 1960. Wildlife management and the customer. Trans. N. Am. Wild. and Nat. Resc. Conf. 24: 472-481.

Case, S. G. and C. Hoffman. 1960. Springboards to community action. Ext. Serv. Bul. No. 18. Colo. State Univ. 16 pp.

Chalk, J. D., D. I. Rasmussen, F. C. Edminster, C. M. Reed, A. Nicholson, and J. P. Miller. 1940. Is the farmer-sportsman council the answer? Trans. N. Am. Wildl. Conf. 5: 54-72.

Cherry, C. 1957. On human communication: a review, a survey, and a criticism. Wiley Pub. Co. New York City, N. Y. 333 pp.

Chester, G. and G. R. Garrison. 1956. Television and radio. Appleton-Century-Crafts, Inc. New York, N. Y. 652 pp.

Christopherson, E. 1952. And they call this sport. Sat. Eve. Post. April 12. 22-23, 104-105.

Cornwell, G. W. 1967. The potential contributions of wildlife extension education. Trans. N. Am. Wildl. and Nat. Resc. Conf. 32: 211-227.

Cosper, P. M. 1958. Selling hunting season recommendations. Proc. W. Assoc. State Game and Fish Comm. 38: 197-199.

Crane, H. S. 1960. Wildlife extension programs: good, bad, or indifferent. 6 pp. (Mimeo).

Culbreath, J. C. 1949. Phase of public relations and their effect upon game management. Proc. W. Assoc. State Game and Fish Comm. 29: 45-51.

————. 1950. Where do we stand on state conservation education programs. Trans. N. Am. Wildl. Conf. 15: 26-31.

————. 1952. The role of public relations in wildlife management. Proc. W. Assoc. State Game and Fish Comm. 32: 54-57.

Cutlip, S. M. and A. H. Center. 1964. Effective public relations. Prentice-Hall, Inc. Englewood Cliffs, N. J. 512 pp.

Davis, K. 1949. Human society. Macmillan Co. New York City, N. Y. 655 pp.

DeBerard, F. 1960. DeBerard tells of eminent domain crisis. Cattle Guard. 5(5): 23.

Derring, P. N. 1967. Propaganda, politics, and persons. Phi Kappa Phi J. XLVII(2): 29-38.

Dunn, R. O. 1961. Ford Motor Company captures annual film audience of 64,000,000. Pub. Rel. J. 17(11): 10-12.

Eastman Kodak Co. 1967. Audiovisual projection. Kodak Pamphlet No. 5-3. Rochester, N. Y. 19 pp.

Flemming, R. 1960. Amendment No. 3 threatens Colorado with absolute czar. Denver Post. Oct. 15.

Flesch, R. F. 1949. How to test readability. Harpers Pub. Co. New York, N. Y. 56 pp.

Foss, P. O. 1960. Politics and grass. Univ. of Wash. Press, Seattle, Wash. 236 pp.

Gerber, J. J. 1960. About who's who in America. Unpub. Rept. 2 pp. (Mimeo).

Gilbert, D. L. 1951. Economics and ecology of the black bear in Colorado. M. S. Thesis. Colo. State Univ. 164 pp.

————. 1956. Television as a wildlife education medium. J. Wildl. Mgmt. 20(4): 456-458.

————. 1960. Successes, pitfalls, and techniques in wildlife television. Trans. N. Am. Wildl. and Nat. Resc. Conf. 25: 444-458.

————. 1962. Public relations and communications in wildlife management. Doctorate Thesis. Univ. of Mich. 201 pp.

————. 1967. A short course for game and fish commissioners. Trans. N. Am. Wildl. and Nat. Resc. Conf. 32: 174-177.

———— and R. R. Hill. 1964. The professional looks at sportsmen's organizations. Colo. Outdoors. 13(6): 33-39.

Graham, J. H. 1960. Business sponsored films—dynamic public relations tool. Pub. Rel. J. 16(5): 12-14, 16.

Graves, H. S. and W. E. Nelson. 1919. Our national elk herds. U. S. D. A. Circ. 51. 34 pp.

Gunning, R. 1952. The technnique of clear writing. McGraw-Hill. New York, N. Y. 289 pp.

Hiebert, R. E. 1965. How public relations is being taught in college. Pub. Rel. J. 21(5): 22-24.

Hjelte, C. 1957. Motion pictures. Proc. W. Assoc. State Game and Fish Comm. 37: 144-146.

————. 1959. Writing effectively. Colo. Game, Fish, and Parks Dept. Ed. Bul. No. 6. 3 pp. (Mimeo).

————. No Date. Tools for teaching conservation. Colo. Game and Fish Dept. Educ. Bul. No. 1. 32 pp.

Hockstrasser, H. 1957. The Morgan Jr. Conservation Club. Trans. N. Am. Wildl. Conf. 22: 594-607.

Hodgson, R. 1958. When should you buy promotional service outside? Industrial Marketing. Chicago, Ill. 2 pp.

Hosie, W. A. and B. Mayer. 1963. Which audiovisual aid for which situation. Pub. Rel. J. 19(12): 14-16.

Hubbell, R. 1959. Television: programming and production. Murray Hills Books. New York, N. Y. 272 pp.

Iowa Agricultural Extension Service. 1955. How farm people accept new ideas. Ag. Ext. Serv. Bul. No. 1. Ames, Iowa. 11 pp.

James, M. L. 1956. Letter to the committee to improve hunting and fishing. Cattle Guard. 1(5): 20.

Johns, W. 1965. Where the livestock, but not antelope can play. Cons. News. Natl. Wildl. Fed., Washington, D. C. 16 pp.

Jones, D. A. 1960. A salable approach to the cattle-elk competition problem. Trans. N. Am. Wildl. and Nat. Resc. Conf. 25: 387-395.

Kilgore, B. M. 1953. A survey of the use of motion pictures by state game and fish conservation departments. Masters Thesis. Univ. of Okla., Norman, Okla. 125 pp.

Klapper, J. T. 1960. The effects of mass communications. Free Press. Glencoe, Ill. 301 pp.

Krech, D., R. S. Crutchfield, and E. L. Ballachey. 1962. Individual in society. McGraw-Hill Pub. Co. New York City, N. Y. 564 pp.

Lahr, L. E. 1953. Fish and game employment relations. Proc. W. Assoc. State Game and Fish Comm. 33: 276-279.

Lane, E. F. 1965. Social science: its lack of application is starving public relations. Pub. Rel. J. 21(2): 8-12.

Lawrie, T. J. 1960. Residents need all-out vote drive. Cattle Guard. 5(10): 3, 34.

Leopold, A., G. W. Wood, J. H. Baker, W. P. Taylor, and L. G. MacNamara. 1939. Farmer-sportsman, a partnership for wildlife restoration. Trans. N. Am. Wildl. Conf. 4: 144-146.

Leopold, A. S. 1956. Hunting for the masses—can game departments supply it? Proc. W. Assoc. State Game and Fish Comm. 36: 59-64.

––––. 1963. Study of wildlife problems in National Parks. Trans. N. Am. Wildl. and Nat. Resc. Conf. 28: 28-45.

Lesly, P. (Ed.) 1962. Public relations handbook. Prentice-Hall, Inc. Englewood Cliffs, N. J. 901 pp.

Levenson, W. B. and E. Stasheff. 1954. Teaching through radio and television. Rinehart and Co. New York, N. Y. 560 pp.

Lively, C. E. 1958. The social side of conservation, some reflections. Trans. N. Am. Wildl. Conf. 18: 36-46.

Madson, J. 1966. The elk. Winchester-Western Press. East Alton, Ill. 125 pp.

Mapes, J. G. 1966. The trouble with employee communications today. Pub. Rel. Speeches. Hill and Knowlton, Inc. New York, N. Y. pp. 96-101.

Mehaffey, J. 1952. Cross examination of the conservation magazine. Trans. N. Am. Wildl. Conf. 17: 519-524.

Mooty, J. J. 1967. License agents as an internal public of the Colorado Department of Game, Fish, and Parks. M. S. Thesis. Colo. State Univ. 150 pp.

Morgan, C. T. 1956. Introduction to psychology. McGraw-Hill Co. New York, N. Y. 676 pp.

Murphy, A. R. 1967. Communications: mass without meaning. Pub. Rel. J. 23(5): 8-10.

Nagle, W. O. 1960. Make your technical writing useful. Am. Fisheries Soc., The Wildlife Society. McLean, Va. 31 pp.

O'Hayre, J. 1966. Gobbledygook has gotta go. Bureau of Land Mgmt., U. S. D. I. 113 pp.

Patterson, P. J. 1960. Ditch and trail. Western Farm Life. (April). 62: 30.

Pengelly, W. L. 1959. Why conservation education for adults? Proc. W. Assoc. State Game and Fish Comm. 39: 335-343.

––––. 1963. Thunder on the Yellowstone. Wildl. and Nat. Parks Naturalist. 14(2): 18-25.

Pfiffner, J. M. 1951. The supervision of personnel—human relations in the management of men. Prentice-Hall, Inc. Englewood Cliffs, N. J. 454 pp.

Reavley, W. L. 1957. Conservation clubs for juniors. Nat. Wildl. Fed. Bul. Washington, D. C. 19 pp.

Reynolds, G. W. 1966. Paths to people. U. S. Bureau of Land Mgmt., U. S. D. I. 57 pp.

Rice, D. 1959. As I see it. Cattle Guard. 4(4): 4, 17.

Rosenthal, H. C. 1967. Create maximum value from your annual report. Pub. Rel. J. 23(11): 37.

Rush, W. M. 1932. Northern Yellowstone elk study. Mont. Fish and Game Comm. 131 pp. (Mimeo).

Samson, N. T. 1965. Films and filmstrips on forestry. Bul. No. 7. Stephen F. Austin State College. Nagadoches, Tex. 78 pp.

Schoenfeld, C. A. 1954. The university and its publics. Harpers Co. New York, N. Y. 284 pp.

———. 1957. Public relations aspects of wildlife management. J. Wildl. Mgmt. 21(1): 70-74.

Scott, R. T. 1960. A successful formula for an open house. Pub. Rel. J. 16(10): 20-22.

Seigworth, K. J. 1960. Communications in a forestry agency. J. Soil and Water Conserv. 15(2): 69-71.

Severy, J. W. and W. L. Pengelly. 1956. Montana's venture in wildlife extension. Trans. N. Am. Wildl. Conf. 21: 596-602.

Shea, J. P. 1948. A new approach to farmer-sportsmen cooperation. Trans. N. Am. Wildl. Conf. 13: 163-169.

Shick, C. No Date. Farmer-hunter relations. Mich. Cons. Dept., Mich State Univ., Coop. Ext. Serv., Unpub. Rept. 3 pp. (Mimeo).

Shomon, J. J. 1952. Education in resource use: our most challenging task in human relations. Trans. N. Am. Wildl. Conf. 17: 525-533.

———. 1959. Effective conservation communications. Doctorate Thesis. Univ. of Mich. 433 pp.

Smits, L. J. 1937. Publicity in wildlife restoration. Trans. N. Am. Wildl. Conf. 20: 603-609.

Starch, D. 1924. Principles of advertising. Show and Sons. Chicago, Ill. 273 pp.

Stephenson, L. E. 1966. The fate of a bill. Colo. State Univ. Unpub. Rept. 21 pp.

Swift, E. 1960. Talking conservationists should first be working conservationists. Conservation News. 25(1): 1-2.

————. 1961. What does conservation education mean? Conservation News. 26(10, 11, 12): 1-5, 4-7, 1-5.

Thomas, K. 1960. Translating you to television. J. Am. Dietetic Assoc. 36: 361-370.

Thompson, W. K. 1958. Fish and game magazines—survey and recommendations. Proc. W. Assoc. State Game and Fish Comm. 38: 361-370.

Throckmorton, M. 1958. Some special educational projects of service to sportsmen. Proc. W. Assoc. State Game and Fish Comm. 38: 348-353.

Titus, H., G. W. Bradt, J. H. Cline, and W. F. Kirk. 1939. Farmer-sportsman, a partnership for wildlife restoration. Trans. N. Am. Wildl. Conf. 4: 176-200.

Tonkin, J. D. and A. F. Skelsey. 1953. Television for you. A handbook for extension agents. U. S. D. A. Handbook No. 55. 24 pp.

Trueblood, T. 1963. Too many elk. Field and Stream. July. 36-39, 78-79.

U. S. Bureau of Land Management. 1965. Position statement on woven wire fencing on public lands in Wyoming. Unpub. Rept. 23 pp. (Mimeo).

U. S. National Park Service. 1964. Long Range wildlife and habitat management plan for the Northern Yellowstone elk herd and its habitat. Yellowstone Nat. Park, Wyo. 88 pp. (Mimeo).

Wagar, J. V. K. 1958. Can weak-kneed public education retain rare wildlife values? Trans. N. Am. Wildl. Conf. 23: 526-532.

Wastcoat, O. B. 1967. The Wyoming fencing controversy. Colo. State Univ. Unpub. Rept. 12 pp. (Mimeo).

Weaver, R. L. 1957. Successful state conservation education programs. Trans. N. Am. Wildl. Conf. 22: 644-651.

Webster's Seventh New Collegiate Dictionary. 1968. Public Relations. G and C Merriam Co., Springfield, Mass. P. 690.

Wells, E. S. 1966. The professional approach to planning. Pub. Rel. J. 22(10): 99-100.

Wildlife Management Institute. 1968. Organization, authority, and programs of state fish and wildlife agencies. 29 pp.

Will, J. W. 1966. The future of public relations. Public Relations Speeches. Hill and Knowlton, Inc., N. Y. pp. 10-20.

Woolf, A. 1967. The Yellowstone elk controversy. Colo. State Univ. Unpub. Rept. 36 pp. (Mimeo).

Youel, K. 1960. Too close to the trees to see the woods. Pub. Rel. J. 16(11): 12-14.

Zelko, H. P. 1970. What's wrong with public speaking. Pub. Rel. J. 26(1): 23-24.

(Where not credited, photographs by the author)

INDEX